THE

EARLY AMERICA: *History, Context, Culture*

Joyce E. Chaplin and Philip D. Morgan, *Series Editors*

The Baptism of Early Virginia

How Christianity Created Race

REBECCA ANNE GOETZ

Johns Hopkins University Press

Baltimore

Johns Hopkins Paperback edition, 2016
9 8 7 6 5 4 3 2 1

Johns Hopkins University Press
2715 North Charles Street
Baltimore, Maryland 21218-4363
www.press.jhu.edu

The Library of Congress has cataloged the hardcover edition of this book as follows:
Goetz, Rebecca Anne.
   The baptism of early Virginia : how Christianity created race / Rebecca Anne Goetz.
     p. cm. — (Early America : history, context, culture)
   Includes bibliographical references and index.
   ISBN 978-1-4214-0700-5 (hbk. : alk. paper) — ISBN 1-4214-0700-0 (hbk. : alk. paper)
   1. Racism—Religious aspects—Christianity. 2. Racism—Virginia. 3. Virginia—Race
relations. 4. Virginia—Church history. I. Title.
   BT734.2.G64 2012
   277.55'07089—dc23   2012001951

A catalog record for this book is available from the British Library.

ISBN-13: 978-1-4214-1981-7
ISBN-10: 1-4214-1981-5

Special discounts are available for bulk purchases of this book. For more information, please contact Special Sales at 410-516-6936 or specialsales@press.jhu.edu.

For my parents, with love

CONTENTS

ACKNOWLEDGMENTS

A friend recently reminded me that all good scholarly work is the result of collaboration. In remembering how within a decade this book went from humble seminar paper to dissertation to actual book manuscript, I am astounded at all the people who helped and influenced me. In the History Department at Harvard, David Armitage, Vince Brown, Joyce Chaplin, Mark Kishlansky, Laurel Ulrich, and the members of Laurel's Early American History Seminar read and commented on this book in its formative stages. Laurel was also my adviser; she encouraged this project from its inception (even when I described my method as "nailing jelly to a wall"). I could not have asked for a kinder or more astute critic. My classmate Louis Hyman coined the phrase "hereditary heathenism" and graciously allowed me to use it. A Graduate School of Arts and Sciences Summer Research Fellowship, a Mark DeWolfe Howe Fellowship in the Study of American Law, and several summer and term-time grants from the Charles Warren Center for Studies in American History at Harvard University made the many months I spent at the Library of Virginia possible.

While I did research in Richmond, Virginia, the Fall Line Early America Seminar allowed me to join the group and present some of my earliest thoughts. Woody Holton, Doug Winiarski, Mark Valeri, Phil Schwartz, and Al Zambone all provided valuable insights. I especially thank Brent Tarter of the Library of Virginia for introducing me to the FLEAS and for assisting me above and beyond the call of duty at the library. The fine folks of the *Dictionary of Virginia Biography* project, especially Brent Tarter, John Kneebone, John Deal, and Sara Bearss, helped me navigate county court records on microfilm and invited me to share many entertaining lunches with them. At the Colonial Williamsburg Foundation's John D. Rockefeller, Jr. Library, a Gilder Lehrman Research Fellowship funded two intense months of research. Jim Horn, Gail Greve, Sam Fore, George Yetter, Del Moore, Juleigh Clarke, and Inge Flester not only were very helpful but also provided me with a calm place to work for two months. At Colonial Williamsburg's Historical Research Division, Cary Carson and Kevin Kelley listened to me patiently and offered helpful suggestions as I floundered through the York County Court Records. Linda Rowe allowed me access to Colonial Williamsburg's painstakingly prepared York County Records transcripts and biographical files and answered all my questions. A Virginia Historical Society Mellon Fellowship allowed me to spend two weeks there combing through the papers of great planters and through parish record books. Nelson Lankford, Frances Pollard, and Greg Stoner made my stay there a pleasant one. The Woodrow Wilson National Fellowship Foundation's Charlotte W. Newcombe Doctoral Dissertation Fellowship for Studies in Religious and Ethical Values allowed me to write for the entire academic year of 2005–6.

At Rice University, I have found a most congenial home in the Department of History. For seven years, I have received research support in the form of a Jon and Paula Mosle Grant, which has enabled travel to archives and conferences. A fellowship from Rice's Humanities Research Center allowed for more writing time over the course of academic year 2008–9. In the history department, the junior faculty writing group has been a supportive place to work out writing problems; I especially thank Lisa Balabanlilar, Kate de Luna, Karl Gunther, Madlene Hamilton, Moramay Lopez-Alonso, Caleb McDaniel, Cyrus Mody, Aysha Pollnitz, and Emily Straus for their insights. My colleagues John Boles and Randal Hall invited me to present portions of chapter 6 at the Houston Area Southern Historians workshop. And Anna Shparberg and Randy Tibbets of the Fondren Library patiently acquired books and microfilm for me. A fleet of Rice graduate and undergraduate students participated in this project as research assistants. I thank Chris Davis, Michael Esquivel, Kelin Herrington, Katie Knowles, Allison Madar, and Ben Wright. Andrew Baker and Sarah Paulus patiently fact-checked the manuscript. Any errors that remain are mine alone.

From 2007 to 2009, I was privileged to be a member of the Young Scholars in American Religion Program at Indiana University/Purdue University Indianapolis, funded by the Lilly Endowment. My colleagues in this seminar helped this project grow and change. I thank Ed Blum, Darren Dochuk, Kate Engel, Spencer Fluhman, Charles Irons, Kathryn Lofton, Randall Stephens, Matt Sutton, Tisa Wenger, and our wonderful moderators, Paul Harvey and Amanda Porterfield, for this great experience.

I have benefited from the help and support of friends and colleagues online and offline. I blogged frequently about aspects of this project from 2003 to 2007 and deeply appreciate all the advice and input from scholars around the globe. My friends Travis Glasson, Heather Kopelson, and Todd Romero read many drafts of this book. I was very happy that Todd and his family wound up in Houston, too! Todd read and reread every chapter. Scott Sowerby and Noah McCormack commented on various parts of the manuscript that deal with seventeenth-century English history. Noah also photographed documents I needed in the British Library and the National Archives Kew. My friend Manan Ahmed read and commented on many parts of this manuscript with his trademark wit and thoughtfulness.

I am deeply grateful to Texas A&M Press for permission to reprint portions of chapter 4. I am also grateful to Jean Niswonger at Rice's GIS lab for making the map. Joyce Chaplin and Philip Morgan were patient and supportive editors as I turned this manuscript into a book.

For a decade *The Baptism of Early Virginia* has been a member of the family, and my closest friends and my relatives have had to tolerate its presence. I thank them all, especially my brother, Joseph Goetz, and my parents, Stephen and Carol Goetz, for their love and their support. I could not have completed this book without them.

A NOTE ON TERMINOLOGY

In the initial chapters of this book I often refer to *English* settlers, but later I refer to the English inhabitants of Virginia as *Anglo-Virginians*. The change in wording indicates that, after the initial decades of settlement, white Virginians created a creole culture, with noticeable differences from English culture, especially as regards religion and race. I refer to native people generically as *Indians*, but where appropriate I refer to the proper names of specific groups, villages, and individuals. Likewise, I have tried to refer to people of African descent at various points as *African* or *African American*, depending on whether I know where they were born.

I have endeavored to preserve the flavor of seventeenth-century spelling and grammar, but I have modernized words, written out abbreviations and superscripts, and placed punctuation where the meaning might otherwise be unclear.

Great Britain did not adopt the Gregorian calendar until 1752; prior to that year, the new year began on 25 March in accordance with the Julian calendar. Therefore I have rendered dates between 1 January and 25 March in this form: 24 February 1624/25.

THE BAPTISM OF EARLY VIRGINIA

Introduction

Potential Christians and Hereditary Heathens in Virginia

When the Reverend Morgan Godwyn arrived in Virginia in the mid-1660s, he was one of the rare Church of England ministers willing to shepherd a colonial parish. Godwyn's later writings suggest a combative personality; appalled by Anglo-Virginians' refusal to proselytize their enslaved property, he challenged his colonial flock on its treatment of enslaved people. He encouraged the baptism of slaves and performed at least two such baptisms himself in Virginia. His actions angered his planter parishioners, Godwyn later recalled. One imagines the officious Godwyn traveling the byways of Virginia, baptizing slaves, and annoying planters who disliked his meddling. He left Virginia (it is possible that his ideas made him so unpopular that he was forced to leave) and wandered to Barbados, a place even more desperate for ministers and as dependent on slave labor for its livelihood. He pursued the baptism of enslaved blacks there as well, and Barbadian planters were equally hostile to the message. Godwyn wrote that he suffered from "hard Words, and evil Language" as a result of his efforts.[1]

Godwyn returned to England and in 1681 penned a stunning indictment of the conflation of religious and racial categories in England's American colonies. In angry tones, he wrote compelling words: "These two words, *Negro* and *Slave*, being by custom grown Homogeneous and Convertible; even as *Negro* and *Christian*, *Englishman* and *Heathen*, are by the like corrupt Custom and Partiality made *Opposites*; thereby as it were implying, that the one could not be *Christians*, nor the other *Infidels*."[2] Godwyn's shock stemmed from the immutability of skin color and enslavement. To say "negro" was to mean "slave," and vice versa. Those identities were self-evident to Anglo-Virginians, who worked hard over the course of the seventeenth century to make sure that various avenues for freedom were cut off and that even free blacks suffered from severe legal disabilities. Morgan Godwyn found that state of affairs disturbing.

1

More shocking was the colonial link between being Christian and being English, and being black and being heathen. "Negro" and "Christian" were opposing identities in Virginia, a distinction that puzzled and angered Godwyn.

Godwyn came from a world that emphasized the universality of Christianity. He believed, along with most Englishmen who had been born in England and lived out their lives there, that any person could convert to Christianity, regardless of their origin. The colonial experience had corrupted that understanding of Christianity. In the New World, Godwyn found, planters believed enslaved blacks were inherently incapable of becoming Christian. This notion apparently extended to native people as well. This new belief was convenient for settlers; dehumanizing Indians and enslaving Africans helped settlers to marginalize and control them. That idea was anathema to Godwyn, who found that these planters abroad held beliefs that were actually quite heathen. After accusing English people of heathen behavior, Godwyn found himself unwelcome in the colonies. Even allowing for Godwyn to exaggerate the situation in Virginia, he was reacting against a trend he observed in the colony, one that separated people on the basis of their Christianity and associated Christianity with English descent and heathenism with Indian or African descent. By describing the "corrupt Custom" that rendered enslaved people unable to be Christian, Godwyn exposed a feature of colonial life: the conflation of religious and racial categories.

Godwyn focused on words: *Negro, Christian, Englishman, heathen, infidel.* These words, gathered together in Godwyn's observations of the religious and racial order in Virginia, prompt questions about how Anglo-Virginians used Christianity to create an idea of race. As Godwyn indicated, English settlers perceived other denizens of the New World— Indians and Africans—as incapable of true Christian conversion, an attitude the English-born Godwyn did not share. How did Anglo-Virginians come to understand *Negro* and *Christian* to be irreconcilable terms? And what did that mean for the formation of racial ideologies in the New World?

This book grapples with these words and their many meanings and how Anglo-Virginians used them to describe and categorize human difference. Over the course of the long seventeenth century, Anglo-Virginians transformed their meanings. Not only did they effectively reimagine what it meant to be Christian but they also invented an entirely new concept—what it meant to be "white." In courtrooms and legislative chambers, in their homes and in their public spaces, and while at war with themselves and with Indians, Anglo-Virginians redefined the meanings of these words and created new racial categories. They increasingly connected physical differences such as skin color with a budding idea of hereditary heathenism—the notion that Indians and Africans could never become Christian. As they began to think of Indians and Africans not as potential Christians but as people incapable of Christian conversion, Anglo-Virginians laid the foundations for an emergent idea of race and an ideology of racism.

This book is also about another word: *race.* Most modern readers of Godwyn's polemics would agree that he was describing the formation of racial difference, and Godwyn himself used the word to suggest common characteristics of people having the same descent. Godwyn wrote of planters who believed that enslaved Africans were doomed to slavery and heathenism because of the biblical Noah's delinquent son Ham "who, they [planters] say, was together with his whole *Family* and Race, *cursed* by his *Father.*" Godwyn here alluded to an interpretation of Genesis that suggested that descendants of Ham were permanently cursed because their ancestor had mocked his father, Noah. Godwyn dismissed this exegesis of Genesis as the result of planters' "wild reasonings."[3] Yet some planters clearly thought in terms of common descent and inherited incapacities. *Race* does have particular modern connotations that early modern people might not have understood. In the sixteenth and seventeenth centuries, race simply indicated common descent (of people, animals, or plants), but by the middle of the eighteenth century, the word had evolved to connote classification by descent, common physical characteristics (e.g., skin color), or common cultural and ethnic traits.

Around this deceptively simple word hovered a whole host of competing ideas about differences among humans. Those differences could be physical, rooted in the body; cultural; religious; or a combination of all three. Underlying the term was an implied sense of heredity and lineage, and a sense of the innateness of certain qualities. Yet the word was flexible, when it was used at all, as was the ferment of ideas that surrounded it. Modern people generally think that *race* describes immutable and ahistorical biological phenomena, despite a vocal and growing chorus of scientific voices arguing that race is a biologically meaningless category. For American scholars especially, even when used historically *race* signals differences inscribed on bodies, whereas cultural or religious differences indicate ethnic rather than racial differences. For early modern people, observable human differences could not be so conveniently split between innate biological and cultural categories. Some cultural attributes—such as Christianity—were perceived as heritable characteristics and contributed to emergent ideas of race in the early modern world. This is why Godwyn's understanding of the planters' designation of Ham's descendants as a race is so significant.

As Godwyn's experience in the New World indicates, Christianity had enormous potential for both defining human difference and reinforcing human unity. Scholars of race have long noted the importance of religious belief to both creating and challenging racial idioms and ideologies of race. The causal link between religion and race submerged and reemerged at various junctures as Europeans encountered the other. The ancient world showed few signs of racial prejudice, and Christianity welcomed black converts in its early centuries. Medieval European Christians, though, held what might be termed protoracial views of non-Christians, especially Jews. Many medieval kingdoms subjected Jews to various legal disabilities, and historical evidence suggests that European Christians saw Jews as subhuman, even demonic. Anti-Jewish and anti-Muslim sentiment took on some racial characteristics in fifteenth- and sixteenth-century Spain. *Conversos*, Jewish and Muslim converts to Christianity, labored under suspicion of a hereditary inability to experience true Christian conversion. Spain emphasized the importance of *limpieza de sangre* (purity of blood, meaning no Jewish or Muslim ancestors), suggesting that at least some Europeans thought religion to be not merely cultural but also hereditary.[4] Godwyn's observation that some Anglo-Virginian planters believed that blacks should remain enslaved and ignorant of Christianity is further evidence that many Europeans thought religion was hereditary.

There were countervailing attitudes as well. Even as Europeans remained suspicious of non-Christians and recent converts, they also continued to believe that all humans could (and should) become Christian. This belief was rooted in the Christian commitment to the notion of a single Creation, and the idea that human diversity was attributable only to the postdiluvian dispersal of Noah's descendants. Godwyn himself sided with the universalizing impulse within Christianity when he quoted Acts 17:26: *"That God hath made [of one Blood] all Nations of Men, for to dwell all upon the face of the Earth."*[5] As Christianity divided into Protestant and Catholic camps over the course of the sixteenth century, Christian belief continued to encompass both a commitment to the unity of mankind and a sense of exclusivity and superiority. In the long encounter between Europeans and the people of the Americas and Africa, Catholic and Protestant Europeans struggled with two competing desires: their missionary impulses to extend the reach of Christendom and their need to justify the enslavement of Indians and Africans. For people who might already be suspicious of recent Christian converts and their descendants, the apparent reluctance of Indians and Africans to completely embrace Christianity aroused severe misgivings. The notion that religion might be hereditary had long roots, but it finally found its full expression in the Americas. Yet although religion was strongly implicated in the construction of racial ideologies, precisely how Europeans mustered religion to make race in the New World remains unexplained.[6] The experiences of Englishmen, Africans, and Indians in Virginia provide a basis for tracing English strategies for using Christianity to create race.

English colonists had brought a firm belief in the unity of mankind with them when they founded a permanent settlement at Jamestown in 1607. They thought of Indians as potential Christians, people who needed only to be taught the error of their heathen ways in order to join English people in fashioning a new society in the New World. Indians, they thought, would make excellent junior partners in an Anglo-Indian Christian commonwealth in the Chesapeake. English colonialism would be a rebuke to the un-Christian, brutal disorder of Spanish colonies to the south. The English belief in the monogenesis of humanity—common descent from the biblical Noah—drove the commitment to a commonwealth of Indians and Englishmen. Early observations of Virginia's Indians, often written by ministers or other highly educated individuals, seemed to confirm Christian elements in Indian culture and Indian receptiveness to conversion. This imagined English world remained a goal for settlers throughout the initial decades of settlement, despite rampant Anglo-Indian violence and obvious Indian reluctance to engage with the English on their terms alone. The English did not anticipate the ferocity of the Indian assault of 1622, and it was that event which brought incipient English ideas about the inability of Indians to become Christian to the forefront. Indians ceased to be worthy of conversion efforts, as far as Anglo-Virginians were concerned.

This episode of brutal Anglo-Indian violence alone did not create hereditary heathenism, but it did portend the separation of English and Anglo-Virginian ideals that so enraged Morgan Godwyn later in the century. Making race was a process, born out of complex interactions between laws passed by the nascent planter elite and the practice of everyday life. Laws proscribing fornication and marriage reflected growing unease about the mixing of Christian and heathen bodies and the status of children produced through these unions. Anglo-Virginians also used the courts and their laws to sever the traditional link between Christian baptism and freedom. Baptism created new Christians, and it ritually created communities and kinship, but Anglo-Virginians changed the meaning of baptism for Indians and Africans, effectively limiting access to Christianity for non-English people. At the beginning of the century, English people did not think of themselves as "white." Anglo-Virginians created whiteness during the seventeenth century and redefined Christianity as a religion of white people. Anglo-Virginians codified the heritability of Christianity and of heathenism, but daily interactions remained fluid. Even as planters used legislation to draw bright lines between Christian English and non-English heathens, court cases show how laws were applied (or not applied) and how ordinary Virginians used (or did not use) the language of hereditary heathenism. Sometimes these new laws appear to have been honored only in the breach, suggesting that some Anglo-Virginians were reluctant to put hereditary heathenism into practice. Enslaved people also resisted, especially by continuing to connect baptism and freedom.

With their words and deeds, Anglo-Virginians gradually created a world where whiteness and Christianity were bound to freedom, political power, and the potential for wealth. Virginia's model of hereditary heathenism proved irresistible as colonial assemblies throughout the English Atlantic mimicked Virginia's innovations, but hereditary heathenism was never monolithic. Protestant Christianity alternately created and undermined race in Virginia. Even as religion was mobilized to provide explanatory power for making race, it could also be used to reassert the unity of mankind and the importance of the spiritual equality of all human beings. Early eighteenth-century Anglo-Virginians thought that their identities as white Christians were secure, but challengers contested this ideology from two fronts. Imperial officials and Anglican missionaries mounted efforts to convert enslaved Africans and Indians in Virginia, much to local planters' disgust, exposing the wide gulf between metropolitan and colonial attitudes. The second challenge came from enslaved people themselves, who began to assert their own identities as Christians and connect those identities forcefully with a right to freedom. As the American Revolution approached, this double assault transformed the ongoing struggle over religion and human difference.

The Virginia colony lacked the hot puritan religiosity of Massachusetts Bay or New Haven, and historians have often assumed that Virginia was a secular place, more concerned with wringing fabulous wealth from tobacco than with enforcing the religiosity of its inhabitants. Yet Christianity was as important to the colonization of Virginia as it was to that of New England.[7] The Church of England was the established church in Virginia, forming a potent point for the enforcement of uniformity among English settlers. Though the Church of England did not produce the angst-ridden sermons and conversion narratives that now serve as windows into the New England soul, Virginia's Christianity found its way into laws, letters, and court records. The Church of England bound settlers together with a common sense of identity. Though historians have had a tendency to focus on misbehaving ministers and the institutional weakness of the church in the seventeenth century, Protestant Christianity remained critical to how Anglo-Virginians saw themselves and others.[8] Sensitive readings of the remaining source materials from seventeenth-century Virginia show that Christianity permeated the daily lives of colonists in ritual, practice, language, and lived experience.

The Church of England was not hegemonic; Virginia contained astonishing religious diversity by seventeenth-century standards. The colony hosted several groups of dissenters: puritans, Quakers, Huguenot refugees, and a handful of politically powerful and wealthy Catholics. In the eighteenth century, small groups of Presbyterians, Baptists, and Methodists began to transform the religious landscape of the colony. Virginia's native people and its enslaved Africans also retained their own religious traditions, even as they adopted aspects of Christian belief and practice.[9] Virginia's religious diversity was critical to the making of race. As Anglo-Virginians confronted the Church of England's detractors, they reluctantly embraced limited toleration for most Protestants. Anglo-Virginians were more willing to accept dissenting white Christians, as long as the benefits of Christianity were not extended to enslaved people. In the advent of religious toleration in the New World, race trumped religion as the most important category of difference.

When the English settled in Virginia, they did so initially under the auspices of the Virginia Company of London, a joint-stock company funded by investors interested in forming a permanent English settlement in the New World. Investors also wanted to gain wealth from pre-

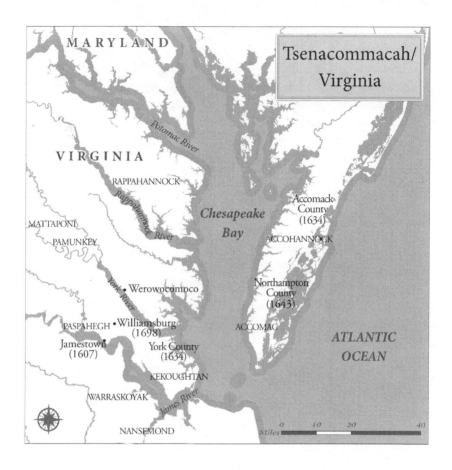

Tsenacommacah/
Virginia

MARYLAND

VIRGINIA

RAPPAHANNOCK

Rappahannock River

MATTAPONI

PAMUNKEY

Chesapeake
Bay

Accomack
County
(1634)

ACCOHANNOCK

York River

• Werowocomoco

Northampton
County
(1643)

PASPAHEGH • Williamsburg
(1698)

ACCOMAC

Jamestown
(1607)

York County
(1634)

ATLANTIC
OCEAN

KEKOUGHTAN

WARRASKOYAK

James River

NANSEMOND

0   10   20   40
Miles

cious metals and other valuable commodities the Spanish had found in
portions of the New World they controlled. Starting in 1614, English
settlers funded in part by the Virginia Company spread out from safe
anchors at the mouth of the James River on the Chesapeake along the
other tidal river systems, building plantations along the York and Rappahannock Rivers as well. The English also spread to the Eastern Shore,
the narrow band of land across the bay from Jamestown and its daughter settlements that separated the Chesapeake from the open ocean. The
Tidewater region of Virginia, even in the midst of its early seventeenth-
century drought, was rich in resources: abundant fish and shellfish,
fertile soil for corn (and later tobacco), and long stretches of navigable
waterways to transport the commodities the English hoped to find there.
In settling in the Tidewater, the English invaded and expropriated land

occupied by Algonkian Indians, who were loosely organized into a confederacy nominally headed by the paramount chief Wahunsonacock
(known to the English, and posterity, as Powhatan).

During the time the Virginia Company controlled English settlement,
records generated by the company, and narratives of English experiences
there, tell the story of the English encounter with the Tidewater Algonkian population. Beginning in 1619, Virginia had its own representative
assembly, and by the 1630s individual counties had formed their own
courts to try local disputes. Court records are notoriously problematic
in any locale and in any century, for they generally highlight only social
anomalies; court cases represent the exceptions to acceptable human
behavior in a given society rather than the rule. But it is through these
transgressions that I am able to trace changing English conceptions of
human difference. In these records, identifiers such as Christian, heathen, pagan, infidel, Negro, and English appear in their everyday usage,
in depositions, wills, and judgments. They therefore show how seventeenth-century Virginians—English, Indian, and African—understood
hereditary heathenism, implemented it, and challenged it. Court records, despite the fact that they generally show people behaving badly,
are therefore invaluable sources for showing the development of the attitudes that so disturbed Morgan Godwyn in the closing quarter of the
seventeenth century.

The seventeenth century was a key moment for the articulation of
race. Many scholars of race argue that new scientific disciplines such as
biology and the classificatory schemes of the Enlightenment in the eighteenth century provided the essential ingredients of race. The invention
of race as a concept required an understanding of biological concepts
of difference that emerged in the eighteenth and nineteenth centuries;
before the 1700s, most Europeans merely described difference in cultural terms. Recently early modernists have challenged that explanation,
arguing that racialized understandings of human difference emerged
earlier and without the assistance of Enlightenment thought.[10] Seventeenth-century Anglo-Virginians developed concepts of heredity and
wide-ranging theories about the origins and descent of Indians and Africans. Religious differences were not merely artifacts of culture but rather
means of assessing the spiritual capacities of Indians and Africans. The
ability of non-Christians to convert was a central question for Anglo-
Virginians. In deciding that Indians and Africans could not truly become

Christian and that their heathenism was hereditary, Anglo-Virginians asserted a new definition of human difference that was written both on the body and in the soul. Christianity was the most important point of comparison as English settlers encountered Indians and Africans, so it is small wonder that religion provided a basis for the Anglo-Virginian articulation of race.

Because the seventeenth century was formative, it laid the groundwork for how planters mobilized Christianity to support race and slavery in the eighteenth and nineteenth centuries. The tropes developed in the seventeenth century, including the full embrace of hereditary heathenism, helped create the idea of white Christianity that undergirded planter identity and power in the eighteenth century. Many seventeenth-century habits of the planter class, including the exclusion of Africans and Indians from marriage, baptism, and other Christian rites and rituals persisted in the eighteenth century as markers of the importance of hereditary heathenism. These ideas spread as well and became dominant in the Anglophone Atlantic world. Planters in the British South and in the Caribbean espoused the ideas of hereditary heathenism that Anglo-Virginians had pioneered. The old vocabulary of English and Christian, black and heathen, retained its potency, and the biblical exegesis of the Curse of Ham enjoyed a resurgence. References to the Curse of Ham as an explanation for blackness, slavery, and heathenism reappeared in a revamped form in the nineteenth century as cotton planters in the American South sought to theorize and historicize their commitment to race-based chattel slavery. The ideas of the seventeenth century survived and supported Enlightenment discourses of race and then supplemented the full-fledged scientific racism of the nineteenth century.

The seventeenth century was also a key moment for the articulation of resistance to ideas of race and of hereditary heathenism. The objections to planter ideology voiced by Morgan Godwyn and a handful of others found purchase in the eighteenth century among both Anglican ministers and enslaved people themselves. Virginia's enslaved population continued to cherish the idea that Christian baptism was a route to freedom, even basing a rebellion in 1730 on the idea that baptized slaves were to be freed by a proclamation of King George II. Enslaved people became the most articulate and dedicated advocates of their own Christianity, reaffirming the unity of mankind and condemning the planter class, all in terms that would have warmed Godwyn's heart had he lived to witness it. By the end of the eighteenth century, a small but increasingly vocal group of white and black abolitionists revisited scripture and mustered versions of seventeenth-century ideas to fight slavery and for the first time define a fully developed idea of Christian abolitionism. The seventeenth century produced strategies for creating and maintaining race as well as the arguments against race that echoed even into the era of the civil rights movement. Understanding this dual (and dueling) role for Christianity in seventeenth-century Virginia should change how scholars frame debates about the historical origins of race as a way of defining and explaining human difference.

The discourse of religion and race in seventeenth-century Virginia might seem foreign to some readers, a mere artifact of the past with no present meaning. Yet understanding the creation of religious and racial categories is relevant today precisely because we have a tendency to dehistoricize these categories and deliberately obscure their past meanings and uses. Americans mute evidence of past grave injustices with upbeat narratives of the formation of an exceptional Christian nation destined to lead the world. The notion of a "Christian" nation flattens intense historical contests over what precisely it meant to be Christian and masks the ways in which categories such as Christian, heathen, black, and white were constructed to render certain groups of people powerless. The problems associated with this simplified past become painfully obvious when presidential candidates sign statements asserting that slavery was good for African-American families or contend that the founding generation "worked tirelessly" to outlaw slavery.[11] The end result is a powerful popular mythology that serves a political purpose but that crushes the ways in which religious and racial identities were contested in the past. This book historicizes these categories by showing who created them, how they were created, and who contested them.

In the aftermath of the tragedy of September 11, 2001, some Americans began to conflate religious and racial categories in ways that are reminiscent of this past. The present propensity to define all Muslims as Arab, for example, conflates specific ideas about religion and race in order to imagine the other as insurmountably different. And the notion that religion is hereditary and predictive of character and behavior persists as well. In August 2010 the Reverend Franklin Graham spoke about President Barack Obama's religion: "I think the president's problem is that he was born a Muslim, his father was a Muslim. The seed of Islam is passed through the father like the seed of Judaism is passed through the mother. He was born a Muslim, his father gave him an Islamic name."[12] The persistent idea that religion is an essential characteristic, inborn, and determinant of future ideas and attitudes is the legacy of hereditary heathenism.

CHAPTER ONE

English Christians among
the Blackest Nations

Like many financially struggling English gentlemen with literary am-
bitions, William Strachey believed he could recover his failing fortunes abroad. Strachey worked for the Levant Company in Constanti-
nople, and he might also have spent time in Ireland. His experiences as a
scribe and secretary eventually led him to employment with the Virginia
Company.[1] Strachey ventured across the Atlantic in 1609, where he lived
and worked in Jamestown for more than two years. In one of his sonnets,
Strachey reminded the "the Lords of the Councell of Virginea" not to
neglect their Christian duty while pursuing colonization:

> imitate your maker in his will
> To have his truth in blackest nations shine
> What had you beene, had not your Ancestors
> Begunne to you, that make their nobles good?
> And where white Christians turne in maners Mores [Moors]
> You wash Mores white with sacred Christian bloud.[2]

Strachey's sonnet, laden with metaphors drawn from his experiences
in the Ottoman Empire and from a Protestant understanding of salvation, signified in verse the English view of their mission to New World.
They were obligated to bring Christianity to a heathen people, a responsibility English people assumed when their own ancestors turned away
from their primitive heathenism and embraced Christianity. Strachey's
description of the heathens ("blackest nations") played on darker skin
tone and what he thought of as their black, devil-captivated souls. The
English, with their comparatively pale skin and even whiter souls, would
be judged not merely by the importation of new commodities and the
generation of fantastic profits but also by the number of heathen people they would save—or wash white. Though at its beginning Strachey's
poem suggested that phenotype predicted the state of one's soul, at the

end Strachey negated that proposition by reminding readers that English Christians could backslide into heathenism. Everyone—"white Christians" and those among the "blackest nations"—could be saved by "sacred Christian bloud." Strachey's poem was a reminder of the potential Christianity of all humans as well as a special statement of English Christian obligations in the New World.

As Strachey's pious sonnet indicates, the impulse to colonize the New World was an expression of English religiosity. In the late sixteenth and early seventeenth centuries, English Christianity functioned simultaneously as a locus of national unity and as a site for intense argumentation and division. English people debated their beliefs in a world threatened by Catholicism in Europe and Islam in the Mediterranean basin. What the English believed at home critically influenced how they thought about the people they found in the New World, where heathens were both an attraction and perhaps a potential threat. In its sermons and documents, the Virginia Company developed an optimistic policy that, like William Strachey's poem, encouraged adventurers and settlers to think of Indians as potential Christians. Most English adventurers believed that the heathens they met in the New World could be made to see the error of their ways and convert to the true faith. What the English believed about themselves, and about Indians, shaped their encounters with Indians in the early years of English settlement in the New World.

What, then, did English people in the early seventeenth century believe? Given the intense and heartfelt debates that surrounded questions of Christian practice and belief in early modern England, the answer is complicated. These debates took place during a confusing time for English Christianity. England had been contentedly Catholic until Henry VIII's break from Rome; it spent the middle decades of the sixteenth century vacillating between Protestantism and Catholicism.[3] Henry's son Edward VI moved English doctrine in a militantly evangelical direction, but his early death brought his Catholic half sister Mary I to the throne. Mary formally reconciled England with Rome and married the Spanish Catholic king Philip II. It was a dangerous time for committed Protestants. About three hundred Protestants were tried for treason and heresy and executed between 1555 and 1558, earning the queen the sobriquet "Bloody Mary," a violent image of Catholicism that proved useful and evocative for Protestant pamphleteers during the next several centuries.[4] In a time before any Europeans seriously advocated religious toleration, the English learned the difficulty of having a "national" church when rulers and subjects alike could not agree what form that church should take. Yet neither could anyone imagine a successful state that did not have religious uniformity.

In 1558 Mary was succeeded by her half sister Elizabeth I. Though not as unequivocally Protestant as her supporters would have liked, Elizabeth recognized the political benefits of resolving the religious question in England as quickly as possible. In 1559 her first Parliament approved the Act of Uniformity, making England Protestant again. Once Elizabeth had established her church, she supported it tenaciously, resisting the recusancy of English Catholics and further purification by the hotter sort of Protestant. While debates about salvation occupied theologians, there were more public arguments about church government, vestments, and the form of services. Hot Protestants, or puritans as they came to be called, denounced the episcopacy, adornments in churches, ornate vestments, and rote preaching as popish corruptions. Nevertheless, Elizabeth's settlement muted theological controversy by enforcing outward uniformity of practice and church attendance while allowing considerable freedom of conscience and individual nuances of belief. James I resisted change to the structure and doctrine of the Church of England just as his predecessor had.

Worship in the Church of England centered on the forms and readings prescribed in the Book of Common Prayer and on sermons from the *Book of Homilies*, both of which made their way in Virginia as well. The Book of Common Prayer's most important purpose was to bind the realm together in one uniform and universal form of worship, declaring that "now from henceforth all the whole realm shall have but one use." The prayer book set readings and ritual (such as marriage and baptism) for the entire church, and the 1559 edition even had a thirty-year almanac to make sure everyone stayed on schedule.[5] The prayer book provided readings for every Sunday and ritual for all religious occasions, and the *Book of Homilies* provided twenty-one sermons for ministers to read cyclically. Some of these approved sermons were doctrinal in nature, such as "Of the Salvation of Mankind," which presented a carefully worded mainstream Protestant soteriology of salvation by faith alone (but did not embrace the Calvinist doctrine of predestination). Others were more prosaic. One was called "An Homilie for repayring and keeping cleane, and comely adorning of churches" (surely absenteeism was at a record high the Sunday that sermon was read). The Book of Common Prayer and the *Book of Homilies* were critical to creating a national church and to ensuring uniformity of doctrine and cultivating subjects' spiritual obedience.

Because the Protestant English embraced the idea that each believer should read and study the Bible enthusiastically, many English families kept a Bible at home. The most popular was the Geneva Bible, an English translation of the Old and New Testament that Marian exiles living in that city had prepared. It appeared in London a year after Elizabeth took the throne. The Geneva Bible went through some 130 editions and remained the most popular household Bible for more than a century, with perhaps half a million copies printed and sold. (It also eventually proved popular in Scotland despite its English origins.)[6] It prefaced each book of the Bible with explanatory notes that were, given the location of its composition, unabashedly Calvinist in nature. The opening of the Geneva Bible's rendition of the Epistle of Paul to the Romans proclaimed that "forasmuche as of his fre mercie he electeth some to be saved, and of his juste judgement rejecteth others to be damned, as appeareth by the testimonies of the Scriptures." It was an overt endorsement of the doctrine of predestination that went beyond the moderate Protestant position endorsed in the *Book of Homilies*. Elizabeth's bishops attempted to forestall the spread of such an obviously Calvinist position on salvation by producing the more mainstream Bishop's Bible of 1568, although it never gained in popularity compared to the Geneva Bible.

The state feared Catholicism more than radical Protestantism and declared that priests could not legally enter the country and that Catholic seminaries were forbidden. The law required frequent attendance at Church of England services. Elizabeth's church rooted out Catholicism whenever it found it, executing 131 priests and 60 lay Catholics between 1581 and 1603.[7] In 1603 there were still as many as forty thousand Catholics living in England, most of whom wanted to be good subjects, but who were also automatically suspect because England had long been at war with Catholic Spain. The introduction to the Geneva Bible helped popularize English anti-Catholicism, calling on the English to stop the "horrible backsliding and falling away from Christ to Antichrist" that had begun under Mary's reign.[8] The association of Catholicism with apocalyptic rhetoric did not ease with the passage of time, for the English considered Catholics generally responsible for some of the greatest threats to the country. Two plots in particular, Spain's infamous invasion by Armada in 1588 and the Gunpowder Plot of 1605, provided more than enough grist for the Protestant conspiracy theory mill. Residual

Catholicism helped create and maintain an environment in which Englishmen self-identified as Protestants, and which united English people under the auspices of one Protestant church. These circumstances elided theological differences between puritans and the mainstream Church of England. Nearly every English Protestant was anti-Catholic, some rabidly so. All combatants in the religious debate saw the value of unity in the church. That was the face the nascent Church of England presented to the world, even as fissures strained it from within.

While it is possible to write about an English "nation" whose complex identities were to a certain degree melded by a common embrace of Protestantism, broadly defined, there is little accompanying evidence of a sense of ethnic or racial superiority.[9] Though many English people believed they had received their faith from the ancient Britons' pure and ancient church, this did not translate into an exclusive church. English people saw their church as a unifier of peoples, for they also believed that the purity of their church and the rightness of its forms and beliefs meant that the English church was the inheritor of God's covenant with Israel. Yet God's covenant with Israel's English heirs was not limited to them and could be shared. The English believed that the rest of the world held the universal capability to become Christian, but that it was also England's responsibility to lead it to proper Christianity. The English considered themselves, controversies and all, to have the purest church, the one closest to the apostolic church memorialized in the New Testament. This overriding sense muted controversies among English Protestants. English Protestantism was as expansive as it was muscular. It sought to evangelize the world, and saw a special and particular purpose in the English venture into the New World.[10]

English people also believed that their religion guaranteed the rights, privileges, and liberties they held so dear. The particular virtue of their country and religion was freedom from slavery as non-Christian (in the English experience, Muslim nations) and Catholic nations practiced it. The English viewed their church and religion as the source of the political liberties they enjoyed. Numerous legal scholars of the sixteenth and seventeenth centuries credited Christianity with the fall of villeinage and a return to pre-Norman Anglo-Saxon freedoms. English legal tradition also held that one could not enslave one's fellow Christians. Membership in the only true church, then, granted specific rights, including freedom from villeinage and enslavement. By implication, those who were not Christians in the English church had no such protections.[11]

Inclusion in this English body of Christ did not require English birth. In 1586 the English celebrated the concept of the universality of mankind and inclusiveness of their church with the conversion of Chinano "by birth a Turke, borne at Nigropontus, hertofore by profession a Saracen, addicted unto the superstitious lawe of Mahomet." In assessing England's religious victory in converting a Muslim, the minister Meredith Hanmer took it as a sign that the tide was turning in the battle against the "face of the earth in manner all covered with heathens, idolaters and false worshippers." England saw itself surrounded not only by false Christians (Catholics) but also by the avowedly non-Christian: "Christian religion is now couched in the North partes of the world, and so far that it seemeth (if we looke for fruits) all frozen." Hanmer reiterated that Christianity was a northern European and specifically an English characteristic throughout his account of the baptism of the "silly Turk." Chinano's conversion also served as his symbolic entrance into the English polity and showed how the English church could be a model for the rest of the world. "The professors (according unto the words of our Saviour) are now a little flock," Hanmer wrote, adding, "It is high time wee should earnestlie pray unto God, that hee wil enlarge his kingdome, that hee will open the eyes of Infidels, that he will direct Idolatrers in the true woorship." The English church was the "true worship" Hanmer had in mind.[12]

Converting Chinano also served a political purpose. Chinano had arrived in England via Francis Drake's West Indian adventures; Chinano, like many of his shipmates, had been liberated from Spanish-controlled Cartagena (present-day Venezuela). Though Chinano had lived among Spanish Catholics in South America for twenty-five years, he had not converted to Catholicism. That the English had convinced him to convert was quite an accomplishment; it showed the fundamental rightness of the English church and the misguided nature of the Spanish Catholic Church. Queen Elizabeth ordered that Chinano be returned to the Ottoman Empire, where presumably he would prepare the ground for further conversions. Chinano the Turk's conversion was a victory for the idea of a universal English church and was a propaganda tool to affirm the rightness of the English church against the perfidy of popery.[13]

Chinano was but one man, and the English were not looking east to the Ottomans but rather westward toward Ireland as the most logical place for spiritual and political conquest and for English expansion. Many English kings had laid claim to Ireland with various degrees of success, but it was Elizabeth who focused her attention there. Ireland remained a Catholic outpost on England's western flank, and therefore Elizabethans viewed its conquest as a geopolitical necessity. The English made it their policy to "civilize" Ireland, whose Gaelic Catholic inhabitants the English found barbarous and uncivilized. Church of England clergymen were instrumental in enforcing imperial Anglicization policies in Ireland, where they tried to introduce English language, dress, and diet. English policymakers experimented with relieving the Irish of the burden of their Catholicism as well as their uncivilized behavior. In the 1590s, English colonizers in Ireland mandated that the children of Catholic Irish luminaries attend the newly founded Trinity College Dublin so they could be educated in "English habit and religion."[14] Education in a college setting was a strategy English settlers and Virginia Company officials would attempt in Virginia as well. Despite the attention paid to the importance of education and civility in subduing the Irish, English conquistadors in Ireland frequently resorted to brute force. Humphrey Gilbert routinely beheaded his adversaries so as to "bring greate terrour to the people when thai sawe the heddes of their dedde fathers, brothers, children, kinsfolke, and friends lye on the grounde before their faces, as thei came to speake with the said collonell [Gilbert]." Though Elizabeth had expressly instructed her lieutenants to treat the Gaelic Irish kindly, her expansionist Protestant deputies were inclined to see the Irish as unregenerate pagans. One witness even claimed that the Gaelic Irish did not know about the sacrament of baptism or the immortality of the soul. This English encounter with a people they believed to be defiantly pagan did not go according to plan. The Irish did not quietly accede to English lordship, culture, or customs. The English viewed the Irish not as racially inferior but rather as culturally inferior—an ameliorable situation.[15]

The English turned a blind eye toward not only the bloody violence of the Irish conquest but also the mayhem in 1586 at Roanoke (which ended with the vicious beheading of the Indian leader Wingina), yet they were quite quick to criticize Spanish conquest and evangelization efforts.[16] They viewed Spanish colonization in the Americas as a gruesome business, an impression encouraged by the writings of the Spanish Dominican friar Bartolomé de las Casas, whose *Brevissima relación de la destrucción de las Indias* (1552) detailed Spanish cruelty toward the Indians. Las Casas's book appeared in English as *The Spanish Colonie* in 1583, spurring anti-Catholic and anti-Spanish sentiment. According to English observers, the Spanish and the Portuguese were cruel and corrupt colonizers who captured ignorant pagans for Catholicism. John Smith, later famous for his exploits in Virginia, described the conversion of some West Africans to Christianity as undertaken by Portuguese Catholics, who "sent for so many Priests and ornaments into Portugall, to solemnize their baptismes with such magnificence . . . that those poore Negros adored them as Gods, till the Priests grew to that wealth, a Bishop was sent to rule over them . . . which endangered to spoile all before they could bee reconciled."[17] Smith made a wider point about the inability of non-English Europeans to colonize and convert effectively. The English, Smith implied, could colonize and convert better than any other European country.

Almost all procolonization literature emphasized plans for stemming the Catholic tide and evangelizing Indians. In 1606 a member of the Virginia Company justified settlement to "deterr, or at least retard ye Spaniard from suddayne attempting us." Detractors warned that such an obvious challenge to the Spanish might create diplomatic trouble for King James, who had made peace with Spain in 1604. The company reiterated the threat posed by the Spanish, who had treated the Indians, "as Barbar's [barbarians], and therby Naturally slaves," and who had claimed "only a Magistracy, and Empire, by which he [the Spaniard] is allowed to remove such impediments, as they had agaynst ye knowledge of Religion." The Spanish, as illegitimate conquerors of the Americas, had mistreated the Indians and made claims to land and empire that could not be supported with religious justifications. The English fear of and disdain for continental Catholicism found an outlet in North America. Virginia was a bulwark for introducing Indians to true Christianity and for guarding against further Spanish Catholic expansion. Small wonder that several years later, another member of the Virginia Company congratulated some Virginia sailors in their recent capture of a Spanish vessel, noting that "the robbinge of the Spanyards (as beinge lyms of Antechrist) is great comended."[18]

England's Protestants drew from the Bible's apocalyptic descriptions of the Antichrist and ascribed its characteristics to Catholics. The Protestant controversialist George Abbot argued in 1604 that "*the Religion of the Papists* is not *that Religion which* Christ *ordained, or left to all generations,* but a meere profanation of his Word & Sacramentes, a horrible abomination, the service of Antichrist, idolatry, and superstition."[19] The prospect of colonizing Virginia suited Englishmen who wanted to extend the reach of the Protestant Church of England while simultaneously resisting Catholic encroachment in the Americas. Virginia's geographic position would hide the English from the Spanish in Florida and the Caribbean, while giving the English a safe stronghold on the vast North American continent from which they could harry the Spanish treasure fleets beating their way back from Mexico. The existence of Virginia and the presence of Englishmen there would restrain the "lyms of Antechrist."

Restraining Catholicism and evangelizing Indians were constant themes in Virginia colonization plans. Indians had once been civil beings and part of a godly community. The English believed in the monogenesis of human origins, as did most Europeans at the time. In the Judeo-Christian scriptural tradition, all human beings descended from Adam, whom God had made on the sixth day of creation. The notion of a united humanity with a single ancestor identified in scripture meant that all humans were related to one another, even if the connections had receded into the mists of the biblical past. It also meant that the English, with their particular brand of evangelical Protestant nationalism, considered themselves morally obliged to reclaim long-lost peoples to the true faith. To explain why some humans retained the proper knowledge of God and others did not, the English (and other Europeans) turned to scriptural tradition related in the book of Genesis about events after the Flood, which only Noah and his wife and their three sons and their wives survived. Noah's sons, Shem, Ham, and Japhet, had each inherited a portion of the postdiluvian world, although there was some disagreement among Christians as to which sons had gone where. Most theologians agreed that Shem's descendants settled Asia, Ham's descendants settled Africa, and Japhet's descendants settled Europe. This left the native peoples of North and South America in a biblical limbo. Because the Bible made no mention of the Americas or the people living there, English theologians decided that Indians must be the descendants of one or another of Noah's sons. William Strachey decided the Indians must be among the descendants of Ham.[20]

The account of the creation in Genesis held sway in an age that was prescientific and lacked modern understandings of biology, genetics, and evolution. During the seventeenth century any espousal of the polygenist origins of mankind was met at best with skepticism and at worst with outright hostility or accusations of heresy among both Catholics and Protestants.[21] The French theorist Isaac La Peyrère posited in 1655 that there had been human beings before Adam and Eve; he used New

Testament sources rather than the standard account in Genesis as his evidence. La Peyrère's work appeared in English in London in two parts in 1655 and 1656, where his so-called pre-Adamite position was roundly savaged by interregnum English intelligentsia. As the Virginia Company was preparing to send its first expedition to the New World, its paid preachers would not embrace heretical polygenist notions of human origins. The English who arrived in Virginia were firm believers in the unity of mankind.[22]

England's expansionist Protestants justified their presence in the New World in explicitly monogenist terms. The puritan minister, controversialist, and Virginia Company supporter William Crashaw affirmed monogenesis and the implicit relationship between Englishmen and Indians in a published sermon in 1610. Crashaw claimed that "the same God made them as well as us, of as good matter as he made us, gave them as perfect and good soules and bodies as us . . . so then they are our brethren, wanting not *title to Christ*, but the *knowledge of Christ*."[23] Crashaw put the best face possible on English colonization in Virginia by publicly affirming that the Indians were just like the English, but removed from the church by means of distance and ignorance. North America's native peoples were among the long-lost descendants of Noah, which for the English meant that they had once known God and that they could and should know God again. Crashaw saw the redemption of Indians as "plainly a necessarie dutie, for every christian to labour the conversion and confirmation of others that are not."[24] No wonder the printed sermon's cover dedication quoted Daniel 12:3: "They that turne many to righteousness, shall shine as the starres for ever and ever," an explicit reference to the rightness of converting the Indians.[25]

The necessity of reclaiming Indians for God and for membership in an anti-Catholic Anglo-Indian commonwealth drove English interest in the origins of Indians and their place in the postdiluvian Noachic dispersal. They asked Indians questions about where they had come from and received sensational yet vaguely familiar answers, perversions of the creation story in Genesis. Thomas Hariot, the mathematician and natural philosopher and client of the famous sponsor of overseas colonies Walter Ralegh, was among the first Englishmen to discuss Indian origins with actual Indians. While visiting Ralegh's abortive colony at Roanoke in the late 1580s, Hariot gathered detailed information from Roanoke Indians about their origins. When he published his account in London in 1590, he noted that the Indians had some religion, "which although it be farre from the truth, yet beyng as it is, there is hope it may bee the easier and sooner reformed," a subtle appeal to the familiarity of Indians and to their ability to be redeemed. Hariot went on to note that Indians believed in "one onely chiefe and great God," a sop to the monotheists looking for a cognate with the Christian God, though Indians worshiped several other "pettie goddes." These gods first "made waters, out of which by the gods was made all diversitie of creatures that are visible or invisible." While not quite the biblical account of creation, this was not far from the details of human origins contained in Genesis, which might have been what prompted Hariot to assert that Indian religion would be easily reformed.[26]

For Hariot, the Indians' creation story lost its cognate status when the Indians told him how mankind came to be: "For mankind they say a woman was made first, which by the woorking of one of the goddes, conceived and brought foorth children: And in such sort they say they had their beginning." In a cultural and religious background that stressed the secondary status of women derived from biblical teaching about Adam and Eve, the idea that a woman had been created first would have been difficult for Hariot to accept. Hariot also noted that the Indians could not say "how manie yeeres or ages have passed since . . . [having no] recordes of the particularities of times past, but onelie tradition from father to sonne."[27] The lack of record keeping was especially difficult for the English to understand, because they came from a religious tradition in which calculating the age of the world and the genealogy of mankind was a spiritually and intellectually important project. (The Geneva Bible ended with a chronological table entitled "A Perfite Supputation of the yeres and times from Adam unto Christ, proved by the Scriptures, after the collection of divers autors.")[28] Nevertheless, Hariot believed that the Roanokes, having witnessed both English piety and English technology and learning, would be able and willing to convert to Christianity, bringing the newly colonized region the stability and security it required.[29]

William Strachey was less understanding than Hariot of Indian origin myths. In 1610 the company instructed Strachey to write a report on conditions in the colony and its future possibilities. He returned to London in 1612 where he worked for some years on his manuscript *Historie of Travell into Virginia Britania*. Although it did not see publication in his lifetime (it did circulate in manuscript), and although it borrowed heavily from previously available accounts of the Jamestown colony, Strachey's *Historie* contains many useful and informative accounts of life in Virginia. In one of the most revealing episodes in the *Historie*, Strachey related an experience he had with an Indian leader aboard a ship sailing around the Chesapeake around Christmas in 1610. The Indian, Iopassus [Japazaws], observed one of the English sailors reading a Bible and asked his interpreter, a young English boy named Henry Spelman, to explain to him what it was. After examining a woodcut in the Bible depicting the creation in Genesis and hearing Spelman's explanation of it, Iopassus related the Powhatan story of creation in return:

[W]e have (said he) 5. godes in all our chief god appeares often unto us in the likewise of a mighty great Hare, the other 4. have no visible shape . . . our god who takes upon this shape of a Hare conceaved with himself how to people this great world, and with what kynd of Creatures, and yt is true (said he) that at length he divised and made divers men and women and made provision for them to be kept up yet for a while in a great bag, now there were certayne spirritts . . . which came to the Hares dwelling place . . . and hadd perseveraunce of the men and women, which he had put into that great bag, and they would have had them to eate, but the godlike Hare reproved those Caniball Spirritts and drove them awaie . . . that godlike hare made the water and the fish therein and the land and a greate deare . . . and then he opened the great bag, wherein the men and the women were, and placed them upon the earth, a man and a woman in one Country and a man and a woman in another country. and so the world tooke his first begynning of mankynd.

The young English interpreter was reluctant to press for more details and feared he would offend Iopassus with further questions. Although Strachey recorded Powhatan mythology with interest, he lent the tale no credence, criticizing the ordering and logic of the storyteller: "Nowe yf the boy [Spelman] had asked him [Iopassus] of what he [the Hare god] made those men and women and what those spirritts more particularly had bene and so had proceeded in some order, they [the Indians] should have made yt hang togither the better."[30]

Perhaps Strachey wanted the Indian creation myth to bear a more recognizable resemblance to the Judeo-Christian story in Genesis, and thus the story would have "hanged togither the better" for him. The story might have served the Powhatans as an explanation for the diversity of human appearances and customs. Although the great Hare made all people, he placed them in separate "countries." Such a tale bore some resemblance to the monogenist position preferred by English intellectuals and theologians of Strachey's time and also served to explain how the globe came to be peopled. (Strachey no doubt would have preferred that there was a flood somewhere in the story.) Strachey found Iopassus's tale heathenish, heretical, and definitely uncivilized, but not necessarily beyond the reach of amendment.

Unsatisfied with the Indians' account of their origins, Strachey sought to use the biblical stories of human creation and dispersal in Genesis to explain where the Indians had come from. He admitted it was a mystery how the Indians had come to the New World, "without furniture (as may be questioned) of shipping, and meanes to tempt the Seas," and also worried over how the American continents had been separated from Europe, Asia, and Africa, and how these continents had come to be populated with animals and plants. On this question he referred readers to the Spanish Jesuit José de Acosta's *Historia Natural y Moral de las Indias*, which appeared in Spanish in 1590 and in an English translation in 1604. Acosta lived and worked in Lima, and his observations on the origins of Indians influenced not only Spanish commentators but also English ones—despite his papist background. Strachey's advice to read Acosta suggests his tacit agreement with Acosta's hypothesis that nomadic Indians had wandered into the Americas via a land bridge at the Bering Strait. Acosta recognized Indians' nomadic qualities and had inquired into the origins of the Inca and other native groups under Spanish control, believing that Indian mythologies would shed some light on how they came into the Americas. Acosta further theorized that Indians might also be the descendants of Noah's son Japhet, from whom Europeans also supposedly descended.[31]

Strachey thought it more likely that the Indians were the descendants of Noah's son Ham, for "yt is observed that Cham [Ham] and his famly, were the only far travellors [among Noah's descendants], and Straglers into divers and unknowne countries, searching, exploring and sitting downe in the same."[32] Hamitic rather than Japhetic descent was a more plausible explanation for the long wanderings and perceived persistent nomadic predilections of American Indians. Indian descent from Ham also made the most sense because contemporary biblical exegesis connected Ham's descendants with a wide range of geographic locations in Africa and Asia, to which Strachey had no trouble adding the Americas as well. The plausible biblical explanation set Strachey's mind at ease on the humanity of Indians, their distant kinship with the English, their

Genesis, Geneva Bible, 1589. This illustration might be the one William Strachey used to explain the Christian creation story to Iopassus. The woodcut was probably intended to give semiliterate or illiterate Englishmen a sense of the story, but one wonders what Iopassus took from it. Courtesy of The Huntington Library, San Marino, California.

potential Christianity, and their potential membership in an Anglo-Indian commonwealth.[33]

Associating Indians with descent from Ham also connected them with a curse. Strachey acknowledged this idea when he wrote about Indian origins, noting that, after Ham had mocked his father Noah's nakedness, he was forced to flee his father's wrath and in so doing "brought to mankynd . . . the Ignoraunce of the true worship of god . . . the Inventions of Hethenisme, and adoration of false godes and the Devill."[34] The so-called Curse of Ham is one of those bits of mythology that, while biblically opaque, existed in a variety of forms in several branches of European Christianity from the sixteenth through the nineteenth century. In the ninth chapter of Genesis, after Noah and his sons had departed from the ark, Noah planted a vineyard, got drunk from the wine, "and was uncovered in ye middes of his tent." Ham, observing his father's nakedness, mocked Noah, but Shem and Japhet covered him. When Noah awoke he knew Ham had mocked him "and said, Cursed be Canaan: a servant of servantes shall he be unto his brethren. He said moreover, Blessed be the Lord God of Shem, and let Canaan be his servant." (Canaan was Ham's son.)[35] Europeans used these few verses to concoct a "Curse of Ham" that not only explained aspects of human origins and diversity, including the darker skin colors of African people (and also sometimes Indians as well) but also served as a biblical justification for slavery.[36]

Medieval Christians most commonly associated the Curse of Ham with sin and heresy rather than with any particular physical attributes (such as skin color). They also associated charges of sexual immorality with the Hamitic curse, attributing the strange sexual behaviors and fleshly sins of non-Europeans to a biblical origin. Noah's curse upon the descendants of one of his sons alienated them from God and made them susceptible to sinful cultural practices.[37] These medieval manifestations of the Curse of Ham were occasionally associated with skin color, as some early medieval commentators associated darkness of skin with sexual license.[38] By the sixteenth century, as Europeans came into greater contact with sub-Saharan Africans, the curse was sometimes associated with darker skin color as well as questionable sexual behavior, and the curse's explanatory power manifested itself in physical ways as well as spiritual ways.

The English explorer and writer George Best's observations about blackness and the Curse of Ham were probably the earliest widely circulated explanations for physical difference in England. He wrote in 1578 that Ham had actually violated Noah's order to abstain from sexual relations while on the Ark and, as a consequence, "a sonne should be borne whose name was Chus [Canaan], who not onely it selfe, but all his posteritie after him should be so blacke & lothsome, that it might remaine a spectacle of disobedience to all the world." Even the briefest of looks at Genesis, as it was translated in the Geneva Bible, indicates that there is no biblical basis for Best's assertion of the sexual aspect of Noah's curse on Ham. Nor is there any scriptural basis for Best's other claim that the blackness of Africans was caused by an "infection of bloud" stemming from the curse.[39] Best was well known for his exploits in the Arctic, not in Africa or the more southerly parts of America, and had probably never encountered Africans, yet here he took the medieval association of Ham's descendants with sexual misbehavior and attached it adroitly to blackness and slavery. Ham's heathenish transgression doomed his descendants not only to perpetual paganism but also to a physical mark of sin (blackness) and to servitude. An Englishman named Richard Jobson who had traveled in West Africa noted in 1623 that "these people originally sprung from the race of Canaan, the sonne of Ham," but as medieval theologians had done, Jobson surmised that the curse had more to do with sexuality. (Jobson thought that Ham's exposure of Noah's genitals had resulted in his posterity suffering from "such members as are after a sort burthensome unto them.") Jobson reaffirmed monogenesis and a common biblical heritage; the Africans he observed had a "wonderous reference to the leviticall law" and had traditions of Adam and Eve, the flood, and Moses.[40]

Best's comments more likely represented a fringe interpretation of the biblical Curse of Ham.[41] Best was probably an innovator in this type of exegesis in limiting the Curse of Ham to sub-Saharan Africans (Ethiopians as he called them) and in implying the curse's effects were both hereditary and unredeemable. Samuel Purchas, a chronicler of England in the New World, collecting and publishing writing about Africa and the Americas and their peoples, explicitly rejected the notion of the Hamitic genealogy's association with hereditary sinfulness, blackness, and servitude. Instead, he pleaded for the unity of humanity, claiming that, "without any more distinction of colour, Nation, language, sexe, condition, all may bee *One* in him that is ONE, *and only blessed for ever.*"[42] Purchas's position was much closer to what most Englishmen believed. The curse was one of heathenism and ignorance of God, which caused Ham's descendants' strange pagan behaviors. Best's scribblings aside, few members of England's intellectual and religious elite believed Ham's descendants could not be brought back into the fold. Nevertheless, Best's writings suggest that ideas about difference, religion, and heredity were on some English minds.

Strachey sided with earlier medieval interpretations of the curse that placed more emphasis on the heathenish practices that cropped up in the Hamitic line. Ham, Strachey explained, had not learned properly from his father "the knowledge and prescrybed worship of the eternall god, the god of his fathers . . . we may conclude, that from Cham, and his tooke byrth and begynning the first universall Confusion and diversity, which ensued afterwardes throughout the whole world, especially in divine and sacred matters." Strachey noted that the descendants of Shem and Japhet had not suffered such spiritual indignities.[43] Ham had neglected to properly teach his descendants, after having been cursed from Noah's sight and destined to wander the globe, and also wandered from the true religion and invented heathenish practices. Strachey applied the Curse of Ham to Indians, but saw it primarily as a cultural curse. The Indians were cursed with ignorance of the true religion, which led to their pagan idolatries and uncivilized customs. Strachey, unlike George Best, did not associate the Curse of Ham with any hereditary and unchangeable physical defects. The curse therefore functioned as a powerful argument in favor of evangelism and the potential Christianity of Indians, rather than as a condemnation to eternal heathenism. Despite the curse of heathenism, Indians were not destined to labor under the Devil's ministrations forever. The English could and should redeem them, show them the error of their ways, and restore them to the true faith.

Strachey maintained that "there is an infused kind of divinities and extraordinary (appointed that it shall be so by the King of kings) to such who are his ymedyate instruments on earth (how wretched soever otherwise under the curse of misbelief and infidelity)."[44] The Indians were potential Christians, having been "infused" with spiritual knowing all along. They merely needed the English to explain to them the error of their ways and they would discover the true path. Strachey endeavored to help them in this project. He learned something of the language, creating a small dictionary, which he appended to the manuscript he sent back to the Virginia Company, perhaps thinking later missionaries would find it useful. "All the injury that we purpose unto them," he wrote, "is but the amendment of these horrible heathenisms, and the reduction of them to the aforesaid manly duties, and to the knowledg . . . of that

God who must save both them and us." The Reverend Alexander Whitaker, who ministered to both English and Indian populations in Virginia, agreed with Strachey's formulation, noting both the Indians' Adamite ancestry and that in the Indians "there bee remaining so many footsteps of Gods image."[45] The Indians were potential Christians both physically and spiritually. The Indians' potential Christianity was not merely an English Protestant conceit. English Jesuits settling in Maryland in the early 1630s also observed the Indians' potential Christianity and Israelite ancestry. Father Andrew White noted in 1634 that "we perceive they [Indians] have notice by tradition of Noah his flood."[46]

In the observations of a company secretary, a trained Church of England minister, and a French-trained English Jesuit, Indians and English alike were cut from the same human and religious cloth. The Indians merely needed to learn better. The problem was not that the Indians did not have religion or that they appeared to be somehow averse to Christianity or incapable of understanding it. The problem was rather how to activate Indians' potential Christianity—conferred by their descent from Noah and Ham—and thereby achieve their conversion. The cognitive dissonance between praise of Indians' potential Christianity as reflected in some of their beliefs and criticism of some of the Indians' more heathenish practices exposes some of the confusion the English experienced when trying to observe, define, and categorize Indian beliefs. The bonds of Noachic brotherhood bridged the intellectual gap between English views of Indians as horrible heathens and devil worshipers and English views of Indians as misguided Hamitic exiles and potential Christians.

The English carefully documented evidence of the Indians' potential Christianity, as measured by Hebraic survivals in their religious practices and in their civil governance. Even among the Indians' vile devil-worshiping practices, the English thought they could discern yet more evidence of a distant proto-Christian past. Thomas Hariot had first noted Indian beliefs about the immortality of the soul from the native people at Roanoke. "They beleeve also in the immortalitie of the soul, that after this life as soone as the soule is departed from the bodie according to the workes it hath done, it is eyther carried to heaven the habitacle of gods, there to enjoy perpetuall blisse and happinesse, or els to a great pitte or hole . . . there to burne continually."[47] Finding such a Judeo-Christian morality among the Indians was no doubt reassuring for Hariot and his compatriots. The English who arrived at Jamestown gathered slightly different information about coastal Algonkian views about life after death.

Virginia Company leader Gabriel Archer's investigations revealed that "they account after death to goe into an other world pointing eastward to the Element [the sun]."[48] John Smith had the opposite take on Indians' belief in life after death, thinking that "their Werowances and Priestes which they also esteeme *Quiyoughcoshughes*, when they are dead, doe goe beyond the mountaines towardes the settings of the sun. . . . But the common people they suppose shall not live after death."[49] Other accounts suggested that souls in the afterlife eventually aged and died as humans do but were then reborn into future generations of Powhatans. That the tricksome werowances should have immortality and that ordinary Indians should not was anathema to the English but formed a basis from which the English could teach the Christian theology of salvation and life after death.[50] Strachey proclaimed the Indians' "error" to be no "more Hethenous then our Ath[e]ists . . . well may these poore Heathen be pytied and pardoned untill they shalbe taught better."[51]

The English also based their faith in the potential Christianity of Indians not only on the Indians' genealogy and evidence of past proper belief but also on their understanding of England's own history of conversion from heathenism and savagery to Christian civility. The English, Strachey noted, had once been heathens, but had been saved first by the civilizing influence of the Romans and then later by Christian missionaries sent by the pope to convert the heathen English. He opened the *Historie* with a piece of his verse:

> ÆcclesiÆ et Reipub [Rei Publicae]
> Wild as they are, accept them, so were we
> To make them civill, will our honour bee
> And if good workes be the effectes of mindes,
> That like good Angells be, let our designes
> As we are Angli, make us Angells too
> No better work can Church or statesman doe.[52]

The title translates roughly as "Church and Commonwealth," and the verse mapped the relationship between the English and Virginia's Indian population as Strachey thought it should be. In his formula, English people and Indians would come together as a church (meaning the corpus of believers) to form a workable polity, a commonwealth. "Wild as they are," the English mission in the New World was to civilize its inhabitants, bringing English norms—including government and religion, which Strachey saw as intertwined—to primitive groups. Strachey reminded readers that the English had been just as wild once ("so were we"). Strachey portrayed the English as angels; they had a divine mission to accomplish in the settling of Virginia, but the word is also a pun on "Angles," the pagan Germans Strachey understood had settled England.[53] While few historians would ever dream of describing European conduct in the Americas as angelic, Strachey expressed in this bit of rhyme important perceptions of the possibilities of cultural interaction in the New World. Strachey's Indians and English were on the same footing: the English had to "accept them." Proper religion brought by English "Angells" would "make them civill." Strachey's view of Indians emphasized their potential Christianity, and like the Angles and native Britons of old, both groups could live together peacefully in a mutually beneficial commonwealth. It was not a racialized view of life in the New World, and it anticipated a utopian commonwealth in the wilderness.

Strachey did not think the conversion of Indians would take long. Everywhere he looked in the New World he saw familiar sights, to which he attributed the Indians' potential Christianity. Some social and religious aspects of the society of Powhatan's people derived from ancient British ones, because an exiled Welsh prince attempted to teach the natives Christianity in the twelfth century. Other, stranger customs were "Turkish" in nature. "Howbeit his [Powhatan's] ordinary correction, is to have an offender, whome he will only punish, and not put to death, to be beaten with Cudgells as the Turks doe."[54] These barbaric practices, including polygamy (another Turkish aspect of Indian society, according to Strachey), were actually a point in the Indians' favor, since the English understood that the Turks could convert to Christianity. Strachey's travels in the Ottoman Empire probably explain his willingness to compare Indian practices with Turkish ones, but they also helped him see the Indians as redeemable. Strachey knew that individual Turks (Turks was a general term for Muslims anywhere along the Mediterranean rim) could be persuaded to leave their pagan worship and convert to the true religion; presumably Indians could as well.

Alexander Whitaker, also observing a form of proto-Christianity in Indian culture, noted that "they have a rude kinde of Common-wealth, and rough governement, wherein they both honour and obey their Kings, Parents, and Governours, both greater and lesse." Whitaker's observation would have been especially important to English colonizers expecting to form their own commonwealth, with Indians eventually taking their place as members. The Indians also had all the marks of Christian virtue: "Murther is a capitall crime scarce heard of among them: adultery is most severely punished, and so are their other offences."[55] He envisioned a plantation in which Indians and English lived together in Christian harmony. The potential for an Anglo-Indian Christian commonwealth existed, and he thought that the English had a responsibility to encourage it. Like Strachey, Whitaker imbued his words with a sense of possibility, as well as a lessening of spiritual differences between Indians and Englishmen. English cultural and political forms would dominate any such English and Indian Christian commonwealth. English settlers were willing to admit their Indian neighbors' potential Christianity, but there was little admirable about Indian society that the English could absorb.

Whitaker also emphatically refuted all English claims that the Indians were incapable of understanding Christianity and therefore incapable of true conversion: "But if any of us should misdoubt that this barbarous people is uncapable of such heavenly mysteries, let such men know that they are farre mistaken in the nature of these men [Indians]," Whitaker scolded. "Let us not thinke that these men are so simple as some have supposed them: for they are . . . quicke of apprehension." Whitaker's pamphlet, the propagandistic *Good Newes from Virginia*, made no mention of the colony's disciplinary troubles among its English residents or its failure to turn a profit. Instead, Whitaker reaffirmed the kinship ties between the English and the Indians: "One God created us, they [Indians] have reasonable soules and intellectuall faculties as well as wee; we all have Adam for our common parent: yea, by nature the condition of us both is all one."[56] Other observers had also noticed that Virginia's Indians were certainly capable of learning Christianity as well. Gabriel Archer noted that the Powhatans he met were "a very witty and ingenious people, apt both to understand and speake our language."[57] English assessments of Indians' intellect were quite optimistic about quick returns in numbers converted. Physically, the Indians even looked like the English. Although the later sensitivity to skin color and complexion was less evident in the early seventeenth century, many observers were careful to note that although the Powhatans dyed their skin and tattooed it, their "tawny skynne" was not so at birth; "they are borne white," wrote John Smith.[58]

The intellectual world of English colonial planners, ministers, and settlers was not fraught with protoracial sensibilities about the denizens of the New World. English people approached Indians as distant reflections of themselves; as primitive people, to be sure, but not as irredeemable pagans. The company's elite and educated settlers drew on a complex theology and a worldview that stressed the unity of mankind and the obligations of Englishmen to recover Indians for Christianity. Though English people were in the grips of their own religious ferment, their Protestant identity shaped how the Virginia Company made policies to acculturate and convert Indians during the initial years of settlement. Yet those years were far from peaceful. The Indians' potential Christianity and the English settlers' own commitment to their Christian beliefs would be tested. In a theater of war, struggle, and starvation, intellectual attachments to monogenesis and common creation mattered little to people concentrating on raw survival. In England's New Canaan on the James River, English doubts about Indians' ability to become Christian awakened protoracialist ideas that suggested Indians were not the close relatives they were supposed to be.

CHAPTER TWO

The Rise and Fall of the Anglo-Indian Christian Commonwealth

The Virginia Company's founding documents emphasized the importance of converting Indians. In its 1606 charter, the crown endorsed "propagating of Christian religion to suche people, as yet live in darkenesse and myserable ignorance of the true knowledge and worshippe of god."[1] This English charter, unlike Spanish charters, did not make colonization contingent on attempts to evangelize native peoples.[2] The English assumed that conversion would be a consequence of colonization. Nevertheless, the king expected efforts to convert, noting that such attempts would be to "the glorrie of hys divyne maiestie." Kind treatment and evangelization of the Indians were points of honor for the English monarch and an explicit rebuke of the Spanish Catholic slaughter of Indians. Conversion would also establish the Church of England's bona fides as the true church and rightful inheritor of God's covenant with Israel. To implement its policies, the company issued "Instructions for Government" mandating that colonists "well entreate those salvages and heathen people . . . [to] the true word and service of God and Christian Faith." Good relations with the Indians would result in the Indians being "sooner drawne to the true knowledge of God, and ye Obedience of us, our heires and successors.[3] The English envisioned a commonwealth in which the Indians would be unequal but willing participants. Indians' conversions would guarantee their cooperation and subservience. Additional advice, while cautioning company leaders in Virginia to be aware of the military dangers posed by Indians, also required them to "have Great Care not to Offend the naturals if You Can Eschew it."[4]

Conversion meant both a knowledge and an acceptance of the Christian God, as mainstream English Christians would describe it, and an acceptance of English government and culture.[5] These two aspects went hand in hand for members of the Virginia Company, who believed that those who assumed the trappings of English civility would soon thereafter convert to Christianity. Successful conversion of the Indians and the economic viability of the colony were inextricably linked. It would be easier for the English to settle and use the land if the Indians were Christian allies and lesser partners in a commonwealth rather than heathen hostiles. Conversion, then, benefited heathen Indians and Christian English—souls would be saved and commercial exchange would prosper, with spiritual and material wealth for all. In 1609 the Reverend William Crashaw preached the connection between conversion and profit still more explicitly, claiming that "he that seekes only or principally spirituall things, God will reward him both with those spirituall and temporall things . . . so though we do not intend our profit in this action, yet, if wee intend Gods honor, and the conversion of soules, God will assuredly send us great profit."[6] Investment in the Virginia Company meant an investment in souls as well as commodities.

The people the company sent to accomplish this gargantuan task were a motley crew of noblemen, the younger sons and brothers of noblemen, wealthy merchants, politicians, adventurers, and gentlemen who hoped to reap riches from the New World. They were not the ideal Englishmen to entrust with the job of forming a working relationship with Indians, building a commonwealth, and earning a profit. Even the clergymen were not suited to the circumstances. The company commissioned Richard Hakluyt and Robert Hunt to minister to the Indians.[7] The ministers were chosen in part for their doctrinal purity. Edward Maria Wingfield had specifically requested Hunt as "a man not any waie to be touched with the rebellious humors of a popish spirit, nor blemished with ye least suspition of a facti[o]us scismatick."[8] Hakluyt, despite his enthusiasm for colonial projects, did not make the journey. Hunt did accompany the first expedition; "scandalous imputations" arose regarding his wife's infidelity and his own tryst with a maidservant. John Smith defended Hunt and his "godly exhortations," claiming that Hunt "quenched those flames of envie, and dissention" on board the ships.[9] Hunt likely volunteered for the voyage to escape his troubles at home, an indication of the difficulties the Virginia Company faced in prioritizing Indian conversion. Highly qualified ministers like Hakluyt avoided Virginia duty even as they advocated it, leaving ministerial disappointments like Hunt to lead the conversion efforts.[10]

That effort began with converting Indian place-names into English ones. On 29 April 1607, the English erected a cross on a promontory they called Cape Henry.[11] The English thus baptized a part of the New World with the name of James I's eldest son, and they commemorated their arrival with a traditional marker of English Christianity. While the English believed that in order to formally claim Virginia they would have to occupy and work the land, the name of an English prince and a symbol of English religion signaled their intent to possess the land. The cross and the name bound together the importance of English government and English religion, both marks of civility that the English wished to bring to the Indians inhabiting the New World. They also warned the Spanish, who had previously founded a mission in the Chesapeake and who had outposts not very far to the south in Florida, that England intended to stay.

Had they seen the cross on the land the English now called Cape Henry, the Algonkian Indians who hunted, fished, and farmed around the rim of the Chesapeake Bay would likely have recognized it and deduced its implications—for Wahunsonacock and his people had encountered Europeans before. In the early 1570s, the Spanish had sent a group of Jesuits to accompany a young Indian man who had been kidnapped a decade earlier. The Indian man, called Paquiquineo, claimed to want to convert his people to Christianity. Within a few months of arrival in the Chesapeake, Paquiquineo led an assault that killed the Jesuits and most of their Spanish servants. In retaliation, Spanish soldiers killed dozens of Indians the following year.[12] The polity ruled by the paramount chief Wahunsonacock (Powhatan) probably formed in response to the Spanish exploits forty years before. It is no wonder then, when the English came to Tsenacommacah in the spring of 1607, the Powhatans were immediately aware of their arrival and promptly attacked. While the first Powhatan attack on the English only hours after their arrival surprised the English, the Indians' action was the result of decades of planning in anticipation of the return of Europeans.

Wahunsonacock's people inhabited the area between the Potomac River and the south bank of the James River, as well as the southern portions of the Eastern Shore of what became Maryland and Virginia. Their territory ran west to the fall line (the point at which the land began to rise and the rivers were no longer navigable, around present-day Richmond). The area encompassed at least thirty groups under Wahunsonacock's control, although the Chickahominy remained independent of Wahunsonacock's authority while living in the midst of Powhatan territory. (The Chickahominy remained friendly with the Powhatans and probably exchanged wives with them.) The Powhatans called their lands

Tsenacommacah, probably meaning "our place." To the west, south, and north, the Powhatans alternately traded and exchanged raids with Iroquoian- and Siouan-speaking groups. The Powhatans retained extensive trading networks with Iroquoians, Siouans, and other Algonkians along the East Coast—which made it easy for them to gather and spread knowledge of Europeans as they acquired it.[13]

The Powhatans might not have seen the cross the English erected on Cape Henry, but they did see a cross that Captain Christopher Newport placed squarely in Powhatan lands during an exploratory venture at the end of May 1607. Newport set up a cross, inscribed with "Jacobus Rex. 1607" and his own name, and proclaimed James I king "with a greate showte." The Indians watched this ceremony with interest and probably some trepidation as well, with the memory of the last Europeans who visited and erected crosses in Tsenacommacah. Newport explained the cross by claiming that "the two Armes of the Crosse signifyed kyng Powatah [Powhatan] and himselfe [Newport] the fastening of it in the myddest was their united Leaug, and the shoute the reverence he dyd to Pawatah [Powhatan]." In Newport's telling, the cross became a symbol of alliance, not of conquest. It is unlikely the Indians were fooled by Newport's off-the-cuff explanation of the cross. Even the English witness who wrote this account felt the need to justify Newport's duplicitous explanation by belatedly adding that Newport had offered to help Powhatan conquer land further upstream belonging to the Siouan-speaking Monacans, which would at least make Newport's metaphor seem plausible to English readers.[14] Nevertheless, the ceremony of the cross was intended to do one thing—to assert James I's authority over the land. Newport also ordered the erection of another cross at the fall line of the James before he and his cohort returned to Jamestown, rechristening the Powhatans' river the James River.[15] The English scattered the religious symbol of their dominion and authority all over Tsenacommacah.

In these initial months the English carefully observed the Indians' religion and governance and evaluated the fitness of Wahunsonacock's people as potential Christians and as potential junior partners in the imagined commonwealth. Though the Indians were "naturally given to trechery," Gabriel Archer hoped that "[God] will make us authors of his holy will in converting them to our true Christian faith by his owne inspireinge grace and knowledge of his deity."[16] George Percy was less optimistic about the Indians' potential Christianity, describing the Indians as acting like "Wolves or Devils."[17] William White, who lived among the Indians for several months in an attempt to learn their language, reported that they engaged in human sacrifice. Though the English later learned that White had misinterpreted a coming of age ceremony, persistent rumors among the adventurers that the Indians practiced cannibalism made it more difficult to see the Indians even as lesser partners in a commonwealth.[18] The colonists also imagined the Indians were respectful and in awe of their religious beliefs and practices. Archer noted that "when they saw us in prayer they observed us with great silence and respect especially those to whome I had imparted the meaning of our reverence."[19] Archer assumed the Indians were impressed with the silent English devotions—a point in their favor. English prayers might have reminded Wahunsonacock and his people of earlier Spanish devotions. By the end of the summer of 1607, Jamestown was under sustained attack.

The fledgling colony at Jamestown seethed with trouble. Having brought few provisions with them and expecting the wholehearted and grateful cooperation of the Indians, the English found themselves short of food. Unable or unwilling to grow and gather their own food and obsessed with finding valuable mineral deposits, the English expected the Indians to provide for them. Their choice of location for their fort was also unfortunate; although the river was deep enough to allow their ships sufficient anchorage, at the end of the summer the water grew brackish and undrinkable.[20] Malnutrition and salt poisoning made the English more susceptible to diseases resulting from poor latrine facilities. Percy reported that the English "were destroyed with cruell diseases as Swellings, Flixes [fluxes], Burning Fevers, and by warres, and some departed suddenly, but for the most part they died of meere famine."[21] By September, only 40 of the original 104 men and boys remained alive—skeletons wandering the confines of the fort. As their numbers dwindled, panic and organizational chaos set in. In mid-September a group of men including John Smith deposed the colony's president, Edward Maria Wingfield. Changing the leadership did not make food appear out of nowhere, though; the Indians brought corn and other food to the starving invaders. Percy explained this critical generosity as an example of divine intervention. God had "put a terrour in the Savages hearts" so that they ceased attacking the English, and "it pleased God, after a while, to send those people which were our mortall enemies to releeve us with victuals."[22] A more likely explanation of Indian generosity lies in

Powhatan political culture. A gift of food, while generous, signaled the subordination of the recipient. For Wahunsonacock, giving food was an act of political supremacy.[23]

In November John Smith voyaged up the Chickahominy River to attempt to barter for corn and other provisions. At first the Indians seemed reluctant to engage in trade but Smith's mission was ultimately successful. He later wrote that "God (the absolute disposer of all heartes) altered their conceits, for now they were no lesse desirous of our commodities then we of their Corne." Smith attributed the Indians' sudden willingness to trade to divine providence—sentiments that would not have been out of place in later colonial settlements in New England. Yet Smith's successes came, as he acknowledged, among the Chickahominy, who were independent of Wahunsonacock's authority. It is likely that the Chickahominy thought to gain some advantage against Wahunsonacock by cultivating a good relationship with Smith and the English. With Jamestown now "indifferently wel provided with corne," Smith resumed pursuit of his true passion: making more discoveries in Virginia.[24] Accordingly, in early December 1607 Smith wandered up the James River in search of adventure.

What followed is one of the most iconic events in early American history: the Indians' ambush and captivity of Captain John Smith. "At each place I expected when they would execute me," Smith later recalled, "yet they used me with what kindness they could."[25] At length Smith was brought before Wahunsonacock himself, who was "richly hung with manie Chaynes of gret Pearles about his necke." Wahunsonacock was surrounded by his wives and his subordinate chiefs, a display of influence and political power Smith misinterpreted when he later referred to the young woman sitting at his side as a "wench."[26] There Smith spun as dishonest a tale as any the English ever told to the Indians, reminiscent of Newport's fib about the symbolism of the cross. When asked why the English had come to Tsenacommacah, Smith replied with a rambling yarn about fighting the Spanish, retreating into the bay, and searching for a passage to the Pacific. Though the tale of seeking a passage to the Pacific was indeed true, Smith's posturing intended only one outcome: Wahunsonacock's subordination to English authority.

Wahunsonacock's response was equally wily. The English were a threat, but they had commodities including metal knives, axheads, and guns that would greatly benefit Wahunsonacock's people. Wahunsonacock offered an alliance on his own terms. Smith thought the offer came from admiration and fear, but more likely Wahunsonacock sought advantages for his people in terms of trade. According to Smith, "hee desired mee to forsake Paspahegh, and to live with him upon his River, a Countrie called Capahowasicke: hee promised to give me Corne, Venison, or what I wanted to feede us, Hatchets and Copper wee should make him, and none should disturbe us."[27] Smith accepted the arrangement with alacrity and returned to Jamestown, but he probably did not understand the terms Wahunsonacock had proposed. What Wahunsonacock wanted was for Smith to live under his protection as a subordinate chief. Just as the English wanted to incorporate the Indians into an Anglo-Indian Christian commonwealth, Wahunsonacock proposed that the English would serve Indian authority and interests. In his later writings on events of late 1607 and early 1608, Smith claimed that a young daughter of Wahunsonacock he knew as Pocahontas saved him from execution; this story is almost certainly a fabrication. The paramount chief would not have risked Smith's life when Smith might be valuable to him; instead, the ceremony Smith recalled in 1624 might have been an adoption ceremony that sealed Wahunsonacock's bargain with the English.[28]

Both sides believed that a bargain had been struck and that the threat from the other had been lessened, if not neutralized. In January 1608 Christopher Newport and Smith made the journey upriver to visit Wahunsonacock with thirty or forty Englishmen accompanying them. Smith characteristically requested food, but Wahunsonacock "expected to have all these men [the English] lay their armes at his feet, as did his subjects."[29] The interaction, fraught with misunderstanding, betrayed how each side saw things. To the English, the Indians were purveyors of provisions; to Wahunsonacock, the English were subject to his authority. It was an uneasy peace. It became ever more clear to the Indians that the English did not intend to live among them, and they did not intend to leave. While Smith remained in Virginia, it was possible for both sides to imagine desirable outcomes. But Smith was sent home in November 1609. By that time the English and the Indians were at war, a five-year conflict that resulted in the deaths of hundreds of Englishmen and Indians directly from the fighting, and more English deaths from starvation and disease. It was not an ideal atmosphere in which to construct a commonwealth of English and Indian Christians.

The desperate need for foodstuffs drove the English to place horrible pressure on Indian communities already suffering from drought. Faced with the potential for food shortages of their own, Indians were understandably reluctant to share with the hairy, smelly, belligerent Englishmen who traversed the James harassing villages and demanding corn. The Nansemonds refused to trade with a group of Englishmen, and in retaliation the men destroyed their village, fields, and holy places, carrying away "their pearles Copper and braceletts." The English who did the raiding were later besieged and more than half were killed in repeated engagements with the angry Nansemonds. The Indians looked on such desperate and counterproductive marauding with scant favor. A short while after the incident with the Nansemonds, a group of Powhatans ambushed another trading or raiding party headed by Captain James Ratcliffe and killed Ratcliffe by scraping his flesh "from his bones wth mussell shelles and before his face throwne into the fyer."[30]

In revenge for Captain Ratcliffe's gory death, in November 1609 George Percy led a raid against a Paspahegh village near Jamestown. After burning the village's houses and cornfields, the English captured the "quene" of the Paspahegh (a *werowansqua*). Debate ensued about what to do with her children; eventually the English decided to dispose of them by throwing them over the side of the boat and "shoteinge owtt their Braynes in the water." That evening another Virginia Company official claimed to have orders to execute the werowansqua by burning her at the stake. Percy demurred and suggested a "quicker dispatche" instead, so another captain "did take the quene with towe sowldiers A shoare and in the woods putt her to the Sworde."[31] The next few years saw several similar incidents. George Percy, from whom we have excellent descriptions of events from 1609 to 1611, had seen military service in Ireland and in the Netherlands. Like his comrades, Percy favored tactics that the English had deployed in Ireland—ambush, deception, and wholesale slaughter of men, women, and children, when possible. If the English had characterized their late sixteenth-century conquest of Ireland as necessary to protect their western flank from French and Spanish Catholic encroachments, then their use of anti-Irish strategies in Virginia signaled a new kind of holy war, one against treacherous heathens.[32] The vision of an Anglo-Indian commonwealth had never seemed less possible.

To make matters worse, there was abundant evidence that the English themselves seemed to be sliding into heathenism.[33] If the English had feared they would find that the Powhatans were cannibals, they must have been horrified to find evidence of such heathenish behavior among their own. John Smith related the incident in his *Generall His-*

torie (1624), describing the manner in which a man had killed, butchered, salted, and eaten at least part of his wife. Smith added that he did not know "whether shee was better roasted, boyled or cabonado'd [grilled] . . . but of such a dish as powdered [salted] wife I never heard of."[34] The starving denizens of Jamestown also exhumed and ate the corpses of Indians slain and buried outside the fort and drank the blood of their own slain fellows (although these transgressions do not seem to have warranted execution, as wife eating did).[35] The English still believed that the Powhatans practiced cannibalism—a heathenish, devil-worshiping behavior.[36] Observing such behavior among the English was a frightening warning. If the Indians were potential Christians who could be returned into the church by English missionaries, then the English were also potential heathens who could backslide from their Christian ways into terrible paganism. English people who lived among the Indians, as Indians, voluntarily relinquished their covenant with God. Such a prospect should have been unthinkable, yet its very reality shocked English observers. When Ralph Hamor met William Parker, who had lived for several years among the Indians, Hamor wrote that Parker had "growen so like both in complexion and habite to the Indians, that I onely knew him by his tongue to be an Englishman."[37]

The English observed creeping heathenish behavior in other ways as well. Some Englishmen fled the confines of the fort and sought out Indian groups with whom they could stay—a good bet, since Indians seemed willing to share food with individual Englishmen. John Smith noted that some among the English would have "sould their soules" for something to eat, even though many considered the food the Indians ate inappropriate for civilized Englishmen.[38] The English construed living among the Indians and eating their food, even in order to save themselves, as an act of potential heathenism. Yet Indians were not always thrilled to have Englishmen among them. In late 1609 seventeen Englishmen from Jamestown stole a boat and sailed to Kecoughtan, apparently to find something to eat. Some of these men were later found "slayne with their mowthes stopped full of Breade beinge donn as it seamethe in Contempte and skorne thatt others mighte expecte the Lyke when they shold come to seeke for breade and reliefe amongste them." The surviving Englishmen were returned to Jamestown, still hungry, "to feede upon the poore store we had lefte us."[39] Percy decided that those Englishmen who died in search of food had been appropriately punished and that those who returned would also be punished in a sense—there was little food at

Jamestown. Instead of being grateful for access to Christianity, the Indians actually seduced Englishmen away with their food and their close proximity. The departure of Englishmen from Jamestown to live with the Indians became a bigger threat than the English had ever thought possible.

There were threats within the palings at Jamestown from Catholic spies and lurking atheists seeking to undermine the struggling colony. Dissension and plotting in the ranks of the ruling council eventually exposed Captain George Kendall, who was executed as a Spanish spy. A Catholic Irishman named Francis Mangel later reported to the Spanish that Kendall had been killed because "they knew that he wanted to come to Spain to reveal to His Majesty what goes on in that land."[40] The threat of Spanish spies brought English anti-Catholic paranoia to the forefront. Archaeological evidence suggests that aside from Kendall's perfidy, the English were right to fear a secret Catholic presence at Jamestown. Most of the religious objects found at the Jamestown site are Catholic: rosary beads, pilgrimage medallions, and crucifixes, suggesting a number of Catholics or Catholic sympathizers (probably Irish sailors) at Jamestown.[41]

Some Englishmen appeared to embrace atheism. One Hugh Pryse "did come openly into the markett place Blaspheameinge exclameinge and cryeinge owtt thatt there was noe god." The denial of God was potentially even a worse transgression than cannibalism or Catholicism, because it went beyond the bounds of misguided heathenism into the realm of atheism. Starvation was no excuse for blasphemy, but the fate that later befell Pryse proved to the colonists that God would strike down blaspheming Englishmen. Pryse left the fort one afternoon in the company of a "Butcher a corpulent fatt man" to seek food in the forest, but the corpses of both men were found later. They were killed and left lying by Indians, but "Pryses Corpes wch was Rente in pieces . . . And his Bowles Torne outt of his boddy." Though Pryse had been "a Leane spare man," Pryse's fat companion "was fownd altogether untouched." George Percy predictably viewed the incident as an example of "gods Indignacyon" at the behavior of Jamestown residents.[42] Fear reverberated within the walls of Jamestown. Surely God would punish the colony for its creeping heathenism, Catholicism, and atheism.

The settlers came to fear the danger of reverting to heathenism more than death. They thought the Indians used their devilish witchcraft to sow dissension and fear among them. George Percy claimed a riot at

Jamestown was "ocasyoned by the Salvages Sorceries and Charmes." Indian witchcraft managed to temporarily achieve a transformation from Christian Englishmen to heathen Indians—a transformation they feared would become permanent. Only God's direct intervention in lifting the "fantasy" prevented total heathen reversion.[43] The Reverend Alexander Whitaker recorded a similar occurrence in 1611. The men, "beinge att praiers," heard odd noises and thought "they sawe one like an Indian leape over the fier." The soldiers suddenly "could speake nothing but 'Oho Oho,' and all generally taking the wrong end of their armes." The episode lasted "not above half a quarter of an houer" and then "the men awaked out of a dream . . . [and] remained ever after very quiett." Another time Whitaker observed Indians dancing along the shore while his ship passed, and within a few minutes there was a violent thunderstorm. Whitaker explained both events by claiming that there had to be powerful witches living among the Indians. Whitaker confided to his correspondent that he supposed that God had avoided the complete destruction of the Indians only because the English could "communicate the most excellent merchandize and treasure of the Gospell with them." He further begged that more "young Godly and learned Ministers whom the Church of England hath not, or refuseth, to sett a worke send them thither."[44] To prevent further bewitched occurrences, the English buried a witch bottle under an entrance to the fort. The glass container contained sharp stones (Elizabethan and Jacobean Englishmen would have used iron nails, but those were in short supply in Virginia), which tradition decreed would ward off the devilish power of witches to enchant and lead good Christians astray.[45]

Anglo-Indian violence, the appalling death rate, starvation, and creeping heathenism among the settlers almost ended the Jamestown venture. The Virginia Company acquired a new charter in 1609, partly as a response to these challenges. Even though it had become apparent that Indian conversion would be neither easy nor welcome, the new charter also emphasized the "conversion and reduction of the people in those parts unto the true worship of God and Christian religion." The second charter also restructured the colony's governance to make authoritarian government possible. Virginia's new governor would have an astonishing amount of power over other Englishmen in the colony, a move that was a concession to both the physical threat from Indians and the spiritual threat of potential heathenism among the English.[46]

In England, the company redoubled its efforts to gain public support for the Virginia venture. In what amounted to a seventeenth-century media blitz, the company drafted London ministers to craft a theological justification for the Virginia enterprise, always being careful to recruit ministers with strong anti-Catholic sentiment. In his 1609 sermon delivered to departing Virginia adventurers, the Reverend William Symonds argued that "Christ our Saviour hath, according to his infinite wisedome, revived the olde law, of filling the earth, in a most excellent manner: *Goe teach* (saith he) *all nations, and baptize them in the name of the Father, the Sonne, and the holy Ghost.*" "Neither can there be any doubt," Symonds continued, "but that the Lord led *Abraham* into another Countrey, doeth also by the same holy hand, call you to goe and carry the Gospell to a Nation that never heard of Christ." Symonds was fond of comparing the voyaging Englishmen to Abraham and his people. God, he said, had promised to make Abraham a great nation, and he would do the same for "all that are of his faith and obedience." Symonds also proposed a method for converting the Indians by taking Indian children captive, converting them, and then sending the young converts back to their families.[47] The Reverend William Crashaw publicly supported the Virginia venture in another sermon. The English in Virginia, he implied, had it much harder than the ancient people of the Old Testament: "The Israelites had a *commandement* from God to dwell in *Canaan*, we have *leave* to dwell in *Virginea*: they were *commanded to kill* the heathen, we are *forbidden to kill* them, but are commanded to *convert* them." The potential rewards, though, were greater than those God had offered the Israelites, because "that land flowed with *milke and honie*, ours abounds with as *good or better.*" According to Crashaw, God had made conversion easier by "inclining the hearts of the Savages, who live in that country, lovingly to call and invite us."[48] Crashaw tapped into long-standing English sentiment that the Indians actually wanted to be converted to Christianity. The Virginia Company's favored ministers emphasized the goal of all good Christians—spreading the (Protestant) faith. Other Virginia Company supporters picked up this rhetoric. The Reverend Robert Gray refuted the notion that the Indians were irredeemably savage; "wee goe to live peaceablie among them, and not to supplant them." Gray described Virginia as at "the beginning of a common wealth" and advocated an apprenticeship program for Indians.[49] The company's propaganda conveniently papered over the previous years of unmitigated disaster and overlooked the Indians' obvious resistance to becoming junior partners in the Anglo-Indian commonwealth.

Crashaw suggested that to strengthen the colony "no sinfull, no leaud [lewd], and no licentious men" should go to Virginia.[50] When new governor Sir Thomas Gates with his vice governor Sir Thomas Dale arrived in the spring of 1610, they worked tirelessly to remedy the problem. Dale worried that the Englishmen at Jamestown were heathen: "I say not many give testimonie beside their names that they are Christians."[51] Gates's solution to the problem of lurking heathenism and colonial failure was to legislate proper moral and religious behavior among the English at Jamestown. Gates's orders included an instruction to defend the Church of England "in all fundamentall pointes" and to see to it that "all Atheisme Prophanes Popery or Schisme be exemplarily punished to the honour of god and to the peace and safety of his Church."[52] The admission that Christianity's hold on Virginia was precarious motivated Gates and Dale to protect English religion. In 1610 Gates promulgated the *Lawes Divine Morall and Martiall*, a comprehensive law code for the English at Jamestown designed to reinforce Englishness and Christianity.

The Lawes enacted an exacting discipline. They prescribed whippings or other physical punishments for some quality-of-life transgressions: casting bath or laundry water into the street at Jamestown, for example, earned a whipping, as did theft of farming tools. Stealing from another's garden was punishable by death.[53] Most significantly, they also reinforced the Christianity of English inhabitants, ordering death for those who took the Lord's name in vain (as Hugh Pryse had) or denied the Trinity and mandating prayer and church attendance on a daily basis. Because the best offense against heathenism was a strong defense, the Lawes also mandated that ministers in the company's employ examine each colonist on matters of faith and religion, that "hee may understand, and gather, whether heretofore they have been sufficiently instructed, and catechised in the principles and grounds of Religion." Those who could not give a good account of their faith were required to receive further instruction from the minister. Those who refused would be whipped until they acknowledged the errors of their ways and begged the congregation for forgiveness. William Strachey noted in his introduction to the London edition of the *Lawes* that evil would come only "if we lived there lawlesse, without obedience to our Countrey, or observance of Religion to God." The Lawes themselves were an observance of God from the English perspective. Their provisions and punishments were deeply rooted not only in the common law but also in biblical law.[54] Gates and Dale saw themselves as Christian magistrates responsible for the material and spiritual well-being of their charges; and they were implementing Crashaw's advice by making "Atheisme and other blasphemie capitall."[55] Success would come only with committed Christian Englishmen converting the heathen Indians.

Dale and Gates hoped to reinforce English cultural and religious identity among the settlers, but they did not intend the *Lawes* to keep Indians and Englishmen permanently separate.[56] The *Lawes* instead reasserted Christian Englishness by bringing English Christians back into the fold, without separating them absolutely from Indians. Once Virginia's leaders reasserted control over the English, Indian conversion would be easier. The *Lawes* seemed to have assumed further contact would be necessary and protected Indians accordingly, prescribing punishments for those who harmed friendly Indians and prohibiting the lunatic piratical actions starving settlers had taken previously against the Nansemond and the Paspahegh. Another law made the rape of Indian women a capital crime. Other regulations prohibited violence toward Indians who came to Jamestown to engage in legitimate trade. Yet another prohibited Jamestown men and women from joining any group of Indians—this law kept Anglo-Indian interactions on English terms, preventing the creeping English heathenism of previous years. It also protected Indians from having to assume responsibility for feeding additional English mouths. Strachey's edition of the *Lawes* concluded with a prayer that the residents of Jamestown were to say every evening, which begged God to "let Satan & his delusions come to nought & as wax melteth before the fire, so let wickednes, superstition, ignorance and idolatry perish at ye presence of thee our God."[57] English discipline and devotion would keep the devil at bay and allow the settlers to work toward the conversion of the Indians.

Close proximity between the Indians and the English sometimes stoked colonial hopes for conversion, as the Indian Kemps demonstrated. Kemps was a Paspahegh man who had been seized during an English raid for corn and other supplies in 1609. John Smith later described him as a prisoner who grew to love his captors, refusing to leave them and teaching them how to plant and care for corn and to hunt deer and turkeys for English consumption. After his release Kemps came and went from Jamestown as he pleased, and sometimes starving Englishmen would seek him out among the Paspaheghs, hoping to be fed.[58] William Strachey wrote that Kemps "could speake a pretty deale of English, and came orderly to Church every day to prayers, and observed with us the keeping of the Sabaoth, both by ceasing from Labour, and repayring to church."[59] While not exactly a convert, Kemps displayed a respect for English religiosity and a willingness to learn and understand Christianity that Strachey clearly found heartening. In the midst of growing war, Kemps was a ray of hope. Unfortunately Kemps could not avoid the ravages of scurvy, and he died at Jamestown in 1611.

Dale drew on his own experience in Ireland and the Netherlands; a strong Protestant identity motivated conflicts in both places. Although the enemies had been Spanish or Irish Catholics in those wars, here the enemy was Indian heathenism. As Dale opined to his superiors back in England, "You have ever given mee encouragements to persevere in this Religious Warfare."[60] And persevere he would. Observers in Virginia increasingly believed that violence would be the only way to subdue the Indians and bring them to Christianity. Dale pointedly advocated the slaughter of Powhatan holy men, called *quiyoughcosoughs*. Richard Hakluyt, from the safety of London, remarked that "if gentle polishing [of the Indians] will not serve, then we shall not want hammerours and rough masons enough, I meane our old souldiours trained up in the Nether-lands, to . . . prepare them to our Preachers hands."[61] A Virginia community that would include both Indians and English remained an important goal for the London investors, but the military men viewed the situation quite differently than ministers comfortably ensconced in their London pulpits.

The *Lawes* did not stop the warfare into which the Indians and the English had settled. Only kidnapping one of Wahunsonacock's daughters while she made a diplomatic visit to the Potomack Indians accomplished that. The English knew the young woman as Pocahontas—a childhood nickname the English translated as "little wanton."[62] As a girl, Metoaka had cartwheeled through the muddy lanes of Jamestown accompanied by English boys.[63] By 1613, Metoaka was a woman—married to one of her father's warriors, a man named Kocoom—with all the responsibilities adult women had, including furthering her father's interests through her marriage and the practice of trade and diplomacy. She might have even had a child at the time of her kidnapping.[64] Ralph Hamor later reported that Metoaka seemed "exceeding pensive and discontented" at her confinement, a reaction that one might well imagine from a young woman torn away from her husband and her people.[65]

Captain Samuel Argall, who masterminded the kidnapping, likely thought of his capture of Metoaka as a stroke of tactical genius. Argall conceived of Metoaka in European terms and erroneously assumed that her father would ransom her as the family of royalty would be ransomed in Europe. Metoaka was not, however, the analog of a European princess. One among a number of daughters from political marriages made to cement alliances, she was not critical to the survival of her father's polity or his political power, however dear she might have been to him personally. To the surprise of Argall and other English officers, Wahunsonacock initially did not respond to English terms for Metoaka's return. Sometime during the summer of 1613, he did send back seven Englishmen with some missing tools and arms and promised to send five hundred bushels of corn upon the return of his daughter.[66] Wahunsonacock did not respond to further English demands in exchange for the return of his daughter until the summer of 1614. By then, Metoaka had lived among the English for a year. "Powhatan's daughter I caused to be carefully instructed in christian Religion," bragged Dale, "who after she had made good progresse therein, renounced publikely her Countrey Idolatry, openly confessed her Christian Faith, was, as shee desired, baptized and is since married to an English Gentleman of good understanding."[67] Metoaka received instruction from the Reverend Alexander Whitaker at Henrico, a minister who was intensely optimistic about the potential Christianity of the Indians.

Metoaka's paramour, the aspiring planter John Rolfe, did not arrive at his "good understanding" with ease. Rolfe justified his choice of bride by constructing a clever and sophisticated theological defense of Anglo-Indian marriage in a letter he wrote to Governor Dale in late 1613 or early 1614. Rolfe wrestled with his attraction to Metoaka, which he thought "toucheth me soe nearly as the tenderness of my Salvacon." Concerned as he was "for the good of the Plantacon, the honor of or Countrye, for the glorye of God, for myne own salvacon, and for the Convertinge to the true knowledge of God and Iesus Christ an unbelieving Creature, namely Pohahuntas [Metoaka]," Rolfe turned to the Bible for guidance. He noted "the heavy displeasure wch Almighty God Conceyved againt the Sonnes of Levie and Israell for marrienge of straunge wyves."[68] The Old Testament, as Rolfe knew, recorded several instances in which the ancient Israelites married their sons to women who were not Jewish with disastrous consequences. Such marriages encouraged idolatry and thereby endangered Abraham's covenant with God—a covenant the English believed they had inherited. Rolfe had likely heard William Symond's 1609 sermon to the departing Virginia adventurers, which reminded them that "Abrams posteritie keepe them to themselves. They may not marry nor give in marriage to the heathen, that are uncircumsized. . . . The breaking of this rule, may breake the necke of all good sucesse of this voyage."[69] Certainly Metoaka qualified as "straunge" in the seventeenth-century sense of the word meaning "foreign" or "alien." Rolfe's own description of Metoaka stressed both her lack of English civility and the inadequacy of her pedigree: "[Her] education hath byn rude, her manners barbarous, her generacon Cursed."[70]

Rolfe initially believed his love for Metoaka would bring disaster to his own soul and on the English covenant with God. "Surely theise are wicked instigations hatched by him whoe seeketh and delighteth in mans destruction," opined Rolfe to Dale. That the devil would happily destroy Virginia through a biblically unlawful marriage was completely clear to Rolfe, and the solution to this problem could only be Metoaka's conversion to Christianity. Echoing William Crashaw's 1609 sermon on the lawfulness of Virginia colonization, Rolfe reminded Dale (and through him other company leaders and investors) that Christian conversion was "the service Iesus Christ requyreth of his best servants." Rolfe artfully turned his original concern about the state of his own salvation on its head. By converting and marrying Metoaka, he wrote, "I shall atayne to that blessed promise pronounced by the holye Prophett Daniell to the righteous, that bringe many to the true knowledge of God, namely, that they shall shine lyke the Starres for ever and ever." Metoaka, he noted in passing, seemed to return his affection and had indicated her willingness to be instructed.[71] In case the readers of Rolfe's letter remained doubtful that the marriage was lawful, Rolfe turned to the New Testament. Rolfe reminded them that "the unbelieving husband is sanctified by the beleivings wyefe, and the unbeleivinge wiefe by the beleivinge husband," thus guaranteeing Metoaka's salvation through his own faith. Rolfe also included Calvin's gloss on Paul to reassure readers that any children produced in the union would be "accompted holye, yea although they be the yssue but of one parent faithfull."[72] Rolfe thus anticipated theological objections and answered them: if one accepted that Old Testament prohibitions against marrying "strange wives" applied in this case, that problem was neatly solved by Metoaka's conversion. And if her conversion were spurious, the marriage bond would still save her soul, and their children would still inherit their father's English covenant with God. Rolfe's letter was the most incisive and theologically sophisticated advocacy of interracial marriage to ever appear in English North America.

Dale seized on the marriage to guarantee the survival of the struggling colony. If life in Virginia was indeed a battle, on both the physical and the metaphysical planes, then the English scored a victory with Metoaka when she was baptized and married Rolfe. The English presented the marriage as a fait accomplit to Wahunsonacock, who acquiesced to the wedding, sending his brother Opechancanough and two of Metoaka's brothers to the ceremony on 5 April 1614. For the English, the marriage represented the revival of the Anglo-Indian Christian commonwealth. Metoaka's conversion showed that such transformations were possible and desirable, and accordingly the English gave Metoaka the baptismal name of Rebecca. After all, the biblical Rebecca was the mother of nations—two nations, the English hoped, that would be united in a new world commonwealth in an inspiring biblical metaphor.

Wahunsonacock and his people did not look on Metoaka's marriage as a way of achieving a peaceable commonwealth. Instead, they probably looked on it as a way of creating the kind of fictive kinship arrangement with the English that Wahunsonacock had attempted to forge through his adoption of John Smith. Though Smith had not cooperated in the way he had hoped, Wahunsonacock thought a marriage in which a woman of his people (less important was the fact that Metoaka was his daughter) lived among the English and bore children there might bring peace and access to trade goods. After all, his people made alliances through marriage with those goals in mind. Those children, he thought, would have dual and dueling allegiances with the Indians and with the English, and would mark a path for a less violent coexistence. It is possible that Metoaka herself consented to the marriage with Rolfe for similar reasons.[73]

The English also thought about the marriage dynastically. Even though they were aware that Wahunsonacock's people passed political power along matrilineal lines, they still thought of Metoaka, or Rebecca as she was now known, as the daughter of a potentate who was therefore available for the sealing of alliances by marriage in the European fashion.[74] The marriage formed an alliance with Wahunsonacock and settled an uneasy peace upon Virginia. On Rebecca's rock would the English build their commonwealth. Yet her name, imbued as it was with biblical symbolism, did not necessarily portend the unity of peoples, as Reverend Whitaker possibly intended when he suggested Rebecca as her baptismal name. The biblical Rebecca, in bearing Isaac's children, favored her younger son Jacob over her older son Esau. The young upstart Jacob stole his brother's lands and inheritance with Rebecca's connivance. In that sense, Rebecca was the mother of warring nations, one of which dominated and dispossessed the other. Perhaps among the English that metaphor of favoritism and dissension was a more accurate prophecy of the future of Anglo-Indian relations. The English saw the marriage as a route to peace and prosperity but also as a victory in placing Indians under English authority. In their view, Christianity had triumphed over pagan savagery. The English thought of Metoaka's conversion and marriage much as John Rolfe did when he wrote to Thomas Dale that "this is ye worke of God and marvelous in our eyes."[75]

Metoaka's conversion and marriage spurred efforts to make the Anglo-Indian Christian commonwealth a reality. In 1617 James I confirmed a charter for the Virginia Company to found a school for Indian children in Virginia "for propagation of ye Gospell amongst Infidells."[76] The following year the Virginia Company set aside ten thousand acres in Henrico County for the formation of the institution and hoped to populate it in short order with children provided by Wahunsonacock's brother and successor, Opechancanough. The company further supported this endeavor by sending fifty men "to beare up the charge of bringing up Thirty of the Infidels children in true religion and civility" and by soliciting donations from wealthy notables to fund the college.[77] Metoaka reportedly lent her approval and support to the college project while she was in England on a sensational tour arranged by the company in 1616. The Reverend Samuel Purchas, who had begun to displace Richard Hakluyt as England's premier chronicler of European adventures in the New World, had described Virginia in 1613 as "not a wanton Minion; but an honest and Christian wife."[78] Metoaka was Purchas's wifely vision made flesh: the Indian woman who set aside her wantonness and had become "an honest and Christian wife." Purchas was delighted to make Metoaka's acquaintance; he noted that she "did not only accustome her selfe to civilitie, but still carried her selfe as the Daughter of a King, and was accordingly respected not onely by the Company . . . but of divers particular persons of Honor in their hopefull zeale by her to advance Christianitie."[79] Metoaka personified the Anglo-Indian Christian commonwealth and the hopes the company and its supporters had invested in it.

Wahunsonacock's brother-in-law, the *quiyoughcosough* Uttamatomakin (also known as Tocomoco), accompanied Metoaka. Wahunsonacock had sent him to gather information about the numbers of Englishmen and how many might be expected to come into Tsenacommacah.[80] At least ten other Indians traveled with Metoaka, an escort intended to do her honor as well as aid her father's trusted adviser Uttamatomakin in finding out what the English intended in Virginia. Uttamatomakin did not make nearly as good an impression on the English as the civilized and Christianized Metoaka did. Samuel Purchas claimed to have spoken with him repeatedly about "his Countrey and Religion" but Uttamatomakin was "but a blasphemer of what he knew not, and preferring his God to ours." Uttamatomakin described ceremonies for invoking the Indians' deity Okeus (whom Purchas assumed to be the devil), and his visits with Purchas must have been quite titillating for the parson. Metoaka demonstrated that Indians could indeed abandon their heathen ways, but Uttamatomakin indicated that more education would be necessary. It was imperative that Indian youngsters be separated from the malign influences of Indian priests like Uttamatomakin forthwith. Uttamatomakin appeared to suggest this course of action himself, telling Purchas the English should "teach the boys and girls which were brought over from hence, be being too old now to learn."[81]

As part of her visit, the Virginia Company granted one hundred pounds to Metoaka and John Rolfe, "to be paid out of the monyes collected for workes to be perfourmed for the planting & propagating of Christian religion in those heathen ptes [partes]." The company wished to honor "that good example of hir conversion, And to encorage other of hir kindred and Nation to doe the like." In return, the Rolfes promised "bothe by their godlye and virtuous example . . . they would imploy their best endevours to the winning of that People to the knowledge of God, and embraceing of true religion." Such a substantial sum signaled the company's seriousness of purpose in converting the Indians but also allowed it to capitalize on her presence in London.[82] Metoaka, on display in the streets and at court, was living proof of the possibility of the Anglo-Indian Christian commonwealth. The money was not well spent: Metoaka did not survive the tour of England. She died, probably of a respiratory illness, at Gravesend as the party was preparing to return to Virginia. An apparently brokenhearted John Rolfe left their young son Thomas in the care of a friend and sailed back to Virginia. Once there, he penned an eloquent letter to Edwin Sandys defending his actions and requesting that Metoaka's "liberalle stipend" might be reserved for the benefit of her son. He also reported that the "Indyans very loving, and willing to parte with their children. My wives death is much lamented [among the Indians]; my childe much desyred . . . [his] life greately extinguesheth the sorrow of her loss . . . but tis enough that her childe liveth." The Anglo-Indian peace of 1614 had hung precariously on the marriage of Metoaka and John Rolfe. He recognized that the continuation of that peace might reside in the figure of their son, Thomas, "the lyving ashes of his deceased Mother."[83]

In Virginia plans proceeded apace for the foundation of the Indian college. Virginia Company leaders had decided one hundred men would support the institution. The company selected men on the basis of their knowledge of trades that would be useful in Virginia and that Indians could learn (including various smiths, carpenters, potters, and other craftsmen).[84] The company would also send a minister to preach to and teach the Indian children and their families at a cost of forty pounds a year. To raise money to send the men and support the minister, the company obtained a patent asking Anglican bishops and priests to take up collections during Sunday services. The company often listed gifts for the "infidles children," in its accounts of meetings, including an anonymous donation of five hundred pounds from a benefactor calling himself "Dust and Ashes" and another bequest from the estate of merchant Nicholas Ferrar to support the college. Another benefactor left books, most notably the works of Saint Augustine and the puritan divine William Perkins, as well as an "exact map of *America*."[85] Dust and Ashes also provided instructions for the best use of his money. Young Indian boys were to learn to read and write as well as learn a trade and thereafter "enioye like liberties and pryveledges wth our native English in that place." Dust and Ashes saw himself as assisting in the creation of the Anglo-Indian Christian commonwealth, so it was no wonder he was annoyed a year later when his donation had been diverted to fund an ironworks. Dust and Ashes wrote another missive to the company suggesting that his money be used instead to bring "male children of ye Virginians (though but a few) . . . over into England here to be educated and taught."[86] The project of converting Indians seized Londoners' imaginations as well as their purse strings.

Wahunsonacock's people resisted English attempts to bring them into the Anglo-Indian Christian commonwealth on English terms alone. In justifying diverting Dust and Ashes' donation to the ironworks, Edwin Sandys noted that a letter written by Sir George Yeardley, then governor of Virginia, explained "howe difficult a thing it was at that time to obtain any of their [Indians'] Children wth the consent and good likinge of their

Parents by reason of their tenderness of them & feare of hard usage by the English."[87] Although John Rolfe had reported that the Indians would gladly give up their children, the Powhatans proved less than cooperative.[88] Yeardley, one of the Virginia Company's representatives in the colony, negotiated a solution with Opechancanough, in which the chief would "apoynt and Cuse [choose] out so many . . . ffamilies that should remove to us."[89] In return Opechancanough selected some weapons and other armaments from the magazine at Jamestown.[90] This compromise solution would theoretically allow Indian and English families to settle side by side on the land, so the Indians could learn English religion, language, and agricultural practices.

George Thorpe, an ardent advocate of Indian conversion who had sheltered some of Metoaka's companions in London, enthusiastically took charge of the college in 1619. He wrote to Edwin Sandys in London in 1621 in a tone of frustration with English settlers' attitudes toward the Indians. Instead of "serious endevours of convertinge the Heathen that Live round about us and are dayly conversant among us," Thorpe reported that "most [English] men wth theire mouthes give them [Indians] nothinge but maledictions and bitter execrations." Thorpe had discovered that not all settlers shared his kind view of the Indians, and many of them preferred the Indians' complete absence from English settlements. Thorpe noted that "if there bee wronge on any side it is on o[u]rs who are not soe charitable to them as Christians ought to bee, they beinge (espetiallye the better sort of them) of a peaceable & vertuous disposition." In Thorpe's telling, those who stood in the way of the Anglo-Indian Christian commonwealth were English settlers who behaved in an un-Christian manner, obstructing Thorpe and his work with the college. The Indians themselves were "peaceable & vertuous" partners with whom the English could work. Of course, Indians themselves probably did not see Thorpe's project as helpful or useful. After all, the college lands were expropriated from Indians, and Thorpe had covered them with more than ten thousand grapevines.[91] Despite his doubts, Opechancanough promised to pursue the exchange system Thorpe envisioned for the college, with some English families living among the Indians and some Indian families sent to "Cohabitt wth us."[92]

Though relations between the English and the Indians were strained by the early 1620s, the council reported to London that the Indians "cominge daylie amongst us and puttinge them selves into our powers."[93] In a census taken in early March 1619/20, four Indians were listed as liv ing among the English in "the service of severall planters." They were not counted with the English but rather in a separate category, "Others not Christians in the service of the English."[94] The tension between including and excluding Indians in the census points to a broader difficulty. What happened when Indians lived among the English but did not become Christian? The four Indians living among the English in 1619 reflected both the promise and the complications of the Anglo-Indian commonwealth: the success of the English vision required Indians to become Christian. Yet few, if any, repeated Metoaka's conversion. The Virginia census taken in 1619 also listed among the non-Christians thirty-two Africans: fifteen men and seventeen women.[95] Enslaved Africans first appeared in Virginia's records in 1619; John Rolfe noted in a letter that the governor purchased "20. and Odd Negroes" from a passing Dutch ship in August of that year; if the date for the 1619 census is indeed March or April 1619, not 1620, those Africans joined an existing population of thirty-six other people labeled "not Christians."[96] Englishmen in Virginia probably looked upon enslaved Africans as potential Christians as well.

Perhaps few Indians lived among the English at Jamestown because they were aware that Opechancanough did not intend to allow the colony to continue expanding. Opechancanough and his brother Itoyatan attacked English settlements on the morning of Friday 22 March 1621/22, in an event variously known, depending on the perspective, as the Great Massacre of 1622, the Coup of 1622, or the Great Assault of 1622. The Powhatans swept through the English settlements along the James and York Rivers to the west of Jamestown, burning fields and houses and killing more than 350 English people (about a third of the settlement's total English population). George Thorpe was among those slain at the college. Later reports indicated his corpse was found severely mutilated, although the writer declined to describe precisely in what fashion, writing only that the body suffered "barbarous despights and foule scornes . . . unbefitting to be heard by any civill eare."[97]

Edward Waterhouse tried to turn tragedy into opportunity in his printed account of the massacre. *A Declaration of the state of the Colony and Affaires in Virginia* spun the bloody deaths of more than three hundred people as a positive event for the company and the colony. According to Waterhouse, the Indians attacked at "the instigation of the Devill (enemy to their salvation)," and because the Indians feared that "we, by our growing continually upon them, would dispossesse them of this Country." Waterhouse wrote that "the houses generally set open to the Sauages, who were alwaies friendly entertained at the tables of the English, and commonly lodged in their bed-chambers . . . and their familiarity with the Natiues, seeming to open a faire gate for their conuersion to Christianitie." The openness that the English believed that they had achieved was their undoing. The massacre fundamentally altered the English colonization project, for "the losse of this blood," Waterhouse wrote, would "make the body more healthfull." Indian violence, betraying the "innocency" of the English, allowed the settlers "by right of Warre, and law of Nations, [to] invade the Country, and destroy them who sought to destroy us." Waterhouse also noted that now the English could merely take the Indians' "cultivated places." Conquering the Indians would be easier than civilizing and converting them, and Waterhouse proposed using the tactic of "Divide & impera" to turn the Powhatans' native enemies against them. Waterhouse further suggested both instigating famine by burning Indians' corn and sending Englishmen with dogs on hunting parties to tear Indians to pieces. Viewing Indians as savage enemies also conveniently solved the colony's perennial labor problems, according to Waterhouse, for "the Indians, who before were used as friends, may now most justly be compelled to servitude and drudgery . . . also some may be sent for the service of the Sommer Islands [Bermuda]."[98]

Waterhouse's counterintuitive conclusion urged readers to consider that "this Massacre must rather be beneficiall to the Plantation than impaire it." Through Waterhouse's propaganda, the Virginia Company repudiated its previous strategy of conversion and commonwealth and abandoned the notion that Indians were potential Christians. Instead, Waterhouse argued for new justifications for the English colonial enterprise that revolved around the intentional dispossession of and enslavement of Indians. The breakdown of the Anglo-Indian commonwealth opened the door to the emerging English ideology of hereditary heathenism. Though Waterhouse paid lip service to the old call for "the propagation of Christian religion" in his concluding remarks, unlike previous company propagandists he offered no specific plans for how to achieve conversion. Instead, he noted that civility was "slow, the effect of long time, and great industry." Waterhouse urged the abandonment of longheld public goals for the company in favor of quick, easy, and violent conquest of the Powhatan people.[99]

Virginians did all they could to extirpate the "perfidious and inhumane" Indians.[100] In 1623 Virginia's representative assembly reaffirmed the religious basis of English identity by emphasizing uniformity of church doctrine, mandating church attendance, and issuing rules for ministers' proper behavior. It also required that "every dwellinge Howse shalbe Pallyzadoed [pallisaded] in for defence againste the Indyans," that every man walking outside his own palisade had to carry a gun, and that all work in English tobacco and corn fields had to take place under the watchful eye of an armed guard. Even the *Lawes Divine Morall and Martiall* had not drawn such a stark line between Indians and Englishmen. Lastly, the Assembly required that "at the begininge of July next the Inhabitants of every Corporatione shall falle uppon their adjoyning Salvages as we did the last yeere."[101] In January 1623/24 the council reported that the Virginians had "to our uttermost abilities revenged ourselves uppone the Salvages . . . cut downe theire Corne in all places . . . [and burned] downe the howses they had reedified."[102] Repression of Indians was the main mode of English engagement with native people around the Atlantic throughout the 1620s. In a violent paroxysm, English settlers massacred hundreds of Caribs on St. Christopher in multiple incidents in 1625 and 1626.[103] Most English people were no longer settling new lands with the expectation of working with Indians.

New England might be considered an exception to this rule. Settlers at Massachusetts Bay incorporated an Indian plea for help and Christianity into their new seal, implying some desire for an Anglo-Indian Christian commonwealth as part of their colonizing venture. New England supporter John White engaged the question of the Curse of Ham and conversion in a pamphlet supporting the venture in 1630. White acknowledged that "some conceive the Inhabitants of *New-England* [Indians] to be *Chams* posterity, and consequently shut out from grace by *Noahs* curse." Even though White recognized that some English people no longer believed Indians could be converted to Christianity, he also argued that there was no scriptural basis for such a conclusion: "It is too much boldnesse then to curse where God hath not cursed, and shut out those from the meanes of grace, whom God hath not excluded."[104]

In Virginia, though, hereditary heathenism was the order of the day. Before its dissolution in 1624, the Virginia Company formally abandoned its efforts to Christianize Indians. A petition signed by planters disputed that the conversion efforts had ever been successful and formulated a new narrative for Anglo-Indian relations.[105] One company member, Alderman Richard Johnson, suggested at a company shareholders' meeting that "as for convertinge of the Infidells itt was an attempt impossible they being descended of ye cursed race of Cham."[106] The change was clear and stark. Where William Strachey used the Curse of Ham to prove the Indians' potential Christianity, Johnson used the curse to prove the Indians' inherent unfitness for Christianity. It was impossible, Johnson implied, for Indians to become Christian. Transformed by violence and English disappointments in their evangelizing mission, the curse of heathenism became a racial marker, one that defined the Indians not by their potential Christianity but by their hereditary heathenism. Although individual efforts to convert Indians would continue off and on during the seventeenth century, this view of Indians—and Africans—prevailed. Hereditary heathenism grew out of the ruins of the Anglo-Indian Christian commonwealth.

CHAPTER THREE

Faith in the Blood

Writing a history of English Virginia in 1705, Robert Beverly gave pride of place to two early marriages in the colony. The first, between John Laydon and Anna Burrows [Anne Burras] in 1609, he described as "the first Christian Marriage in that Part of the World: and the Year following the Plantation was increased to near Five Hundred Men." Although the Laydons were not personally responsible for the colony's burgeoning English population, Beverly cleverly postulated a connection between this first Christian marriage and the growth of the colony. Marriage, Beverly thought, had been key to the colony's success. The second marriage Beverly included was that of Metoaka and John Rolfe in 1614. Beverley reproduced for his eighteenth-century readers John Smith's letter of introduction for Metoaka to Queen Anne, which emphasized Metoaka's status: "The first *Christian* ever of that [Indian] Nation: The first *Virginian* ever spake *English*, or had a Child in Marriage by an *English* Man. A Matter surely, if my Meaning be truly consider'd and well understood, worthy of a Prince's information."[1]

The marriages Beverley recognized in his history thus provided two models for the stability of the colony. In one, the colony's population increased through marriage between English men and women. The other featured the conversion and absorption of Indians into an English polity, through Christian marriage of English men to heathen Indian women. Both Smith and Beverley understood Metoaka's importance to the English colonial project: the information most valuable to Queen Anne was not necessarily that she had converted or that she spoke English, but that she had "had a child in Marriage by an *English* man." The production of legitimate heirs within marriage was crucial to the colony's survival. English children inherited their parents'—most critically their fathers'—property, wealth, and the privileges of free Englishmen. Any reproduction that took place outside the confines of duly sanctioned marriage threatened the legitimate lineages upon which status and privilege were built. Beverley was quick to praise Metoaka's issue, "one Son, nam'd *Thomas Rolfe*, whose Posterity is at this Day in good Repute in *Virginia*."[2] The descendants of Metoaka and John Rolfe could claim the benefits of their paternal lineage—Englishness and good reputations. Implicit in Beverley's account of the union of Metoaka and John Rolfe was the idea that Rolfe's children inherited his Christianity. Legitimacy, lineage, and Christianity were indicators of status in England's old and new worlds. Lineage, determined through marriage and legitimate reproduction, defined heritable privileges as well as heritable taints. For seventeenth-century English people, lineage was both familial and collective; it determined the status of individuals and of nations.[3] The marriage of Metoaka and John Rolfe was built in part upon the notion that Christianity was transmissible from parent to child.[4] In this understanding of lineage and heritability, Metoaka's marriage subsumed her Indian heathenness and that undesirable quality was not transmitted to her offspring.

For the English, Metoaka's marriage symbolized heathen submission to proper religion and to English gender norms. Yet would unions between English people and Indians or Africans continue that pattern? It was a particularly pressing question in Virginia after the collapse of the Anglo-Indian commonwealth, and after 1660 increasing numbers of births resulted from illicit relationships between English and non-English partners. By the early eighteenth century, almost a third of prosecuted fornication cases were between English women and African men.[5] Children from these relationships endangered English gender norms and flouted conventional ideas about legitimacy.[6] How Anglo-Virginians came to understand these unions, between Christian and heathen, slave and free, was integral to the process of making race in their new world. Over the course of the seventeenth century, English people living in North America forbade access to Christian marriage for people they defined as heathen and devised new punishments for illicit sex between Christians and heathens. Christianity was a matter of lineage and blood as well as belief, and by the end of the century the English had condemned offspring produced in a union of one Christian and one non-Christian to perpetual paganism. Regulating sex and marriage was therefore a mechanism for defining and controlling lineage and for linking religious affiliation and race.

While in England ideas about lineage, blood, and religion were in large part uninterrogated, in Virginia these amorphous beliefs about heritability of Christianity became mechanisms for defining people perceived as irretrievably heathen. If membership in the Christian community was hereditary, then perhaps heathenism was also hereditary. As minister and controversialist Thomas Blake put it in 1644, "The *priviledges* or *burdens*, which in Family or Nation are hereditary, they are conveyed from parents to posterity, from Ancestors to their Issue: As is the father, so is the child, as respecting these particulars: The child of *a free-man* with St Paul is *free borne*: The child of a *Noble* man is *noble*. The child of a *bond-man* (where servants were wholy their masters to dispose) is a *bond-man* likewise." Blake also extended his analysis to include the heritability of religion: "So the child of a *Turke* is a *Turke*; The child of a *Pagan* is a *Pagan*; The child of a *Jew* is a *Jew*; The child of a *Christian* is a *Christian*." Blake carefully enumerated those characteristics that were heritable and those that were not. Scars and other bodily wounds, or peculiar talents like a gift for art or prophecy were not heritable. "The *priviledges* or *burdens*, which in Family or Nation are hereditary," such as membership in the Christian community, were heritable. According to Blake, "This Scripture hold therefore firme for proofe of the assertion, That Christians have their Birth-right Priviledge, that they transmit a Covenant Holinesse to their Issue, even to their whole posterity." God had a Covenant with Christians, and that Covenant was passed from parent to offspring as a heritable privilege (or burden), and moreover, that Covenant was particular to English people. The nation of the Elect passed their collective Christianity on to future generations. Christianity itself was a birthright for English children.[7] Blake was not alone in his characterization of Christianity as a heritable characteristic. In 1678 Massachusetts minister Increase Mather famously wrote that "God hath been good to cast the line of Election so, as that it doth (though not wholly, and only, yet) for the most part, run through the loins of godly parents." Mather thought of Christianity and salvation as heritable, and he implied that at some future date Christians would only be born of other Christians. Mather did allow that there were some Christian children who were "not born of Elect Parents."[8]

Thinking about Christianity as a heritable condition, as Blake and Mather did, did not necessarily connote theological opposition to the idea of common descent from the sons of Noah for all human beings. Yet theologians increasingly argued, as Mather did, that being human and claiming a place in Noachic genealogy did not necessarily mean that one could become Christian. As the Presbyterian minister Richard Baxter wrote in 1683, "We are all the offspring of Righteous *Noe* [Noah], and yet that maketh not the Infants of *Heathens* baptizable or pardoned."[9] The idea of universal ancestry favored by almost all Christians that emphasized all living humans as the descendants of Noah after the Flood did not make pagan children able to become Christian. It was this nascent idea about the heritability of Christianity and heathenism that gave English colonists in the New World an opening to deny Christianity and its associated privileges to Africans and Indians.

English concern about the suitability of Indian women for marriage surfaced soon after their arrival in Virginia. William Strachey described Indian women as "most voluptious" and eager to "embrace the acquaintance of any Straunger, and it is accounted no offence."[10] Though Strachey recognized that the English and Powhatan's people subscribed to vastly different mores regarding sex and marriage, the dissimilar cultural expectations for the appropriate behavior between men and women helped the English separate themselves from the Indians.[11] Indian women's openly flaunted sexuality disturbed him. Strachey caustically noted that in consequence of what he considered to be their intemperate behavior, Indian men and women alike "are full of their own country-disease (the Pox)." Strachey also remarked upon Indian marriage practices, especially the custom of polygyny among male political leaders. Some Indian men had many wives, Strachey thought, "because they would haue many Children," but he did not believe the Indians' polygynous system achieved its object. "[Y]t may be a Probleme in Philosophy, whether [a] variety of women be a furtheraunce or hinderaunce of many Birthes?" Strachey answered his own question, noting that "many women deviding the body, and the Strength thereof, make yt generally vnfitt to the office of Increase." Polygynous marriage, Strachey believed, had resulted in what he observed as stunted population growth among the Indians. Non-English, non-Christian marriages were not suited to a thriving populace. Strachey concluded his musings on Indians' marriage practices and population increases by recommending that "they keepe a stricter Ceremony in their kynd of Marriages."[12]

English visitors among the Powhatan had also observed that, in addition to their odd marital arrangements, the Indians had a different way of defining lineage and of determining inheritance of status and political power.[13] Powhatan matrilineality would have been strange to English observers, whose patrilineal inheritance patterns gave little thought to mothers' status. In Virginia, Algonkian women were the primary caretakers of the cornfields surrounding their villages as well as the custodians of lineage, heritable privileges, and status—all male prerogatives in English society. A corollary horror to the matrilineal nature of Powhatan society was the perceived sexual looseness of Indian women; Strachey was not the only English observer who found the mostly unclothed Indian women to be licentious and sexually available. Powhatan women picked their sexual partners and easily arranged and dissolved marriages. English men in Virginia, coming as they did from a society that regulated sex, marriage, and lineage through social, legal, and religious strictures, found these social characteristics to be distasteful signs of heathenism and barbarity. Most appallingly, Indian women's sexual licentiousness confused English notions of patrilineality: if women could pass from man to man easily and by choice, how could legitimate heirs of property, wealth, political power, and status be properly determined? Strachey's protoethnographic interests in sex and marriage among the Indians notwithstanding, it was clear to most Englishmen in Virginia that the Indians desperately needed to emulate Christian English patterns of marriage and lineage.

Nevertheless, the dearth of English women at Jamestown in its early years and the close proximity of Indian women probably made intimate relationships between English men and Indian women inevitable. Don Pedro de Zúñiga, the Spanish ambassador to England between 1605 and 1612 and accomplished spymaster, reported to the king of Spain that as many as fifty Englishmen had married Powhatan women.[14] (This indication of friendly relations between the English and the Indians alarmed the Spanish and added to the Spanish fear that stable English settlements in the Chesapeake could eventually threaten Spanish Florida and the Caribbean.) Zúñiga's spies, however, were not witnessing liaisons that either the English or the Indians would have described as marriages or even as permanent partnerships. Algonkian sexual mores permitted informal pairings that either partner could dissolve after a short period of time, which were certainly possible in the early days of the settlement when Indian visits were welcome at Jamestown. Archaeological evidence suggests that in its early years the Jamestown fort sheltered Indian women weaving traditional grass mats and manufacturing shell beads and Indian men making arrowheads, thus increasing the likelihood that sexual relations between English men and Indian women took place in greater numbers than historians have previously supposed.[15]

Virginia Company officials might have been aware of Indian women at Jamestown. The *Lawes Divine Morall and Martiall* of 1612 sought to control interaction between English men and Indian women, by making the rape of "any woman, maid or Indian" a capital crime and fornication punishable by whipping and begging "publique forgivenesse."[16] The law simultaneously protected Indian women from ravishment and regulated English men's interaction with them by threatening punishment of the men. Indeed, when the law used the word *maid* to describe the few English women in the colony at the time, which indicated in its seventeenth-century usage a virgin or unmarried woman whose chaste behavior was a commendable indication of Christian virtue, it implied that Indian women did not conform to the ideal of a chaste, virginal English woman.[17] It was the first antifornication statute in Virginia, and one that even in the absence of ecclesiastical courts continued the English tradition of public humiliation and contrition. Although the *Lawes* intended to cut off unsanctioned sexual contact between heathen Indian women and Christian English men, the English did see officially sanctioned Anglo-Indian marriage as a tool of both conversion and assimilation. Only when English men reduced Indian women to their proper place in Christian marriage were Anglo-Indian sexual relationships acceptable. Marriage became the only religiously and legally sanctioned way to cross those boundaries.

Though the marriage of Metoaka and John Rolfe is the most famous Anglo-Indian marriage, there were others preceding the devastating violence of 1622. Two female attendants accompanied Metoaka to London and remained there for some time at the Virginia Company's expense, eventually converting to Christianity and taking the names Mary and Elizabeth. The company opted not to return them to Virginia but instead sought to provide them with English husbands in Bermuda. Company leaders might have feared the two young women might revert to heathenism unless they were married to pious English men and kept permanently separate from bad influences in Tsenacommacah. As marriageable English "maids," they made ideal wives for planters newly arrived in the Somer Isles, but even if the Englishmen there did not consider them attractive wives, their respective dowries of "one servante apeec" meant they came with wealth in the form of labor, making them irresistible to planters in that island's growing tobacco economy. They were also given a Bible and a psalter to share. In Bermuda, the governor and his council received special instructions for the "carefull bestowinge" of the two women—in other words, their husbands were to be carefully selected.[18] Though Mary died en route to Bermuda, Elizabeth survived and more than one hundred people feted her at her wedding. She and her husband might have eventually relocated to Virginia.[19]

The conversion and subsequent marriages of Metoaka and Elizabeth (who might have been Metoaka's half sister) were the substance of their transformation—in English eyes—from heathen, sexually licentious Indians to proper Christian "maids." Properly reduced to Christianity and assuming their places in Christian English households in Virginia and Bermuda, these women became for the English the ideal outcome of the conversion program—both civilized and married to English men. These marriages opened the door to other Anglo-Indian dynastic marriages: marriages that brought converted Indian women into the English orbit and ensured that the children born of these unions would share an English Christian lineage.

Despite the two Anglo-Indian marriages the Virginia Company orchestrated, intermarriage was not an immediate solution to the dearth of marriageable women. After 1618, the Virginia Company mandated that land be privately held. Planters now had to marry to establish New World family lineages, produce legitimate heirs, and make the land inalienably English. With Wahunsonacock's successor Opechancanough reluctant to pledge more Indian women as wives, English women were necessary to accomplish this task. By 1619, the company had begun recruiting English "maids" and widows to travel to Virginia and there marry English men. As a pilot project, one company investor proposed that one hundred women, "young and uncorrupt" should be sent to Virginia to "make wifes to the Inhabitantes and by that meanes to make the men there more settled & lesse moveable who by defect thereof . . . stay there but to gett something and then to returne for England, w[hi]ch will breed a dissolucon, and so an overthrow of the plantacon."[20] Making English men more settled would make the colony more successful. Thus, the Virginia Company pursued the point that Robert Beverley wrote about almost a century later: marriages between English men and English women would ensure the continued growth and success of the colony as well as the Anglicization of the land itself. The presence of women as wives both settled men and made them less susceptible to wandering and rebellion. To make profits and ensure stability, the company needed English women.

By 1620, at least ninety women had journeyed from England to Virginia for the express purpose of marrying men there, and the company wanted to send one hundred more.[21] These potential wives were not a free commodity the company provided for its settlers; planters were expected to reimburse the company for the costs of transporting their wives, a charge that varied between 120 and 150 pounds of tobacco. Planters were to receive the women "with the same Christian pietie and charitie as they are sent from hence." The marriages were integral to maintaining English Christianity, but the women themselves were offered to a limited number of planters—that is, men of property, not indentured servants. The company paid lip service to the right to choose one's marriage partner, at least, but the intent was clear: women were a product, not unlike tobacco, for whom able planters had to pay. Poor indentured servants who managed to attract the interest of the company's maids were discouraged and would have to pay for their wives later. The system seemed to work: at the end of May 1622, observers at Jamestown reported that "57 young maids have bin sent to make wives for the Planters, divers of which were well married before the coming away of the Ships."[22]

The scheme was not perfect. There were still not nearly enough potential English wives to go around in Virginia, a state of affairs that prompted the company to declare that women indentured servants could not promise themselves in marriage "without either the consent of her parents, or of her Master or Mistress, or of the magistrate and minister of the place both together." Apparently women with contractual obligations to provide labor for planters for a term of years were reducing or outright evading their service through marriage. And not all the women who arrived in Virginia were the pious maids planters expected. A 1623 complaint about the company's governor claimed, "He sent but few women thither & those corrupt." The corrupt women might have been among those who in 1624 had taken advantage of the imbalanced population to promise matrimony to two or more men. Such women were sentenced to a whipping or a fine, "according to the qualitie of the p[er]son so offending." Despite the problems, Virginia's settlers continued to demand that English women be sent, if not as wives, as laborers to nurse sick men or to do washing. As one plaintive comment on English women in early Virginia acknowledged, "Women are necessary members for the Colonye," but the women who lived there "doe . . . nothing but to devoure the good of the land without doing any dayes deed whereby any benefit may arise either to ye Company or Countrey."[23] Wives were both a blessing and a curse.

The dissolution of the Virginia Company in 1624 and Virginia's new status as a royal colony ended the tobacco-for-wives scheme, but finding enough English women to sustain the colony's stability and to ensure its growth remained a challenge. One Englishman chose the option of Anglo-Indian matrimony when it served the greater economic and geo-political interests of both the English and the Indians. In 1638 John Bass, a minister squatting south of the James in what would shortly become Surry County, married the daughter of the Nansemond werowance. The marriage guaranteed his family's security, all of whom were settled ille-gally in a territory whose native residents paid tribute to Opechanca-nough. The union benefited the Nansemonds as well, who likely used the kinship ties formed through the marriage to loosen their dependence on Opechancanough and to trade and to treat with the English. The Basses gained access to land south of the James River, as well as security against possible attack by Opechancanough.

Bass chose his bride with English religious strictures in mind. His wife Keziah was identified in Bass family records as "a Baptized Xtian [Christian]" whom Bass married in the Church of England. (Keziah was the name of one of Job's daughters, suggesting that she chose this particular name to symbolize her conversion and marriage as the end of a period of tribulation. The biblical Keziah also received an inheri-tance from her father—unusual in the Old Testament, which suggests that both Keziah and John Bass expected some support from Keziah's father.) The couple lived together for forty years and had at least eight children—a much longer and more successful marriage than that of Metoaka and John Rolfe, if less well known.[24] Though this union post-dated the ferocious violence of 1622, it followed the same general guide-lines John Rolfe established years earlier. The bride was a converted Christian, and the children themselves carried the name and lineage of their father John Bass. Yet, unlike the Metoaka-Rolfe marriage, this one received no fanfare in England and no official recognition, reflecting the post-1622 ambivalence toward Anglo-Indian marriage. Indeed, unlike Thomas Rolfe, the Bass children enjoyed no special privileges as scions of a noble union and lineage; they faded away from the territory around Surry County only to resurface as members of the Monacan nation in the early eighteenth century.

In newly settled Catholic Maryland, the proprietary government under the Calvert family had also instituted a program to convert the Pis-cataway Indians they encountered there. English Jesuit Andrew White soon converted the tayac (a title the English translated as "emperor") and his wife. Governor Leonard Calvert and Margaret Brent oversaw the baptism of the tayac's daughter and probably served as her god-parents as well. After the tayac's death, Margaret Brent kept the little girl, whom the English called Mary Kittomaquund, in her custody to guard against attacks by the Piscataway and to preserve English claims to land in Maryland. Sometime in late 1644, Margaret Brent permitted the girl, then probably eleven or twelve years old, to marry her brother Giles Brent. In marrying Mary, Giles Brent probably thought he could gain title to Indian lands, believing that property would descend to Mary after her father's death. Lineage worked this way in English law but the Piscataways, like the Powhatans, ceded power between genera-tions matrilineally. Giles Brent failed to gain political power or land in Maryland, and after the anti-Catholic and antiproprietary Ingle's Rebel-lion of 1645–46, the Calverts forced the Brents to leave the colony for the Northern Neck of Virginia, where Mary gave birth to at least two children before her early death. The Brents remained in Virginia, where they were known for decades as a recusant Catholic family in unabash-edly Protestant Virginia. Anglo-Virginians long distrusted Giles Brent and Mary Kittomaquund's descendants because of both their Catholi-cism and their Indian heritage, suggesting that the Brent descendants were as ostracized as the Bass descendants.[25]

The English were willing to tolerate the Anglo-Indian marriages of Metoaka and John Rolfe, Elizabeth and her unnamed husband, Keziah and John Bass, and Mary and Giles Brent because the Indian women had converted to Christianity (although Mary was still suspect because of her Catholicism). Their Christianity rendered the women acceptable, but the English also knew that most Indian women did not convert to Christianity. The English also could derive geopolitical benefits only from a limited number of these marriages. These English men married converted Christians, Indian women who had been transformed through conversion into "maids." Bound legally and religiously to English men in godly marriage, these women had ceased to be threats and had become English in their sexual mores, and their children were born into English notions of heredity and patrilinity. The women's Indian heritage was effectively subsumed by Christian marriage, and their children's Indian heritage was overwhelmed by English blood.

The Bass and Brent marriages show that English settlers in Mary-land and Virginia tolerated Anglo-Indian marriage only within certain strictures. Whereas marriage at least could subsume a woman's Indian-ness into her husband's Englishness, fornication and adultery, whether among the English themselves or between settlers and Indians or Africans, remained unacceptable. The *Lawes* of 1612 did not make distinctions about fornication; miscreants were to be whipped regardless of whether they were English or Indian. Indeed, Anglo-Indian fornication in this early period was punishable in precisely the same way as fornication between English people—by whipping. Later, punishments for fornication evolved to include traditional English acts of public humiliation and contrition, usually involving public penance during Sunday services, for which the perpetrators stood in front of the congregation wrapped in white sheets and carrying white rods.[26] Although ecclesiastical courts performed the function of enforcing moral discipline in England, that institution was never introduced in the English New World. Thus the regulation of sexual behavior in early Virginia was haphazard as well. Though the records contain many references to illicit sexual behavior— usually fornication and its attendant problems, bastardy, adultery, and even occasionally sodomy—it is impossible to discern a pattern of accusation, conviction, and punishment. Most colonies in the English Atlantic enacted laws regarding behavior (or neglected to do so, providing no guidance), and the civil courts of the counties were responsible for prosecuting fornication cases, a state of affairs unknown in England before the Interregnum. For example, in 1619 the new Virginia Assembly required ministers to report "ungodly disorders" such as "whoredomes, dishonest company keeping with weomen and suche like," but it did not specify particular punishments, saying only that the miscreants "be presented and punished accordingly." (The law did suggest that repeat offenders might be excommunicated.)[27] As practice varied from jurisdiction to jurisdiction, a hybridized system developed, in which perpetrators were sometimes fined, sometimes whipped, sometimes required to do the traditional penance, and sometimes required to perform some combination of all these punishments. Occasionally courts even discharged offenders with no punishment whatsoever.

The problem was particularly acute in Virginia, which suffered an unusually high rate of illegitimate births to English women.[28] In 1638, for example, John Holloway and Catherine Jones, both English people, were convicted of fornication. John had to pay two hundred pounds of tobacco and "acknowledge his Fault before the Congregation the next Sabboth day," while Catherine had to submit not to public penance but rather to thirty lashes across her back. In 1639 one English couple was convicted of fornication without ever being made to stand in white sheets before the congregation. Instead, John Pope and Elsie Kotton were each given forty lashes. That same court session, three married couples who presumably had borne children too soon after their marriages were all convicted of fornication; these couples stood "in the Church three severall Sundays doinge penence accordinge to the Cannons of the Church."[29] In 1641 Elizabeth Storkey suffered twenty lashes for fornication, but mysteriously her parish's vestry specifically requested that she "be Cleared from standing in a white sheete."[30] In 1645 Alice Staples escaped her fornication charge without any punishment; her paramour John Jewett was fined one thousand pounds of tobacco.[31] Before new legislation in 1662 whipping was the most frequent punishment, followed by public penance, additional time on an indenture, and fines.[32] The explicit exemption from standing in white sheets in some of these cases raises an intriguing possibility: perhaps the shame and humiliation of begging penance before an audiences of fellow Christian English was more of a social stigma than fines or a whipping. Or perhaps the geographic distance between parishes and the frequent lack of ministers and Sunday services meant that justices occasionally ordered a whipping for public humiliation because standing before the congregation was not an option. Nevertheless, the law was ambiguous and punishments varied among Anglo-Virginians.

The discovery and punishment of Anglo-Virginian fornication was a confused affair, perhaps because there was less confusion when it came to what was coming to be seen as a greater crime: illicit Anglo-Indian and Anglo-African sex. The rising incidence of both transgressions brought the English a new problem—the mixing of Christian and heathen bodies outside the bounds of marriage. Enslaved Africans lived among the English, usually as indentured servants with a fixed period of servitude rather than as slaves for life, and after they gained their freedom they continued to live among the English, pursuing their own livelihoods as planters and tradesmen. Unlike the Tidewater's Indians, Africans had to settle for living among the English—there was nowhere else for them to go. Thus, as the opportunities for Anglo-Indian sex dwindled, opportunities for Anglo-African sex burgeoned, prompting the English to judge those relationships in religious terms as well. Punishments for Anglo-African sex varied as well, although the accusations and the punishments were often described using religious language, unlike those for English couples engaging in illicit sex. If deciding how to punish fornicating English couples was a problem for Virginia's infant judicial system, Anglo-African couples caused even greater problems. It was a given that English couples could be punished with public penance in church—they were all Christian.

Hugh Davis's case in 1631 was the first recorded prosecution for Anglo-African sex in Virginia, and it illustrates the quality of English anxieties about these liaisons and the precarious religious position of enslaved Africans in the community. Davis's case was also the opening salvo in a long and bitter battle over the mixing of English and African bodies. David was "soundly whipped, before an Assembly of Negroes and others for abuseing himself to the dishonor of God and to the shame of Christians, by defiling his body in lying with a Negro; which fault he is to acknowledge next Sabbath day."[33] Intercourse with an African body defiled Davis's Christian English body, suggesting the presence of a color line for religious affiliation in early Virginia. To add to this, Davis's crime was to the "shame of Christians"; in other words, he implicated an entire community while he was "abusing himself." Juxtaposing the Christian Davis and his presumably heathen African partner pointed to a widening gulf between English people and enslaved Africans. Davis was not in trouble with the law simply for having committed fornication, as was the case for so many of his fellow settlers. He was also in trouble for mixing his Christian body with a heathen one.

Not all Anglo-African fornication cases produced such hostile language; ten years later, another Anglo-African fornication case came to a similar conclusion but without the religiously descriptive language. In October 1640 Robert Sweat and an unnamed African woman were convicted of fornication. Robert was sentenced to "do public penance for his offense at *James* city church in the time of devine service according to the laws of *England*," while the anonymous woman was publicly whipped.[34] Which was the more humiliating punishment is an open and possibly unanswerable question. It is likely, though, that Sweat's partner was not Christian and therefore ineligible for punishment and penance before the congregation.

Describing sexual intimacy between heathen and Christian bodies as an act of defilement occurred elsewhere in the English Atlantic as well. In 1644 the assembly of Antigua in the Leeward Islands laid out punishments for "any Christian man or woman that be Lawfully Convicted to have had Carnall Copulation with A heathen man or woman." Penalties differed according to marital status, status as a free person, servant, or slave, and whether a child was conceived; punishments ranged from fines to hard labor and from whipping (for those unable to pay) to banishment or enslavement with offenders being made "a Slave ffor his or her Life to the Collony." (It is not clear if English people could be punished with enslavement.) Enslaved people convicted of breaking the law were whipped and branded. The harshness of the penalties indicates how threatened English people felt by the rise in bodily mixing through "carnall coppullation" around them and the increase in mulatto children whose lineage, and therefore their social position, was difficult to determine. English paternity was critical to clarifying the status of children resulting from these unions; illegitimate children who had English Christian fathers were brought up as indentured servants and gained their freedom when they reached the age of majority, but the mulatto illegitimate children of English Christian mothers received no such benefit, remaining enslaved for life. If accused fathers disputed paternity for these children, a special jury was impaneled once the infant reached one month old to determine if "the Child to have bin beggotton by A white man Indian or negroe." Presumably the delay allowed skin tone to become more obvious, and if the child did not survive, local institutions would be saved the cost of the investigation. Establishing lineage was as crucial to maintaining the social order as was punishing any "man soo defiling himselfe with any heathen."[35]

In Bermuda English paternity was also sometimes critical to determining the status of children born out of wedlock to an English father and an Indian or African mother. When the father was an indentured servant and the mother was enslaved, it seems that the parents' master generally took responsibility for the child, as in 1649 when William Johnston gained custody of a "Mallatto child reputed to be the child of John Browne begotten of Mr. Jonston's negroe." That child was indentured until the age of thirty. Similarly in 1651, another child "begotten by an Englishman of the body of one of the Companyes Negroes" was indentured for twenty-eight years.[36] Like the Virginians and the Antiguans, Bermudians took a dim view of fornication and were inclined to punish such activities in public. In 1657 several "negros [were] presented for fornication and adultery [and] were ordered to have 39 lashes upon the naked backe, at the publicke meeting places where the Minister preacheth."[37]

In Virginia, even the rumor of interracial fornication was sufficient to cause an uproar. In November 1646, at the Accomack County Court, Stephen Carlton testified "that he hard [heard] Rowland Mills say that

Martin Kennett should say that Goodwife Hinman had layen with an Indian." Charlton, who as a member of the court was a prominent person socially and politically in the county, sensed that someone was trying to slander the Hinmans and so replied "lett them have a care what they say." Rowland Mills answered that "it is generally Spoken of." That Goody Hinman had had sex with an Indian was so "generally spoken of" that it had reached the ears of one of the more illustrious planters in the county.[38] The court records say no more about Goody Hinman and her alleged Indian partner until February 1646/47, but by that time the story moved beyond errant gossip of the slanderous sort—that is, rumor passed orally from person to person—to a libel case, one in which demonstrably untrue statements were written down and passed from person to person. The libel took the form of a 125-line poem that was conveniently recorded by the justices, beginning, cryptically, by describing a wild boar breaking a pipkin: "The Boare did strike it with his Tush [tusk] / but did not enter farr."[39] The poem goes on to record the various attempts of English tradesmen ranging from a blacksmith to an innkeeper to repair the damaged pipkin. (A pipkin is a small, delicate pot used for making sauces or, in this case, a metaphoric representation of a dainty, innocent woman or maid.)[40] John Hinman thought that the pipkin represented his wife Sarah and that the savage boar alluded to in the poem was an Indian, who had violated his wife with his "tusk." The libel, Hinman said, had turned up at the same time someone stole clean laundry drying on the hedge outside his home. John Hinman apparently woke up one morning to find his favorite "Holland shirt & smocke" missing and the libelous poetry left in its place.[41]

Hinman sued Richard Buckland, John Culpepper, and Roger Johns for defamation. Hinman alleged that the three men had "scandalized & defamed" both his wife and his stepdaughter Ann Smyth through spreading both the rumors and by dropping the libel. Libeling Sarah Hinman implied two things about her daughter: one, she was illegitimate, and two, she was half-Indian. No word existed to describe such a person in the Anglo-American world. Although the Spanish had coined the term *mestizo* to describe persons of mixed European and Indian descent, Virginians had no identifying term, so despite their discomfort Anglo-Virginians could not fix a label on Sarah Hinman's progeny. John Hinman's response to the libel suggested that he thought his neighbors derided his ability to govern a Christian English household, enforce gender norms, and beget legitimate heirs. His English masculinity was called into question. Yet when John Hinman sued the alleged destroyers of Sarah Hinman's reputation in county court, his most forceful, most emotional claim was that they had "barbarusly Scandalized & defamed yo[u]r pet[itioners] wife by sayeinge that she defyled her body with a pagan in your Pe[itioners] owne howse insomuch that she hath . . . lost her Credit & her fame by the s[ai]d Aspcon [aspersion]."[42]

As if the accusations of the libel were not enough, some of the witnesses called by Buckland, Culpepper, and Johns to show that they were not the originators of the slander or the libel demonstrated how far-reaching the rumor was. One deponent testified that she "did heare speeches that an Indyan did lye with an English woman And that the woman was with child." Another deponent agreed that there were rumors of an English woman having sex with an Indian but could not remember who the woman was. She posited that it might have been Goodwife Howse or Goodwife Booth or maybe even Goody Hinman.[43] "She defyled her body with a Pagan." These words were powerful for what they suggested about English Virginians' perception of themselves and their perception of the Indians who lived near them. To defile her body intimated that she had rendered herself "foul and filthy," and she had desecrated herself. Thus, the punishments visited upon the three offenders were also serious. Richard Buckland was ordered to "stand att ye Church doore . . . with a pap[er] upon his hatt" with his crime written upon it. The humiliation of public penance "in the tyme of divine service" served as the communal, public agent of punishment and forgiveness. John Culpepper was sentenced to a similar fate as well as a hefty fine.

Although the breadth of the accusations that came to light in the Hinman case was not common, county court records reveal other rumors of illicit Anglo-Indian sex. Farther north on the Eastern Shore in Maryland, Mary Edwin sued her neighbor for slander, "saying she hath lyen with an Indian for peake or roanoke."[44] Just as the Hinmans believed that even the rumor that Goody Hinman had "defiled her body with a pagan" was damaging to her reputation, Mary Edwin saw the potential damage to her reputation if she allowed rumors that she had slept with an Indian to go unchallenged. Actual illicit relationships with Indians also earned opprobrium from the English as well. In 1655 the wife of merchant and Indian trader William Clawson was granted a divorce from her husband after she was able to prove he had abandoned her to live with an Indian woman from a Delaware band. Although divorce was next to impossible in English society, the county court took William Clawson's abandonment of his wife in favor of a "pagan" very seriously.[45] The self-identification of the English as Christian and their identification of Indians as heathens in these cases show that the mixing of Indian and English bodies caused substantial anxiety among the English. If the Hinmans' reaction seems like overkill (prosecuting three people), the threat to Sarah Hinman's and Ann Smyth's reputations and, by extension, to John Hinman's reputation, was serious. The insinuation that Goody Hinman had "defiled" herself with a pagan Indian was devastating—not in the least because it called into question the lineage and Christianity of her children.

An Anglo-African fornication case occurred in 1649 and was punished quite differently. One Will Watts, presumably an Englishman, and Mary, "Mr Cornelius Lloyds negar woman," were required to acknowledge their fornication by standing before the congregation of Elizabeth River Parish swathed in white sheets and carrying a white rod on the Sabbath.[46] In this case, a white man and a black woman were punished together and equally, in the church, for their offense. The case implies that Mary was in some way a member of the congregation, as does the fact that she had a Christian name. Indeed, Christianity seems to have been a factor in deciding how to punish two Africans for fornication. In 1654 "Richard Johnson Negroe, & a Negroe woman [Mary Gersheene]" were presented, along with an English couple, for fornication and required to attend the next court.[47] Johnson was Christian and Gersheene almost certainly so; those facts together with their presentment alongside an English couple suggests that their Christianity was what allowed them to be prosecuted in the same manner as English couples. (Unfortunately the outcome of their trial was not recorded.)

Similarly, in York County in 1658, Thomas Twine, an indentured servant, was found by "Circumstantial Evidence" to be the father of an African woman's child. The woman, unnamed, apparently belonged to Twine's master. He was ordered "att next publique meeting at Marston Church hee doe open pennance," but there was no punishment noted for the woman in question.[48] In early 1662 the court ordered Alice Miles, a servant of John Hill, to suffer an unspecified number of lashes but she apparently evaded the punishment. A later entry requiring her master to produce her for punishment clarified her crime: "fornication with a Negro Mr John Hills servant."[49] Twine could be punished before the congregation at Marston Parish; he was undoubtedly considered Christian, but his partner was not and therefore was not included in the punishment. Yet Alice Miles was ordered whipped for a similar infraction, showing the ambivalence and confusion in the courts. The English were uncomfortable with Anglo-African fornication, especially since the punishment of non-Christian perpetrators was difficult to effect.

In 1661 the New Poquoson Parish churchwardens presented Thomas Heyrich and Rebecca Noble for fornication and adultery. The county court convicted Noble and sentenced her to "ten stripes on her bared back" and that she "do penance in the s[ai]d poquoson pish [parish] church by standing in a white sheet & asking open forgiveness on hir knees of God almighty for hir s[ai]d offence before the whole Congregation and also that shee forthwith aske forgiveness of the Court." Heyrich, on the other hand, escaped punishment by claiming that Noble "kept company with a Negro man of Coll Mathewes & would have had him had it not been for Collonell Carey and that shee was to have Maryed a Negro of Coll Reads." By the early 1660s, then, even the unproved accusation of interracial fornication earned Noble a whipping and two forms of public punishment, one in church and one in court. The growing English anxiety about the mixing of pagan and heathen bodies extended to Anglo-African marriages as well as Anglo-African fornication; the court considered itself fortunate that it obstructed Noble's marriage. (She was also a servant; her marriage would have been illegal without her master's permission even if it had been to an English servant. Yet nowhere did the court imply that her marriage would have been illegal on the basis of her paramour's African descent.) Heyrich also accused Noble of having an "evill life & conversation"—not an ordinary sort of moral fallibility.[50]

In 1662 Virginia made its first attempt to standardize the criminal prosecution and sentencing of fornication cases. The General Assembly could now do this legally because the Restoration permanently gave civil courts jurisdiction over moral offenses, essentially the judicial power of the Church of England. The new law stipulated: "Whereas some doubts have arisen whether children got by any Englishman upon a negro woman should be slave or ffree, *Be it therefore enacted and declared by this present grand assembly*, that all children borne in this country shalbe held bond or free only according to the condition of the mother, *And* that if any christian shall committ ffornication with a negro man or woman, hee or shee soe offending shall pay double the ffines imposed by the former act."[51] The first part of the law referred to an "Englishman" and a "negro woman," clearly showing "English" and "negro" as marks of identity, one implying slave status (although the law did not discount the idea that a black woman could be free). The second part of the law, the part dealing with fornication, complicated these two identities substantially by adding a third: Christian. "If any christian shall committ ffornication with a negro . . ." The law was not gender specific, but it expressed a clear assumption: English people were Christian; people of African descent were not. The Virginia planters who enacted this law did more than define who was a slave and who was free. They also used religious criteria both to codify perceived differences between English bodies and African bodies and to judge the appropriateness of interracial sexual contact. In doing so, they automatically defined Africans as non-Christians, despite the fact that many Africans arrived in Virginia already Christian or shortly thereafter converted. What makes this act— and the cases surrounding it—so fascinating is its mix of religious and racial language. Though the Antiguan law from 1644 had pioneered the connections among lineage, religion, and race, Anglo-Virginians were poised to irrevocably racialize religion, sex, and reproduction.

The act also set up a bifurcated system of punishment. Servant women who were convicted of fornication had actually committed two crimes and therefore suffered two punishments. The first transgression was a civil crime, her violation of her contractual agreement with her master, which the act punished by the fine, usually assessed through extra time on her indenture to recompense her master for time and effort lost during her pregnancy and delivery. The second crime was her moral offense against the community, punished, as was traditional, by a public whipping. Although there was no further ecclesiastical component to this, public whippings of male and female fornicators on court days stood in lieu of white sheets and white rods in front of the congregation. Indentured servants and free English alike could find themselves whipped for fornication. Convicted servant women could waive the whipping by paying a fine, which they paid not to their masters or to the county, but to the parish. (Often masters paid their servants' fines in exchange for yet more years of service.) The Virginia legislature cleverly retained the tradition of communal punishment for moral offenses, and masters could still recover damages for lost time when their servant women became pregnant. Shortly after the passage of the act, a court assigned two punishments to Ann Roberts such that "at the Expiration of hir time by Indenture shee make satisfaction to hir s[ai]d Master according to Act of Assembly either by service or paymt of tobacco And also that for hir offence against God shee be taken into the Sherriffes Custody and receive 10 stripes on hir bared back."[52] Roberts's offenses against her master and against God were separate transgressions and thus merited two separate punishments.

Other colonial legislatures approached the problem of interracial and interreligious fornication in different ways. In 1663 Bermuda simply prohibited marriages between "ffree borne subiects" from marrying "any negroes molattoes or musteses [mustees]" with banishment from the colony as a possible punishment.[53] This law did not address fornication, however, which remained a problem. In 1670 an English indentured servant named Judith Porter was whipped in "the churchyard after the Evening Sermon" after she gave birth to a "Blacke Childe."[54] The child's status (servant or slave) was not recorded. Bermuda struggled with the same issue that plagued Virginia: how could the lineage of mixed-race children be established, especially when there was no marriage to clarify matters? In Judith Porter's case, public humiliation and whipping seemed to be the answer.

Marylanders approached the problem from a slightly different perspective, especially as it respected the children of interracial marriages and illicit interracial unions (the Virginia law did not address marriage at all). In September 1664 the Maryland Council presented the lower house with a problem, wanting to "knowe what the lower howse intends shall become of such weomen of the English or other Christian nacons being free that are now allready married to negros or other Slaves." Marylanders framed the issue in religious terms also, although at issue there was the marriage of "Christian" English women to non-Christian Africans or Indians ("other slaves"). In wondering what to do about these women, the Maryland Council asked three questions: "Shall such weomen be forced to serve as long as their husbands liue? . . . shall the issue already borne of such marryage be bond or free? . . . shall the issue hereafter to be borne of such marryage be bond or free?" The lower house answered that women need not serve with their husbands but that children of those unions, both before and after the debate, would serve thirty years. The law that resulted, though, looked a little different. It stipulated that all African slaves were to "serve Durante Vita"—for life—and that children born to slaves would remain enslaved. The law also addressed the problem of "freeborne English women forgettfull of their free Condicon and to the disgrace of our Nation doe intermarry with Negro Slaues" by mandating that the woman serve her husband's master, and all children born in the union would be slaves like their fathers. Children already born were exempted from this requirement and instead were to serve thirty years. The women concerned, initially identified as free women from "Christian nations," were participating in "shameful matches." By marrying presumably heathen African men, they shamed their Christianity and lost the freedom that English residents of the Chesapeake associated with their religion. The loss of their children's freedom compounded the women's loss of freedom. Although in Virginia slave status was inherited from the mother and in Maryland from the father, the outcome was more or less the same—the children of interracial unions now lost their freedom as well, in effect inheriting a pagan identity.[55]

In Virginia, it took some time for servants to suffer the effects of the 1662 law. In York County, there were no interracial fornication cases between 1662 and 1683; for two decades, then, the harshest provisions of the 1662 act lay moribund. While women servants found themselves serving extra time for producing bastards, the county courts still made an effort to identify and punish fathers as well. Of the twenty-one fornication cases brought in that twenty-year period, eight involved free English women. In those cases, the court pursued the man involved as well. The remainder involved English servant women.[56] Between 1683 and 1691, when a further law penalizing interracial fornicators was passed, there was only one such case in York County. In 1683 Elizabeth Bancks was presented for "fornication & Bastardy with a Negro slave" and was ordered to pay her master with extra time and to suffer thirtynine lashes. There are odd gaps in the York County records; for example, there were no fornication presentments of any type between 1665 and 1671. Perhaps churchwardens were not as energetic in reporting cases as they were supposed to be; in 1682 the churchwardens were censured by the county government for being "very remise in presenting such persons as have comitted misdeamenoars in their precincts contrary to their duty."[57] It might also suggest that the residents of York County viewed the provisions of the 1662 law not just with laziness but with skepticism and ambivalence.

Although presentments and punishments appear fairly relaxed in York County, elsewhere the religious tensions in interracial fornication cases continued. In Accomack County, Elizabeth Lang, an indentured servant, gave birth to an illegitimate child she readily admitted had been fathered by an Indian she called Oni Kitt. In January 1671/72 she agreed to three years' extra time on her indenture, declaring that she "humbly desireth that the Indian may not have the bringing up of my child, nor anything to do with it . . . a Pagan may not have my child." In an ordinary fornication case, the child's father would be required to pay some sort of maintenance for his child—but sheriffs were unable to locate Oni Kitt. Elizabeth's strong words might have been a ploy to keep her child with her by saying what the court wished to hear, but the court and the mother were worried about a non-Christian having some control over the upbringing of an English woman's child.[58]

In 1691 Virginia passed yet another law regulating interracial fornication: "That if any English woman being free shall have a bastard child by any negro or mulatto, she pay the sume of fifteen pounds sterling."[59] Those unable to pay would be sold into indentured servitude for five years. The law was the same for servant women, only those women were not afforded the opportunity to pay the fine; their servitude was extended for five years. In York County, again, punishments were seldom in accordance with the new law. In 1694 Judeth Clarke was convicted of "the sinn of fornication with a negro." For the sin portion of her crime she received twenty lashes, and then she was assessed two years' extra service (the standard time since 1662) for inconveniencing her master.[60] At the same legislative session, the burgesses passed another act mandating exile for "whatsoever English or other white man or woman being free shall intermarry with a negroe, mulatto, or Indian man or woman bond or free."[61] The act, while not forbidding interracial marriages, made them economically unfeasible for most planters by requiring couples to leave the colony. Not all English Virginians found this new law acceptable. A planter named George Ivie, who was presumably married to a black or mixed-race woman, petitioned the Virginia legislature for the "Repeale of the Act of Assembly, Against *English* people's Marrying with Negroes Indians or Mullattoes." Though the council referred the matter to the House of Burgesses, the Burgesses instead supported a rival petition from Surry County that laws against Anglo-African and Anglo-Indian marriages be "inforced and Strengthened." The House concluded that no changes to the law of 1691 were necessary.[62]

By the early eighteenth century, there was a strong cultural stigma against interracial liaisons, even if the legal penalties remained what they had been in the 1660s. In Accomack County, Mary Newman was presented for fornication and bastardy in December 1704, and the informer in her case declared her illegitimate child to be "a bastard child by a Negro." Mary disagreed vehemently, saying that, while her child was illegitimate, it had not been fathered by a black man, and "she offered to take her oath that ye s[ai]d child was not got by a Negro, but yt it was got by one William Edgg, a white man. She going to kiss ye Book [the Bible], Col Robinson as informer, out of a tender care, fearing she should forswear herself, prevented her."[63] Newman's willingness to admit to fornication while insisting that the child's father was white is telling, as is Colonel Robinson's refusal to allow her to swear the oath, implying that it was obvious her child was mulatto. The greater transgression was not simply having a bastard child; it was having a *mulatto* bastard child. (Interestingly, the county court dismissed the charges against Newman without explanation.)

In 1705 the legislature promulgated a new Law of Servants and Slaves that reinforced the distance between black and white, Christian and heathen. The act protected indentured servants "of christian parentage" but condemned non-Christians to slavery. "Christian parentage" was critical to freedom in this brave new world. The law also revisited the antifornication and antimarriage law of 1691, this time reviling the children from these unions as "abominable mixture and spurious issue." The law sought to prevent "unlawful coition" through hefty fines and a prison sentence, and it also punished any minister who might "wittingly presume to marry a white man with a negro or mulatto woman; or to marry a white woman with a negro or mulatto man" with a fine of ten thousand pounds of tobacco. (The law did not clarify how such a thing could happen "unwittingly.") The sections on marriage and fornication did not, however, engage the language of religion and race, instead using purely racial descriptors to identify miscreants: "white," "negro," and "mulatto." The language was probably deliberate; in this way, none of the parties to such a marriage could claim that Christian conversion was grounds for allowing the marriage to proceed.[64] The seventeenth-century conflation of religion and race made the codifications of the Law of Servants and Slaves possible.

The difficulties and ambiguities of punishing interracial fornication in the wake of the new law were still evident in the seven different county court entries of the action brought by Mungo Ingles against his servant Rachell Wood. Hearings about *Ingles v. Wood* straggled on for more than two years through multiple issues of arrest warrants for Wood, continuances, and contradictory judgments, only to end in a manner completely inconsistent with the 1705 Law of Servants and Slaves. On 24 June 1707 the court ruled that Wood, having borne a "bastard mulata female child . . . she is ordered to serve the s[ai]d Mungo one whole yeare after her time by indenture or custome be expired for the trouble of his house & it is allso ordered that after ward she be sold by the church Wardens of Bruton parish as the law directs." Although neither the county grand jury nor the Bruton Parish churchwardens had actually prosecuted the case, Ingles had made the case known and pursued it, and predictably the court's ruling included the traditional compensation for the master, who lost time and revenue to a pregnant servant ("the trouble of his house"), and the provision for sale of servants producing mulatto bastards detailed in 1705. But York County had successfully sentenced and sold only one woman, Rebecca Stephens in 1706, since the law was enacted, and apparently Rachell Wood would have none of it. In February 1707/8 Mungo Ingles was back in court presumably because Wood had not begun her extra year's service, but she did not come to court. The following May Wood was again sentenced to an extra year of service in Ingles's household, but there was no mention of the mandatory sale. A year after that, in May 1709, Wood still had not returned to Ingles to serve out her extra year. Wood did not come to court that session or in the June 1709 session. In July 1709 the county court, clearly growing tired of Ingles's repeated complaints, dismissed the petition, noting that "on consideration of the law in that case & the advice of the Councill at the Barr thereon are of oppinion that (the s[ai]d Woods time by indenture being expired) there is no service due to her master." Wood had been free for some time without having been sold by the churchwardens, and the court seemed to have had no intention of actually returning her to Ingles. Then, six months later in the January 1709/10 session, the court reconsidered its verdict at Ingles's request and ruled that "the Court took . . . into consideration again this day as also the law laid before them & s[ai]d Woods confession are of opinion that s[ai]d order formerly made disallowing service on a petition than refered by the s[ai]d Ingles is erronious & do therefore order that she the s[ai]d Wood serve her s[ai]d master in consideration of the loss of time & trouble of his house 1 whole year." Wood had to return to Ingles's service for a year, but she never appeared in the court records again. There is no evidence that the court followed through on its order to the churchwardens to sell her for a further five-year indenture as the law required.[65]

If application of the 1705 law did not always result in the sale of English women servants for five years following the illegitimate birth of a mulatto child, it was not because the county court usually acted in an opaque manner, as it did with Rachell Wood. More and more women found the solution to their problems in escape. In Accomack County in 1708, an English servant woman accused of fornication with a free black man named James Longo simply left the county after dragging the case out over a year and a half.[66] As English control over Virginia extended past the fall line of the James and new counties formed, it became easier for servant women facing punishment in the form of a further five-year indenture to run to the frontier and start new lives.

The 1705 act was the culmination of a process in which Anglo-Virginians defined themselves by their religion and defined others—Africans and Indians—as incapable of it. By regulating sexual activity, especially in fornication cases, but also in forbidding marriages and refusing Africans and Indians the civil and religious protections of Christian marriage, Anglo-Virginians linked their Christian lineage with heritable privileges. They effectively defined the children born of both licit and illicit interracial unions as hereditary heathens. Yet, despite the legal bright lines drawn by planters jealous of their power and privileges, the actual experiences of Anglo-Virginians and their African or Indian partners suggest that many people were ambivalent or even contemptuous of legal enforcement of race and separation. Making race legal was easy, but forcing people to live race the way it was written into Virginia's laws was a more difficult prospect. The resistance of individuals—from planters such as George Ivie and from indentured servants such as Rachell Wood—undermined the neat legal boxes planter-lawmakers created. Indians and Africans also resisted, increasingly using Christianity—and, more specifically, Christian baptism—as a means for undermining racial differentiation.

CHAPTER FOUR

Baptism and the Birth of Race

L ate in September 1667, Virginia's burgesses passed legislation governing a serious matter of bondage and freedom and of religious
inclusion and exclusion. The act began by exploring a critical question:
"Whereas some doubts have risen whether children that are slaves by
birth, and by the charity and piety of their owners made pertakers of the
blessed sacrament of baptisme, should by vertue of their baptisme be
made free." The assembly answered this question firmly: *"It is enacted
and declared by this grand assembly, and the authority thereof,* that the
conferring of baptisme doth not alter the condition of the person as to
his bondage or ffreedome; that diverse masters, freed from this doubt,
may more carefully endeavour the propagation of christianity by permitting children, though slaves, or those of greater growth if capable to be
admitted to that sacrament."[1] The burgesses thus closed a legal loophole
and negated a widely accepted tenet of Christian practice that had formerly awarded freedom to enslaved converts. This law allowed Anglo-
Virginians to create a Christianity in which the traditional privileges
of an Englishman, most notably freedom, were denied to Africans and
Indians.

Baptism and the Christian conversion it conferred had been an accepted route to freedom in the English Atlantic during the sixteenth
and early seventeenth centuries.[2] While this 1667 law is critical to understanding the legal development of slavery, baptism also played a sin-
gular role in defining the English understanding of human difference.
Although the law did not prevent the baptism of Africans (it probably
meant to encourage it), it had the practical effect of discouraging English
slave owners from baptizing their slaves. The law did not apply to Indians and was not intended to alter Indian policy, but it probably had a
chilling effect on Indian baptism as well, because Anglo-Virginian masters probably still feared that Indian indentured servants (who served
terms much longer than English servants) could successfully sue for
their freedom on the basis of their baptisms. Thus, the ambiguities of

the law shaped the servitude and freedom of Indians and Africans in ways the burgesses had not anticipated.

The law also had other unintended consequences. It engaged competing ideas about the nature of baptism that transformed how Anglo-Virginians thought about the sacrament. It also allowed Anglo-Virginians to assess the "capability" of individuals for genuine baptism, allowing them to flout centuries of Christian custom to argue that some, if not all, Africans might not be capable of Christian conversion at all. In the two generations following the passage of the law, Anglo-Virginians manipulated the meaning of baptism and controlled access to baptism to redefine their own Christianity and to racialize Indians and Africans as non-Christians, a process that reverberated throughout the greater English Atlantic. Passing the 1667 law was an exercise in self-definition and in racial categorization for the English; Virginia's legislature thus accomplished a legal redefinition of what it meant to be Christian. It was a decisive step in the English quest to comprehend and regulate human difference.

Baptism was a certainty in the life of almost every European child born into a Christian family (although some radical Protestant sects practiced adult baptism). Europeans strongly and sometimes even violently contested the meaning of baptism. Should only infants be baptized? Or should one be baptized as an adult capable of understanding the Christian faith? Was baptism the primary route to salvation, or did it signify only a covenanted relationship with God? In the early modern European world, questions about baptism took on enormous cultural, social, and theological significance. The fundamental differences in the ways Catholics and the emerging Protestant denominations viewed baptism fueled bitter controversies about the nature of the Christian community and how one became a member of it. The result was endemic and acrimonious debate about who was Christian, how one's membership in the Christian community was properly designated, and to what extent baptism conferred an undeniable Christian identity. Even more puzzling for Europeans was the question of what rights and responsibilities baptism conferred on its recipients.

Early in the Reformation, Protestants upset what had been a universally accepted baptismal culture when they began to question baptism's efficacy in both fighting sin and incurring eternal salvation. Animated debaters argued whether baptism was essential to salvation (as Catholics believed) and when it should take place: shortly after birth as a matter of course or after some education in Christian doctrine or a profession of faith (as some Protestants began to insist). The baptism debate between Protestants and Catholics and even among different groups of Protestants centered on one overriding controversy: Did baptism result in salvation and faith, or did salvation and faith result in baptism? Catholics held the former position, and Protestants usually held the latter, with varying degrees of radicalism. Some Protestants even denied the necessity of baptism.

The English waded into the resulting theological quagmire with enthusiasm. The Church of England, with a monarch at its head rather than a pope, functioned as a state church designed to make the religion of the people and the government of the people a single entity. The theology was an ambivalent mixture of Continental reforms and residual Catholic folk practice, but the government prized conformity with the doctrines and practices of the new, national church, punishing those who remained Catholic and those who wished to further reform Church of England practice with varying degrees of severity. In the English church, secular and spiritual loyalties were indivisible: to be English was to worship exclusively in the Church of England and to accept its tenets. Those who were outside the established church were generally deemed to be outside the English polity as well. An Englishman could not simultaneously serve two masters—monarch and pope.[3] This expectation led to hostility toward not only Catholics but also radical Protestants and Presbyterians and, by the 1650s, Quakers. Those who refused to participate in Anglican services faced certain legal strictures, social censure, and a decrease in their rights as Englishmen. By attaching rights within the English polity to support participation in the English state church, the English were implicitly excluding those who were outside the church either by choice or by circumstance—a state of affairs that had a great deal of influence on the religious and legal status of Africans and Indians in the New World.

The Church of England sailed carefully between the Scylla of Catholic belief and the Charybdis of radical Protestant belief on baptism, retaining the infant rite and mandating it for all children born in the country. For the English, baptism was both a sign and a seal of a covenant with God, a Protestant belief characteristic of Continental divines, and a sacrament that eased faith and salvation, with a nod to residual Catholic belief and practice. In other words, Anglican baptism had something for everyone, reluctant Anglicans and budding Calvinists alike. For the faithful of the Church of England, baptism of infants allowed these children to join the spiritual community of Christian believers. People who rejected baptism were feared in England: among the Christian sects active there and in the New World, only Quakers refused infant baptism, which earned them at best contempt and at worst criminal prosecution and even execution. Even puritans generally allowed their children to be baptized, although they rejected the traditional language of godparentage in favor of "witnesses," "guardians," or "sureties." Refusal to baptize a child and delaying baptism were both legally condemned.[4] Baptism was a spiritual "mark of difference, whereby Christian men are discerned from others that be not christened" that signaled exclusion from the Christian community.[5] In other words, baptism was a crucial building block of English community—it defined groups of Christians in both the temporal and spiritual worlds and cast suspicion on those who did not partake in the ritual.

While successfully negotiating the difficulties of baptismal theology in the Reformation by adopting the most appealing notions about baptism from all sides of the debate, the English satisfied traditionalists and reformers alike. The very flexibility that allowed the English state to survive the tumults of the Reformation in the sixteenth and early seventeenth centuries relatively unscathed eventually led to diverging ideas about what being both English and Christian meant in a world the English perceived to be threatened by both unreformed Christians and infidels and heathens (Turks and other Muslims as well as Africans and Indians). The English viewed their church as a beacon for the rest of the Christian community, as a role model to be emulated. In that sense the English saw themselves as leaders of a universal church that anyone who professed faith could join—even Catholics and other heathens. This unified vision of the church came into conflict with the contradicting vision of the English as a particularly blessed nation of the Elect. A sense of superiority warred with the sense of universality in ways that had profound consequences in the New World.

From the start of the English colonial adventure in North America, Christian baptism was a tool of conquest. Baptizing the Indians they encountered would allow the English to number the Indians in the Christian community; as we have seen, it was generally believed that conversion would bring the Indians to civility—a term that indicated to English ears the acceptance of English language, land tenure, agriculture, animal husbandry, and clothing as well as religion. In addition to being a tool of salvation and assimilation, baptism also meant inclusion in the English political community. Baptism had political as well as theological implications; the baptized were members of a congregation that transcended time and place.[6]

In Virginia as in England, infant baptism was a legal necessity. Virginia's General Assembly condemned the "new fangled conceits" and "hereticall inventions" of those Virginians who refused to baptize their children (most likely Quakers, who had begun to enter the colony in small numbers) and leveled the hefty fine of two thousand pounds of tobacco for each offense.[7] In 1665 the Northampton County Court fined Ambrose London (probably a Quaker) at least that much for not baptizing his children.[8] There was at least one acceptable reason for not baptizing a child. In 1690 Christopher Blith was summoned before the Surry County Court for not baptizing his children but "now makeing it appear that he was soe bare of Clothes that he could not, & that as soon as he could gett any he Carried his s[ai]d Childe to be baptized . . . he is discharged from the s[ai]d presentment paying his fees."[9] In Blith's case, extreme material poverty, not spiritual poverty or nonconformity, excused his failure to baptize his children.

The actual ceremony of baptism as performed in Virginia had been in use almost continuously since 1552 and was adapted from the previously used Catholic version of the rite. Virginians seem to have taken the ritual seriously; numerous court records show the purchase and maintenance of fonts in churches. In 1672 Surry County accounts noted a payment of eleven hundred pounds of tobacco to a Mr. Caulfield, reimbursing him for expenses incurred acquiring a "bason" for the church in which to baptize newborns.[10] The ritual of baptism, in addition to welcoming a new member to the community, was an opportunity to establish secular social ties for children through the selection of godparents. Godparents often provided livestock—usually cows or pigs but sometimes a horse—to godchildren in their wills. Some godparents even gave their godchildren gifts of livestock before their deaths, as John Wilkins did when he gave his godson Fisher a cow in 1639.[11] John Broch gave his two godsons a more unusual gift, deeding to brothers Joseph and Benjamin Croshaw "a stocke of bees" in 1646.[12]

In the Chesapeake, godparents also took on the role of caring for orphaned godchildren—although often these children were not actually blood kin. This was a common arrangement throughout the seventeenth century. In 1648 Stephen Gill took custody of his orphaned godson, John

Foster, promising to keep him for nine years and to teach him to read. Elizabeth Lang's godmother successfully sued in Northampton County Court in 1677 to gain custody of her goddaughter by promising to care for and educate Elizabeth. In a similar case, when Hannah Harlow insisted in orphans' court that she be placed with her godfather John Tatum, Tatum readily agreed to assume his social and spiritual obligations. Sometimes wills even explicitly stated that godparents should assume guardianship of their godchildren upon the death of the parents. In 1672, worried that after his death his wife would marry a "cross man" who would abuse his daughter Anne, Jarrett Hawthorne specified that Anne's godmother Margaret Wyld would have custody of her.[13] Godparents incurred serious social and spiritual obligations, and they were important elements that helped to bind this new English society together. The traditional rituals of baptism held together a sense of family even in the face of appalling mortality in the Chesapeake.[14]

Godparents also reinforced the Protestant English Christianity of their godchildren. In 1691, when Peter Blake, "a professed Papist & contemner & slighter of ye Publick worship of God" won custody of the orphan Christopher Homes in Nansemond County, Christopher's godfather protested vigorously. He wished to have custody of Christopher so that he "may better performe those duties doth become him as a Godfather, Christian & a friend to ye afores[ai]d Childe, that hee may be brought up in ye Knowledge and feare of God, & in ye true principalls of Christian Religion." Blake had already taken Christopher into Maryland, and his recovery to true Protestantism would be all but impossible to achieve.[15] Most godparents viewed their obligations in less drastic terms. Godparents who wished to be involved in their godchildren's education as English Christians left them Bibles and other religious tracts in their wills. The English used baptism as one means of creating and reinforcing their Christianity in a religiously diverse colonial world.

The English also used baptism as a tool for converting Indians and Africans, as a means of forcing diplomatic exchange with Indians, and for exercising control over their new lands. After the ferocious Anglo-Indian violence in 1622, Indian converts remained few and far between. Yet baptism and the Christian conversion it signified seem to have granted some rights to Indians living as servants or slaves in Virginia after 1622. The muster list taken in January 1624/25 recorded not only the number of able-bodied men and the number of weapons that could be used against the Indians but also interesting tidbits about the denizens of Virginia. Of the two Indians listed as living with the English, one of them lived on Captain William Tucker's plantation and was listed as "William Crashaw an Indian Baptized." (William Crashaw was also the name of an evangelizing minister who vigorously supported the conversion of Virginia's Indians from his London parish, suggesting a connection between the minister's efforts and the Indian's conversion.) Another Indian lived on Thomas Dunthorne's Elizabeth City plantation and was listed as "Thomas an Indian Boaye."[16] That the muster listed a baptism for the Indian William Crashaw but not for little Thomas suggests that Indian baptism remained exceptional but that those who underwent the ritual gained some recognition from the process—otherwise the Virginia Company's census takers would not have recorded it. Unfortunately, neither Thomas nor William appears in any Virginia record again, making it impossible to assess their success or failure in living among English Christians.

William Crashaw's baptism was not the only post-1622 Indian baptism. To facilitate more Indian baptisms, London merchant and Virginia enthusiast Nicholas Ferrar provided three hundred pounds for the college for the conversion and instruction of Indians.[17] Although the Anglo-Indian agricultural utopia of the college never materialized, the Ferrar endowment supported Indian children who lodged with English families and were thereby converted. In 1641 George Menifye presented to the General Court an Indian boy who had been "christened and for the time of ten years brought up amongst the *english*" by Menifye and William Perry, who apparently served in godfatherly capacities by undertaking the religious education of their charge. The court questioned the Indian boy closely and was satisfied that the boy was sufficiently familiar with Christian doctrine. Menifye went home that day with eight pounds for his troubles.[18] This is quite possibly the only recorded situation in which a godfather benefited materially from his godson—not the other way around.

In 1655/56, in exchange for killing wolves, the English gave the Indians cows, which was to "be a step to civilizing them and to making them Christians."[19] Because the cow-to-Christian progression did not work out as well as the Assembly hoped (probably because rather than raising dairy cattle Indians used cows for meat), the burgesses passed laws to encourage Indian parents to send their children to live with English families, where the children would learn about English religion, language, and other customs. Not all English families were as scrupulous about their Christian responsibilities as the Assembly had anticipated. In 1657 the court had to reiterate that Indian children thus adopted were to be freed at twenty-five.[20] Other English colonies had similar problems. In 1655 Bermuda planters were chastised for enslaving "30 or 40 Indians wch were freeborn And ther made into perpetual slaves to the great dishonor of God." The Indians were freed, possibly because they were baptized.[21] Some English planters found conversion programs an easy way to acquire unfree labor.

Even voluntary conversion of Indians to Christianity without the coercion of cows or training in a specific trade seems to have been met with some hostility. Francis Yeardley wrote in a 1654 letter to English merchant John Ferrar, whose family remained interested in Virginia and in the conversion of Indians, that in a visit to South Virginia (now North Carolina) he had spent time among the Roanoke Indians. The Roanokes' "great man" requested that his son be sent to live among the English, learn to read and write, and "serve that God the Englishmen served." When the Indian man and his son arrived in Virginia, they attempted to attend church with the Yeardleys, but the members of the congregation "carried themselves uncivilly towards them, forbidding their coming in any more . . . [and] after [the] sermon, threatened to whip him, and send him away." Only the presence of Mrs. Yeardley, who insisted on remaining with the visitors, prevented violence on that occasion. The Yeardleys eventually had their way; in May 1654 "the Rowanoke presented his child to the minister before the congregation to be baptized, which was solemnly performed in presence of all the Indians, and the child left with me to be bred up a Christian." Yet the threatened violence against the Roanokes in opposition to their presence in the English church suggests that by the 1650s many Englishmen in Virginia resisted extending baptism to Indians, even children, thereby making them a part of the English Christian community.[22]

Though relationships between the English and the Indians like the one between the Yeardleys and the Roanokes were uncommon on the mainland, they were more common on the Eastern Shore. There, Indian children were brought before the county court. Their ages were judged, and ceremoniously their Indian names were recorded along with new English names. Renaming implied a godparent-like relationship between English masters and Indian adoptees, because one of the godparent's responsibilities was to name his godchild. Assigning an English—that is, Christian—name implied that baptism was the intent, if not the actual outcome, of this ritual renaming. Renaming assigned a fresh identity to Indian children—which they might have embraced, because Algonkians often took new names during certain life transitions—and from the English perspective it brought them into the Christian spiritual community. In 1667 at least thirteen Indian children were presented before the Accomack court and renamed—the same year as the baptism law.[23] The English settlers of the Eastern Shore were slower to abandon this interaction with Indians than were their counterparts on the mainland. Nevertheless, adoption of Indian children waned after 1680. Thereafter, Indians who appear in court records were identified not by proper English Christian names but by the diminutives increasingly also common among African slaves: Jenny Indian, Dick Indian, and Charley Indian, for example.[24] Even in the relative absence of Anglo-Indian violence, English people on the Eastern Shore repudiated baptism for Indians.

The muster list of 1624/25 also recorded the existence of twenty-two people of African descent: ten men, ten women, and two children (the list identifies them variously as "negroes" or "negars"). Of these men, women, and children, only seven are named, and all of these have English names, which indicates they were probably Christian. It is likely that the unnamed Africans did not have English names, or any record of their conversion, and therefore might have been held even at this early date as slaves for life. Those with English names probably had some previous experience with the English or other Europeans and were able to take advantage of that knowledge. Certainly at least three came in ships from England.[25] But the baptism of only one—a child—is recorded. The list of people at Captain William Tucker's plantation in Elizabeth City includes "Antoney Negro: Isabell Negro: and William theire Child Baptised."[26] Perhaps William, Antoney and Isabell's son, was named for his master, William Tucker. And since English practice urged that godparents bestow their own names on godchildren, it is possible that William Tucker was little William's godfather. The recognition in the muster list of a baptized black child suggests that that baptism meant something to both the English master and the child's African parents. Antoney and Isabell knew that baptism and a godfather secured some rights and protections for their son. And it seems that William Tucker was the kind of master who encouraged these kinds of arrangements for his non-English servants. As the infant William's situation suggests, Africans in Virginia knew that baptism granted membership in the established church and that most Englishmen believed that being Christian brought freedom and certain liberties. They could not fail to see the advantages of baptism, especially in the emerging hardscrabble world of the English Chesapeake, where most of the first African slaves were almost certainly Atlantic creoles who were familiar with European languages, cultures, and religions.[27] The causal connection between baptism and rights correlated clearly in the experience of one African baptized in the Church of England who came to Virginia in 1624. John Phillip, "A negro Christened in *England* 12 yeers since," was permitted to testify in court about the improper seizure of a Spanish ship by the English ship in which he was traveling.[28] In recording his testimony, the clerk was careful to note Phillip's baptism and Christian conversion, suggesting that had Phillip not been able to demonstrate his Christianity, his testimony would not have been accepted.

Those Afro-Virginians living as Christians in early Virginia commonly made sure their children were baptized and used godparentage as a way of building community networks. The experience of the Johnson clan demonstrates this admirably. Anthony Johnson arrived in Virginia in 1621, numbering him among the first Africans to arrive in the colony (Africans had first been sold in the colony in 1619 from Dutch ships).[29] He was known only as "Antonio a Negro" and resided, probably as a servant, on the Surry County plantation called Wariscoyack. In 1622 an African woman named Mary came to the plantation. At some point, Antonio married Mary, gained his freedom, Anglicized his name to Anthony Johnson, and acquired property on Virginia's Eastern Shore. Johnson established himself as the patriarch of a large family.[30]

Johnson and his family were not the only free, property-owning, moderately prosperous blacks on the Eastern Shore. The families of Francis Payne, Emmanuel Driggus, William Harmon, King Tony, and Philip Mongum joined the Johnsons on the Eastern Shore in a close-knit black Christian community held together by bonds of marriage and of spiritual kinship. With the exception of King Tony, all of these men have "Christian" first names as well as surnames, which indicate a conversion to Christianity. Some of these men might already have been Christian on their arrival in Virginia: "Antonio" is an Iberian name, and Emmanuel Driggus's name could have been a corruption of "Rodriguez." Johnson and Driggus had contacts at some point with the Spanish or the Portuguese, and probably the English as well, in the Caribbean before their arrival in the Chesapeake. This might explain why these families became so adept at moving in the English legal world. The court records of Accomack County and Northampton County are full of lawsuits, criminal cases, debt actions, and other materials such as wills and notices of lost livestock generated by these families. Through these documents, it is possible to see how connected these families were by bonds of spiritual kinship. That their practices continued long after the 1667 baptism law indicates that that law had little effect on Afro-Virginians who had already learned to use English religion to their advantage.

When Francis Payne died in 1673, his will was a testament to his Christianity: "I bequeath my Soule to my lovinge ffather my creator and to Jesus Christ whereby his blood and passion suffered for my Sinns & all ye world trustinge through his merits to injoy that heavenly portion prepared for mee and all true believers." Payne's pious phrases in the preamble reflect more devotion than the usual formulaic sentences that precede most English wills of the time. More importantly, he went on to oblige his wife to "give unto each of our godchildren a Cow calfe a peece when they attaine to lawfull age." Payne observed the time-honored tradition of providing godchildren with the means of corporeal as well as spiritual sustenance, adopting the English practice with ease. One godchild had done something to anger Payne: "But as for Devrax [Devorax] Dregus [Driggus] hee is to have nothing by this Will."[31] By naming the black sheep of his spiritual family, Payne helpfully tells us that the Paynes and the Drigguses were joined by bonds of spiritual kinship. Probably other Drigguses and possibly Johnsons as well were numbered among Payne's other godchildren. The Drigguses did not limit themselves to kinship with the Paynes. When King Tony's will was probated in March 1678/79, he left his godchild Sarah Driggus a cow.[32] These two wills demonstrate that these Afro-Virginian families were committed to reciprocal spiritual and social obligations, just as English families were. They had embraced English Christianity in its full meaning, even as English Christians rejected the possibility of spiritual kinship with and among Africans slaves in the baptism law of 1667.

Their Christianity allowed the Eastern Shore's black families to participate in the broader English political community. Christian ties to English people also permitted Africans to protect themselves and their families in times of trouble. In 1645 Emanuel Driggus signed an indenture with his master Francis Potts consigning his two daughters Elizabeth and Jane to indentured servitude. Although the length of their service was uncommon (Elizabeth had to serve until she was sixteen and Jane until she was thirty), the indenture specified that the girls were to be brought up "in the feare of god and in the knowledge of our savior Christ Jesus."[33] Such long indentures were unheard of in England, but what is clear is that Potts had a clientage relationship with the Drigguses, which might explain why the indenture made specific religious references and why Potts was assigned a role in the girls' lives that looked remarkably like that of godfather. Emanuel Driggus later "bought back" the younger girl Jane, whose indenture had been the longest. In essence, Potts protected the two girls in the same way an English godfather might look after his goddaughters if their natural parents were unable to do so. Emanuel Driggus had learned to use an English institution to his and his family's advantage.[34]

Nevertheless, the Afro-Virginian families of the Eastern Shore were exceptional. By 1677 free blacks made up 16 percent of Northampton County's population.[35] No counties on the mainland ever saw such a flourishing of free black planter families. Possibly Northampton County's distance from the mainland and a soil type less suitable for commercial tobacco production allowed for other customs to develop, because there are no other examples of black families so entwined. Gradually the fortunes of these families fell, probably as a direct result of legislation in the General Assembly that continually chipped away at the privileges enjoyed by free blacks all over Virginia. Late in the century, the Johnson family moved to Maryland. Christianity had ceased to be a protection, even far away from the center of political power in Virginia.

Elsewhere in the English Atlantic it was more difficult for enslaved Africans and their descendants to gain access to baptism, conversion, and freedom, and therefore it was more difficult for them to form networks of free black Christians. Richard Ligon, an Englishman working in Barbados in the late 1640s, reported a long conversation about the use of compasses with an enslaved man named Sambo. Sambo, Ligon wrote, marveled at the compass "and desired me, that he might be made a Christian; for, he thought to be a Christian, was to be endued [endowed] with all those knowledges he wanted." Ligon spoke to Sambo's master, who argued that the laws of England forbade making Christians slaves. Ligon responded that "my request was far different from that, for I desired him to make a Slave a Christian. His answer was, That it was true, there was a great difference in that: But, being once a Christian, he could no more account him a Slave, and so lose the hold they had of them as Slaves, by making them Christians; and by that means should open such a gap, as all the Planters in the Iland would curse him." Ligon's argument for converting the enslaved man was certainly a sly one; he supposed the argument for making a heathen slave a Christian, rather than enslaving someone who was already Christian, would sway the sugar planter. But the planter's response mirrored the fears of Virginia planters: that baptism would lead to freedom. Unlike the Virginians, though, Barbadian and other Caribbean planters never attempted the kind of legislation that simultaneously encouraged baptism while disconnecting conversion from freedom. Ligon was shocked by the Barbadian planter's attitude, as many Englishmen who traveled in the English Atlantic were. Ligon remarked several times on the denial of Christian conversion to enslaved people, noting that some "earnestly sought it." Ligon reproached those planters "professing the names of Christians, and denying to preach to those poor ignorant harmless souls the *Negroes*, the doctrine of Christ Crucified, which might convert many of them to his worship." Ligon's pleas apparently fell upon deaf ears; the Barbadians made even fewer attempts at conversion and seemed less troubled by their actions than mainland planters.[36]

By the time the baptism law passed in 1667, English Virginians lived in a world in which Indians and Africans alike comprehended the many meanings of baptism and took advantage of them to build their own communities and gain a place in English society. Yet Virginia instituted a law barring baptized slaves from gaining their freedom, and it was not the only colony to do so. Bermuda actually banned the baptism of "Bastards and Negroes Children" in 1647 as part of a law meant to encourage infant baptism in the face of apparent Anabaptist sentiment.[37] Maryland first considered such a law in 1664, when some legislators asked for legislation stating that baptized slaves did not get their freedom, "they thinking itt very necessary for the prevention of the damage of such Masters of such Slaves may susteyne by such Slaves pretending to be Christened."[38] The danger as Marylanders saw it was not from actual Christian slaves but those who pretended conversion for their own nefarious purposes. No law was passed in Maryland explicitly stating that baptized slaves could not gain their freedom until 1671; Marylanders, like the Bermudians, did not even bother to encourage planters to baptize their slaves.[39] The Virginia planters innovated legally with their law of 1667, even if they were anxious about the idea of holding Christian slaves.

The text of the 1667 law implied both that African slaves demanding their postbaptismal freedom was a common occurrence before the law's passage and that many English Virginians must have been expressing doubt about the wisdom of baptizing their slaves. The burgesses began their new law by acknowledging the delicate question of Christian conversion and slavery: "Whereas some doubts have risen whether children that are slaves by birth, and by the charity and piety of their owners made pertakers of the blessed sacrament of baptisme . . . be made ffree."[40] The burgesses were eager to show both their own Christianity and their commitment to converting their slaves by illustrating the fact that slaves converted frequently enough to cause comment. Their own "charity and piety"—two key Christian attributes—were undeniable. The preamble to the law also underscored the ongoing importance of baptism as both a social and a religious marker of Christian identity in Anglican belief and practice. But it also betrayed a budding sense of discomfort within English planters' Christianity: while they were committed to their spiritual obligation to convert the heathen, they also recognized that the act of baptism essentially depleted their captive workforce.

But did baptism frequently result in freedom for slaves prior to the Virginia law's passage? The available evidence suggests a much more complicated picture of the role of baptism in pre-1667 emancipations. Cases were highly individual, often reacting to specific sets of circumstances, and most baptismal emancipations seem to have been the result of careful negotiation among enslaved people, planters, planters' heirs, and the courts. Enslaved people sometimes sued for their freedom but were more likely to negotiate for it within carefully formulated networks of masters, overseers, ministers, lawyers, and godparents, and sometimes enslaved people even arranged for some sort of monetary compensation for their masters. Baptism was usually just one of many criteria for freedom that slaves advanced, and only one of the strategies they used. But it also seems that very few slaves were actually attempting to gain their freedom in ways that involved the courts at all. Some of the records that indicate emancipation were presented to the court only for record-keeping purposes, not because the court had any role in emancipation. Instead, the surviving records reveal the ingenuity of slaves who negotiated freedom for themselves and their families, using English attitudes toward conversion and baptism as an important way of differentiating themselves from non-Christians. But it is almost certain that large numbers of slaves were not single-mindedly pursuing freedom through baptism. Instead, baptism functioned as both a mechanism of freedom and a consequence of it; there was no explicit causal relationship between the two concepts that led directly from baptism to freedom. The correlation between baptism and freedom was too complicated for the simple statement forbidding the freedom of slaves on the basis of their baptism at which the burgesses finally arrived.

In 1641, for John Graweere, the freedom and subsequent baptism of his child were intimately connected events. Graweere, a black man who was either a slave or an indentured servant, had a child with an unnamed black woman from a neighboring plantation. He told Virginia's General Assembly that "he desired [the child] should be made a Christian and be taught and exercised in the church of *England*, by reason whereof he . . . did for his said child purchase its freedom." The court duly noted this arrangement, acknowledging that "the child shall be free . . . and remain at the disposing and education of the said Graweere and the child's godfather who undertaketh to see it brought up in the Christian religion aforesaid."[41] Although the godfather is not identified in this record, it is clear that Graweere truly understood the religious underpinnings of English society in the Chesapeake: a godparent served the dual purpose of helping to educate the child and providing him with access to the Anglo-Virginian Christian community. There is no evidence that Graweere's child was freed because of its incipient baptism and acceptance into the wider Christian community. Baptism was not a precondition for freedom but rather a consequence of it—one that Graweere probably understood would confer status on his child and entail opportunity. And perhaps Graweere's English coconspirators were more likely to accept Graweere's purchase of freedom for his child once they understood that Graweere intended that the child be brought up in ways familiar to the English. And perhaps the child's freedom did not disturb the English because Graweere apparently made no attempt to free himself or his child's unnamed mother.

Graweere's actions are interesting precisely because of their ambiguities. There was an implied link between baptism and freedom, although one did not flow directly from the other. In a time when the status of blacks was contingent on a number of factors and unclear legalities, religion and not physical appearance (e.g., skin color) was a more powerful and evocative way of categorizing people and of moving through the malleable barriers between slavery and freedom. For John Graweere, the baptism and godparentage of his child was part of a process of acculturation in which Christianity was open to all and religion was a possible way to avoid or to mitigate bondage.

Graweere apparently did not need to sue either to gain his child's freedom or to enforce it; his was an arrangement carefully negotiated in which his child's baptism and incipient Christianity were decisive factors. Graweere was not unique; Mihill Gowen made an arrangement similar to John Graweere's for his own child in York County in 1657. Gowen had been granted his freedom by his master Christopher Stafford's will, which required him to serve only a further four years after Stafford's death. Stafford's heirs honored the agreement and had Gowen's bill of freedom entered in the county court records (possibly to prevent his reenslavement at a later date). At the same time, Stafford's niece Anne Barnehouse also recognized the freedom of Gowen's son "borne the 25 Aug 1655 of the body of my Negro Posta being baptized by Edward Johnson 2 Sept 1655 & named William & I the said Anne Barnhouse doth bind my selfe . . . never to trouble or molest . . . or demand any service of the said Mihill or his said sone William." As in John Graweere's case, Gowen seems to have made no effort to secure Posta's freedom, but he did use the Christian establishment to secure notice of the freedom of his child. Edward Johnson, the minister who had baptized William two years before, was the signed witness on little William's bill of freedom. Although this notation does not list a godfather for the child, as Graweere's did, Gowen used Johnson similarly to the way Graweere used his son's godfather as a guarantor of freedom. Again, there is no evidence to suggest that William Gowen was freed on the basis of baptism; rather, his baptism was one of a number of factors that allowed his father to negotiate his freedom among Christopher Stafford's heirs and the local minister.[42] Networks of religiously based freedom of the kind Graweere and Gowen set up for themselves and their sons could also protect their baptized children from illegal or unfair servitude. While these situations might simply indicate the malleability of status for blacks in the early years of settlement, it is telling that each child's Christianity clearly played such a visible role in his freedom. An unbaptized child, with no network of protectors connected through the ancient traditions of baptism followed by most English Virginians, might not have fared so well.

Enslaved people who failed to negotiate such contractual arrangements with their masters sometimes availed themselves of the courts and governing institutions of Virginia. In 1654, when Elizabeth Key, who was probably the daughter of an English father and an African mother, sued for her freedom partly on the basis of her baptism, her English godfather was a crucial witness. Shortly after her reputed father Thomas Key's death, Elizabeth and her brother John Key found themselves sold to the

Estate of Colonel John Mottrom. Initially in court documents deponents called Elizabeth a Negro, and then later "Molletto," indicating confusion about Elizabeth's status and parentage. Elizabeth's paternity became crucial to her case for freedom. One deponent claimed that Thomas Key could not be her father, since "a Turke of Capt. Matthewes was Father to the Girle." Another deponent noted that she had heard that Thomas Key had been fined for fornication with an African woman in another parish and that Elizabeth was the product of that relationship. The deciding factor in Elizabeth's suit for freedom was her Christianity. Colonel Humphrey Higginson claimed that he had an agreement with Thomas Key to look after Elizabeth and take her back to England with him and give her a portion of her father's estate when she came of age: "That shee hath bin long since Christened Col. Higginson being her God father and that by report shee is able to give a very good account of her fayth." Higginson accepted the obligation of being Elizabeth's godfather and affirmed her Christian ties. She gained her freedom, but instead of sailing to England with Higginson, she married the lawyer who argued her case.[43]

Enslaved people also used Christianity in the courts to gain their freedom when, presumably, careful negotiation with their masters and a network of kin and contacts had failed them. In 1644 a mulatto slave named Manuel sued successfully before the Virginia Assembly in Jamestown to be "adjudged no Slave but to serve as other Christian Servants do." Manuel made an explicit connection between his Christianity and his right to serve a lesser term as an indentured servant, not as a slave for life. His master William Whittacre was not pleased with the deal, however, writing in 1666 that he had purchased Manuel "as a Slave for Ever" and that he eventually had freed Manuel in September 1665 (making Manuel's term of service still significantly longer than that of most English servants). Whittacre maintained that Manuel had been sold to him under false pretenses and petitioned the governor and his council for "satisfaction from the Levy being freed by the Country and bought by your Petitioner at £25 Sterling." The Assembly denied Whittacre's petition to be reimbursed for the loss of his slave; the Council of Virginia— an institution dominated by the wealthiest and most powerful planters in the colony—did not acknowledge "any Reason why the Publick should be answerable for the inadvertancy of the Buyer or for a Judgment when justly grounded as that Order was." The entire sequence—Manuel's suit for freedom, Whittacre's response to it, and the Assembly's reaction to Whittacre's petition—all suggest that even slaves who did not work within their network of contacts and used the courts instead were able to use evidence of their Christianity to gain their freedom, and that the council (whose members stood to lose the most from allowing a precedent for freeing Christian slaves) recognized claims to Christian freedom as just—even when the original order was more than two decades old. Only two years before the Assembly passed the baptism law, the Council of Virginia upheld a precedent that freed enslaved Christians, obligating them to serve their masters as would an indentured servant.[44]

Indians who found themselves unexpectedly in servitude for life also used baptism as a justification for freedom. In 1661 an Indian boy was able to gain his freedom in a manner reminiscent of John Graweere's strategy. Metappin, called a Powhatan Indian in court documents, was ordered freed, "he speaking perfectly the English tongue and desiring baptism." Technically it was illegal to enslave Tidewater Indians, but the circumstances of Metappin's enslavement were peculiar. Surry County documents there show that an Indian identified as "a Kinge of the Waineoakes" sold Metappin, "a boy of his nacon . . . untill the full terme of his life" to Elizabeth Short, accepting a horse as payment.[45] Metappin's sale into slavery did not resemble George Menifye's earlier experiment with Indian servitude and conversion. Under what pretense the king of the Waineoakes sold Metappin (also called Weetoppin in Surry records) is unclear, but Metappin fought back almost immediately, bypassing the Surry court and suing for his freedom directly in the General Assembly. His status as an Indian was not what explicitly resulted in his freedom; his promise of conversion as well as his proficiency in English accomplished that task. In other words, it was his status as a proto-Englishman and potential Christian that allowed his freedom. Even the planters of Surry County, a prosperous and chronically labor-short tobacco-growing area on the south side of the James, had to acquiesce to the freedom of an Indian who could be bound to them by ties of conversion.[46]

The experiences of Manuel, Metappin, and their predecessors were soon to become the exception rather than the rule. In 1667 the Lower Norfolk County Court was not interested in entertaining the free, Christian aspirations of a black man. At that court, "Fernando a Negro" sued his master Captain John Warner for his freedom. Fernando cleverly amassed a series of arguments in favor of his freedom: he claimed he was Christian and that he had lived in England, and he produced documents to support his claim. One can imagine Fernando's impassioned pleas before the court. Lower Norfolk County's judges were unconvinced. To them, Fernando merely was "pretending he was a Christian and had been severall yeares in England." The qualifications that had served Africans from John Phillip to Mihill Gowen well were now cause for doubt. Additionally, the magistrates noted that Fernando's documents were "in Portugell or some other language which the Court could not understand." The judges rejected Fernando's appeal, and declared "the Court could find noe cause wherefore he should be free but Judge him a slave for his life time."[47]

There are many reasons the court ruled against Fernando. Perhaps he overwhelmed the court with his protestations, which combined several different avenues of argument for his freedom. It is also possible that by claiming Christianity and by providing documentation in an Iberian language, Fernando left the inadvertent impression that he was Catholic—an affiliation unlikely to win him any privileges in Protestant Virginia. And after all, from the judges' perspective, anyone could claim to have been in England and therefore be subject to the English customary law regarding the limited term of indentured servitude. But Fernando did not give up. He appealed his case to the General Assembly of Virginia (though the outcome remains unknown). Whether or not the Assembly freed Fernando, though, Anglo-Virginians were increasingly wary of blacks who pressed for freedom on the basis, in whole or in part, of their Christianity.

It seems likely that Fernando's case was one of the precipitating factors in the passage of the 1667 law. Faced with the tenacity of slaves such as Manuel and Fernando and the increasing reluctance and fear of masters like William Whittacre, Anglo-Virginians faced the tension between their beliefs and obligations as Christians and their need to maintain control of a captive labor force. In one swift stroke, the Virginia legislature undid centuries of English and Christian custom. A close reading of the language the burgesses used in the law reveals two innovative threads in their thinking about the sacrament of baptism: that they ought to take more care to determine that only sincere converts received baptism, and that many enslaved people might not be capable of baptism at all. Virginians were to "more carefully endeavour the propagation of christianity," which might in this instance mean that slave owners should more "discerningly" determine who among their human property should receive baptism, rather than offering the sacrament to all comers without regard to the possible consequences. The burgesses suggested that children might be appropriately targeted for instruction and baptism while at the same time questioning the capability of adult black slaves to adequately comprehend Christianity and therefore be completely converted. "[T]hose of greater growth," meaning adult enslaved people, should in the burgesses' new legal formulation be baptized only "if capable to be admitted to that sacrament."[48]

What precisely did the burgesses mean when they referred to who was "capable" of receiving baptism? Contextually, the burgesses explicitly meant that children might be able to learn about and accept Christianity, but adults would not likely be receptive. Yet "capable" also indicated in seventeenth-century usage a legal or moral qualification or ability.[49] This usage then implied that adult enslaved people were morally incapable of learning about and accepting Christianity and thus excused planters from pursuing Christian education and baptism for those individuals. For most planters, though, this situation was not limited to adults; there is little evidence suggesting that planters pursued baptism for enslaved children in the latter half of the seventeenth century. Having been "freed from this doubt" that baptism equated freedom, slave owners chose not to baptize their slaves but to systematically exclude them from this rite of Christian initiation and membership. Indeed, slave owners' behavior suggests that to them Africans were innately and irrevocably non-Christian, an attitude that the law unintentionally fostered.

Imperial officials had a much more ancient view of the matter rooted in traditional ideas about the potential Christianity of all humans, even those unregenerate heathens. While not challenging the legality of slavery as an institution per se, officials chose instead to attack the enforced and hereditary heathenism of enslaved people that colonials had invented. In December 1660 Charles II charged the newly formed Council for Foreign Plantations with taking "an effectuall care of the propagation of the Gospell in the severall Forraine Plantations . . . and you are to consider how such of the Natives or such as are purchased by you from other parts to be servants or slaves [enslaved Africans] may be best invited to the Christian Faith and be made capable of being baptized thereunto."[50] While the instructions mimic earlier charter language requiring conversion of heathens in the New World, it is significant that the council was to oversee that process and suggests that the newly restored monarch wished to involve himself more directly in colonial religious affairs. A year later further instructions from the council reminded Governor William Berkeley to persuade English residents of Virginia to effect "winning such as are purchased by you as Slaves to the Christian Faith and to the making them capable of being baptized thereunto."[51] Proposed Parliamentary legislation from the reign of Charles II or James II asserted that enslaved people were interested in Christianity and advocated baptism and Communion for converts, while also emphasizing that conversion would not result in freedom. Though the act never passed Parliament, it suggests the growing gulf between colonial and metropolitan ideas about race and religion.[52] In 1685 the renowned diarist John Evelyn noted that the newly crowned James II argued against "that impiety of their masters prohibiting it [baptism], out of a mistaken opinion that they would be *ipso facto* free."[53]

Anglican ministers who came to the colonies to minister to their flocks found colonial attitudes toward enslaved blacks and Indians not just misguided but also offensive and incomprehensible. The Reverend Morgan Godwyn served in Virginia, probably in York County, during the 1660s before departing for Barbados in 1670. Godwyn was so horrified by planter attitudes toward enslaved people he wrote two treatises on the importance of conversion efforts after his return to England in the late 1670s. Though Godwyn's keen powers of observation and indignation were unusual among ministers, his tales of Virginia planters resisting the baptism of their slaves are suggestive of how metropolitan observers saw provincial attitudes. Godwyn tried to baptize slaves while in Virginia but found the task difficult simply because many slave owners thought their slaves lacked the ability to become Christian. Godwyn did not believe them: "As to their [slaves'] (alike pretended) *Stupidity*, there is . . . little truth therein."[54] Yet when he tried to baptize African slaves, even in the wake of the 1667 law that should have permitted such baptisms, he ran into stubborn opposition. One woman informed Godwyn that he "might as well Baptize a Puppy, as a certain young *Negro*, the Mother whereof was a *Christian*, and for ought I know (notwithstanding her Complexion) *as dear to God as her self*." Godwyn could not comprehend why a planter would refuse to baptize the child of a baptized mother, regardless of "complexion." Another slave owner was even more hostile, telling Godwyn that baptism was "*was to one of those* [slaves] *no more beneficial, than to her black Bitch*."[55] Applying bestial characteristics to African slaves was a convenient mechanism for Virginia planters to protect their property from baptism—after all, dogs could not be baptized; they had no ability to comprehend any sacrament.

Godwyn later lamented the "Hellish Principles, viz. that *Negroes* are Creatures destitute of Souls, to be ranked among Brute Beasts."[56] "Creatures destitute of Souls" had no ability to be included in the community of Christians, even as slaves. The planters Godwyn encountered upped the ante by suggesting that enslaved people were not human beings at all. If Godwyn is to be believed, planters resisting the baptism of their slaves by arguing that "[b]ecause they are *Black*, therefore they are *Cham*'s Seed; and for this under the *Curse*, and therefore no longer *Men*, but a kind of *Brutes*." Godwyn vehemently denied that the Bible sanctioned anything like the popularly used Hamitic curse to justify enslavement and denial of Christianity. Other planters argued that enslaved blacks were not part of the Noachic genealogy at all and, as such, were created separately from English Christians and therefore not able to become Christian. One imagines a purple-faced Godwyn sputtering with rage at the polygenist conceits of Virginian and Barbadian planters. As Godwyn noted, "The *Pre-Adamites* whimsy, which is preferred above the *Curse*, (because so exceeding useful to undermine the *Bible* and *Religion*, unto both which they have vowed never to be *reconciled*)."[57] In other words, planters were advancing religious arguments in favor of blackness as a curse or as a sign of separate creation (the pre-Adamite argument), both of which were presumed to be hereditary conditions and which were justifications for racial slavery. Though those arguments found little favor in late seventeenth-century England, they were undergirding the construction of race in colonial slave societies. If Godwyn correctly represented the views of colonial planters, then planters completely rejected that late sixteenth- and early seventeenth-century consensus on the potential Christianity of all human beings and had conveniently adopted fringe ideas like the curse of Ham and polygenesis to justify their budding racial ideologies. It is possible that Godwyn influenced the passage of the 1667 law, seeing it as a way to counter the heathenish behaviors and heretical racial ideas of Virginia planters.[58] Yet the very language of capability, which Virginia's burgesses perhaps thought would mitigate the issue of freedom by encouraging slaveholders to baptize at least children, paradoxically encouraged planters to think of their slaves as completely incapable of ever being Christian—as hereditary heathens. The law's language might have reinforced the very ideas Godwyn hoped to combat. Godwyn had even less luck in Barbados, which passed no law similar to Virginia's. Instead, he confronted Barbadian planters whose "common *Affirmation*, That the *Baptizeing* of their *Negro's is the ready way to have all their Throats cut*."[59]

Outside the Anglican establishment, Protestant dissenters also challenged the colonial practice of denying access to Christian conversion to enslaved people. Nonconformist minister Richard Baxter's enormous *Christian Directory* affirmed Godwyn's goals when it directed slave owners to treat their slave property kindly and encourage conversion: "Make it your chief end in buying and using slaves to win them to Christ and save their souls."[60] And Thomas Tryon, the vegetarian and radical writer, wrote a pamphlet aimed at planters after a trip to Barbados, lecturing slave owners from the perspective of a fictional enslaved Barbadian named Sambo. Tryon's ventriloquized Sambo told the planters that they "are drunk with our Blood and Sweat," a sin compounded by the fact that planters "desire and endeavour to keep us *Heathens*, that we may continue their *Slaves*, and thereby are Guilty not only of oppressing our Bodies, but (as much as in them lies) of *damning our Souls*."[61] Though English monarchs, colonial officials, Church of England ministers like Morgan Godwyn, and others such as Baxter and Tryon were not assaulting the legal institution of slavery, they were expressing a genuine moral outrage against colonial efforts to deny enslaved people Christianity (though Baxter was a mainstream figure and Tryon was definitely on the fringe). In this way, the debate between the imperial metropole and its colonial peripheries was fundamentally about the definition and legal construction of race as a concept. Tryon's Sambo denied the very idea of race when he asked his master if it would be fair that "a man be made a *Slave* forever, meerly because his Beard is *Red*, or his Eye-brows *Black*? In a word, if our *Hue* be the only difference, since *White* is as contrary to *Black*, as *Black* is to *White*, there is as much reason that you should be our *Slaves*, as we yours."[62] For the Londoner Tryon, skin color was irrelevant both to slavery and to Christian conversion. But the planters were reaching the opposite conclusion and defining racial boundaries based not just on skin color but on lack of access to Christianity. By condemning enslaved people to hereditary heathenism, planters could ignore arguments made by men such as Godwyn and Tryon in favor of a colonial system that used baptism, that universal right of Christians, to uphold slavery and to create race.

Yet despite the planters' legal power play, enslaved people in Virginia were still using baptism as one among many reasons for freedom, despite the 1667 law to the contrary. Court records from 1695 described William Catillah, a mulatto, as "servant to Mrs Margrett Booth," and it seems, from the terms described in his lawsuit, that he had been indentured to Booth as a small child. Having turned twenty-four, he demanded his freedom because he was "the son of a free woman & was baptized into the Christian faith." Booth was unable to prove to the court why she continued to hold Catillah, and he gained his freedom. The court probably did not regard Catillah's Christianity as a reason for his freedom; more likely the court freed him on the basis of an indenture guaranteeing his freedom. Nevertheless, it is significant that Catillah himself considered his baptism and his Christian identity as contributors to his freedom.[63]

Baptism was probably a factor that protected some mulattoes—people, like William Catillah, of English and African descent—from perpetual servitude. In 1683, for example, Elizabeth Banks, an English indentured servant to James Goodwin, was whipped for "bastardy with a Negroe slave." Nineteen years later, her daughter Mary (probably the child for whom Elizabeth was whipped) made indenture arrangements for her own bastard child Hannah Banks to another member of the Goodwin family. Hannah had to serve until the age of twenty-one, and Peter Goodwin was required to "see the child baptized into the Christian faith & (as soon as she comes to majority) to teach or cause her to be taught her the creed the Lords Prayer & the Tenne Comandments in the Vulgar tongue if she be capable to attaine unto the same." Peter Goodwin had duties similar to those of a godfather according to this indenture; even if he was not Hannah's actual godfather, it still fell to him to educate her in the Christian faith. Unlike most other servants and slaves of African descent, Hannah would be brought up Christian, perhaps because she was also of English descent. Claiming that descent entitled the Banks children to baptism and its privileges—privileges that slaves did not get. But Hannah's indenture also reflected another growing assumption about the ability of blacks and mulattoes to become Christian; it mandated that she ought to be taught the catechism only if she proved herself "capable." Implicit in that requirement is the acknowledged possibility that Hannah Banks, mulatto indentured servant, might not have the innate capability to understand her catechism and truly be Christian. Only her English blood gave her the opportunity to try.[64]

Other mulatto servants' indentures also specified education. In 1703 John Bayly specified in his will that his "Mulatta Boy named William" be given both his freedom and fifteen pounds sterling. Bayly ordered that William stay with a Major Buckner "untill he Arrives at the Age above named [twenty-one] and also requested that the said Major to take care that the s[ai]d Boy be kept to School and brought up in the feare of God and Protestant Religion." At twenty-one, William was to use the money to leave the colony.[65] Like Hannah Banks, William's master allowed for his education, although he did not seem to doubt that William would be capable of learning "Protestant Religion." Like Hannah Banks and William Catillah, William's knowledge of Christianity served to include him in the Christian community, not exclude him. William's status as a mulatto was helpful rather than harmful. Not every mulatto servant's indenture specified education in the Christian religion as a requirement of the agreement. Abraham Royster, a mulatto bastard whose mother had apparently left York County while her son remained, signed a standard seven-year indenture to learn the trade of boatwright without any religious education at all.[66] Mulattoes, in other words, fit into a liminal space in which they sometimes could call upon their English heritage and their Christian ties for some protection, even after the 1667 baptism law discontinued the connection between baptism and freedom.

Slaves who were Christian seem to have had some other privileges, or at least, their masters noted it as important. Anne Trotter left a slave to her godson Richard Dixon, identifying the slave as a "Negroe Girle named Elizabeth And Christned in Charles Parish Church to him and his heires for ever."[67] It seems likely that Elizabeth was intended to be a personal servant for Richard or eventually for his wife, suggesting that slaves who were actually part of the household were more likely to be baptized or accorded some Christian education. (It is also possible that Elizabeth was mulatto, though a slave, which might explain why she was baptized so readily.) Nevertheless, by the beginning of the eighteenth century, Elizabeth's experience was by far the exception rather than the rule. By then, not only had the English rejected the connection between baptism and freedom, but they also had rejected the notion that baptizing Indians and Africans was necessary, right, or proper.

In so doing, English people in the Atlantic littoral created a creole idea of race and Christianity that strongly rejected metropolitan ideas about the potential Christianity of all people. By the end of the seventeenth century, colonial legislatures were willing to disregard imperial instructions regarding the conversion of enslaved people. In 1698 Bermudian legislators listened to an address by newly appointed governor Sir Richard Robinson in which the governor asked that they "find out means to facilitate and incourage the Conversion of negroes and other Slaves to the Christian Religion." The Bermudians replied that they had "[l]ong endeavoured the Conversion of our negroes and Slaves to Christianity . . . our too constant experiences plainly evince unto us that such is their general Contrariety thereto: That the better they are Instructed in Religion the ffurther they are from Conversion thereto."[68] By emphasizing enslaved people's "general Contrariety" to Christian conversion, Bermudians adopted the racialized language of hereditary heathenism.

By rejecting the connection between baptism and freedom for Africans and Indians, colonial English people were doing more than just perfecting the law of slavery. By questioning the ability of Africans to become Christian, settlers defined both their own religious and cultural identity and the identities of the Indians they lived beside and the Africans they owned. The 1705 Virginia *Law of Servants and Slaves* reiterated that baptism of "servants" could not result in freedom at any age.[69] Only the English could be truly Christian—a New World innovation that would have profound consequences. In this sense, the 1667 law and its successor legislation was a crucial step in the English quest to comprehend and regulate human difference, by identifying themselves as Protestant Christians and their slaves as heathens incapable of Christian conversion.

CHAPTER FIVE

Becoming Christian, Becoming White

I n 1667 Governor William Berkeley wrote a letter to King Charles II
on the challenges of governing Virginia, asking him to "consider us
as a people press'd at our backes with Indians, in our Bowells with our
servants ... and invaded from without by the Dutch."[1] Berkeley might
have added that also rootling around in the innards of Virginia's body
politic were a growing number of African slaves and religious dissenters. Berkeley's Virginia was a colony under siege from within and from
without. The acts of 1662 and 1667, which regulated reproduction and
baptism, had defined religious belonging and connected belief to emergent racial categories. They also began to create a social order in which
being both white and Christian were critical to having access to political
power. But what did being "white" and "Christian" mean in the context of
the colonial social order? At the time of Berkeley's complaint to the king,
few Anglo-Virginians identified themselves as white; they were far more
likely to use words such as "English" or "Christian" to describe themselves. "Christian" was also a disputed term; Indians and enslaved people
were not Christian, and yet English Quakers were also suspect. With its
insecure frontiers and belligerent religious dissenters acting as diseases
on the Virginian body, Anglo-Virginians saw the maintenance of their
social order as the only cure for their situation. Challenges abounded.
They increasingly relied upon enslaved Africans for labor, and struggled
with religious diversity. By the end of the seventeenth century, Anglo-
Virginians had confronted these problems by redefining the meanings of
"English," "Christian," and "white" in their colonial context.

A functional social order began in the household. The English political thinker Robert Filmer argued that the household governance and
the governance of the state mirrored one another. Kings were fathers of
their people, and fathers were the undisputed masters of their households. The analogous structures of individual households and of states
were, Filmer thought, divinely ordained and embedded in Christianity. The good order of society depended upon masters controlling their

households and upon kings controlling their states. Though other English political theorists found Filmer's ideas (especially those that negated the concept of natural rights) overstated and repugnant, most English people believed that order in the family was critical to order in the state.[2] In Virginia, many households included indentured servants and African slaves, and it is not surprising that planters emphasized the importance of masters' controlling their households.

To maintain the supremacy of the master of the household, violence within undefined but generally accepted limits was commonplace and expected. Masters and mistresses kept children, indentured servants, and slaves in their proper subservient place through strategic and controlled beatings. Limitations on beatings were malleable and hard to discern, and while servants expected some correction from their masters, neighbors and courts frowned upon excessive beatings.[3] One law in 1642/43 condemned runaway servants but acknowledged that some servants had legitimate grievances. Some masters employed "harsh or unchristianlike usage or otherways for want of diet, or convenient necessaryes."[4] What behavior precisely constituted "unchristianlike" usage was left undefined, though perhaps there was unwritten cultural agreement on what treatment met that criterion. Another law a little more than a decade later condemned "harsh and bad usage" and required county courts to take care that "no servant or servants be misused by their master or mistresse."[5] The legal standards were vague, and apparently masters continued to treat their servants badly, and servants had little recourse.

In March 1661/62, the Virginia Assembly addressed what it saw as a problem of both household governance and public relations. The "barbarous usuage of some servants by cruell masters bring soe much scandall and infamy to the country in generall," the burgesses wrote. They then enacted legislation mandating the good and fair treatment of all indentured servants, guaranteeing them "competent dyett, clothing and lodging" and limiting the severity of the punishment masters could visit upon their servants. Indentured servants who could prove their masters had violated this law could make a complaint to the county court and could expect "remedy for his grievances."[6] The shoe was on the other foot as well: while forbidding maltreatment of servants and limiting the scope of corporal punishment, the burgesses were also wary of servants who challenged their masters' authority. The "audatious unruliness of many stubborne and incorrigible servants resisting their masters and overseers have brought many mischiefs and losses to diverse inhabitants of this country," they wrote, and such servants were to serve one year after the expiration of their indentures.[7]

Though the Assembly intended the laws to result in better-regulated households and plantations, the language was characteristically vague. The burgesses left definitions of what exactly constituted "competent dyett, clothing and lodging" and what constituted servants' "mischiefs" out of their attempt to regulate the relationship between planter and indentured servant. What constituted unacceptable behavior toward a servant was opaque, and thus it was difficult for maltreated or abused servants to protest their treatment.[8] English law and tradition provided some guidelines governing the reciprocal relations between masters and servants. Masters were legally obligated to treat servants well and according to the terms of their contracts, and likewise servants were obligated to honor their masters. Abusive masters in England could be deprived of their servants, and the quarter courts could punish unruly servants. The invaluable guide *The Countrey Justice* contained tables detailing appropriate wages and also admonished masters with biblical verses to treat servants well. *The Countrey Justice* also advocated that local magistrates and constables prevent "many other . . . abuses and disorders both in Masters and Servants."[9] Virginia practice toward servants departed from this model in some significant ways, as planters depended on servants in ways that English masters did not, making laws that protected masters' interests over servants' interests popular in Virginia. Yet the same underlying expectations of mutually Christian behavior underlay indentured servitude as it developed in the Chesapeake.

Some indentured servants perished from beatings, for which there seem to have been few legal ramifications. In March 1672/73 planter John Watts's young servant Anne Dupper died. Although a servant's death was not normally recorded in the county court records, Dupper's was cause for suspicion. Before her death, she had filed a complaint alleging brutal treatment at Watts's hands, and the court had ordered him to cease his abusive conduct. The court ordered Watts to post bond to ensure his good behavior. If Watts bought another "Christian servant" at a future time, he was to return to court and post bond to ensure "Christian-like usage" of that servant, suggesting that the court surmised that his treatment of Dupper might have contributed to her untimely demise.[10] When Watts beat Dupper, he departed from accepted norms of "Christian-like usage." Normal, acceptable household violence crossed the line to "unchristian" behavior when masters forgot their responsibilities toward their servants and caused permanent damage or death. That the court did not prevent Watts from keeping non-Christian dependents—Indian or African slaves—suggests that blacks and Indians had fewer protections against abuse than English indentured servants did.

Some servants were quite savvy about asserting their rights within the household. In 1661 Mary Rawlins sought out the protection of Governor William Berkeley to escape the beatings her master John Russell insisted on giving her. Her earlier attempts at redress in York County Court had been unsuccessful, for she fled to the governor's estate at Green Spring to directly enlist his help (an unusual move for an indentured servant). Berkeley sent her back to York with a note for the county magistrates telling them that Rawlins had been "most unchristianly and cruelly used by hir master" and that Russell should be required to post bond "for his better using of hir." Berkeley took the sting out of his missive by assuring the York County commissioners that "I doubt not but the Comrs will take care that servants shall be christianly used."[11] Back in York County, a magistrate questioned Rawlins and those who had witnessed the beating that sent her to Green Spring to seek out Governor Berkeley. The depositions reveal what sort of beating a servant had to endure for it to be deemed "unchristian." First, the beating had to have been public in some way, with witnesses to observe the abuse and to find it excessive. One witness, a free Englishman named William Parman, testified that John Russell and his wife Bridgett had beaten Rawlins with a switch, chasing the fleeing woman out of the house until they caught her and resumed their blows. When Parman attempted to stop the beating, Russell attacked the well-meaning Parman as well, striking him across the back of his hand with the switch.[12] Excessive passion or rage accompanied the un-Christian beating; it was more than a mere corrective to insubordinate behavior. Second, witnesses had to examine the victim's body to ascertain that bodily injury had indeed occurred. A group of York County matrons examined Rawlin's body, finding her "very much bruised and black and blew [blue] over her shoulders and Arms to the Elbows."[13] Third, the damage inflicted on the servant had to be lasting in some way. Henry Blagrave, a doctor, examined Rawlins again a few weeks later, revealing further bruising along her chest and midriff, and that one of Rawlins's breasts was "blackish."[14]

Rawlins had been treated in an "unchristian" manner: her beating had been public and the correction humiliating; the beating itself was excessive, causing visible bruising and some impairment; and her injuries were lasting. York County magistrates eventually found that Russell had used "unchristian-like usage & unlawfull correction" and required him to post forty pounds as bond for his good behavior toward his servants (which Russell promptly forfeited "by using uncivill contemptuous & rude language" in the court).[15] John Russell sold Rawlins's indenture to Andrew Lather, a man it appears she had wanted to marry.[16] Though Rawlins's story, unlike Anne Dupper's, had what can be described as a happy ending, it also illustrates the difficulties servants faced in enduring and proving "unchristian" treatment.

Later cases show that a masters' right to beat his servants at all could be rescinded entirely if the court found it necessary. When Mary Adney sued her master the Reverend John Wright, this is precisely what happened. Adney complained of his "barbarous usage," and "good & credible witnesses" affirmed that Wright "had by beating & whipping treated & used the s[ai]d Mary Adney after a most grosse, inhumane & barbarous manner." The court required Reverend Wright to post bond in the incredible amount of five hundred pounds that he would not "beat strike whipp or any other ways evilly intreate any Christian serv[an]t or serv[an]ts whatsoever." Wright could no longer beat recalcitrant servants at all. Instead, county magistrates would undertake that responsibility should it be required.[17] Though cases like Rawlins's and Adney's were difficult to prove, when they were proved, magistrates had a strong interest in making sure that English indentured servants were treated in a commonly accepted manner.

Masters received more legal protection from their servants than servants from their masters. When indentured servants beat their masters, it was an event that upended the traditional and widely accepted household hierarchy. In 1662 Thomas Morley presented his servant John Shelton at the county court, alleging that Shelton had "took the sticke out of his Masters hand twice (correcting him)" and that Shelton had also hit Morley's son William with the same stick. Shelton was sentenced to an extra year's service in the Morley household.[18] There was no suggestion that Morley was wrong to beat his servant, but resisting and then reciprocating a reasonable beating were certainly illegal.[19] In 1682 Joseph Stookley beat his master Robert Pritchard with a tobacco stick. A bystander, Jane Sturlin, attempted to protect Pritchard but the "Barbarous Creature [Stookley] did lay abt. him as if there was no master or woman in the case." Stookley, Sturlin testified, did not like Virginia food, which

Sturlin characterized as "pone & hominy salt & fat."[20] The detail about Stookley's dislike of the food his master served him only underscored the viciousness of his attack. Sturlin's obvious contempt for Stookley's disdain for "the good ordinary faire of the Country" implied that Pritchard actually fed and treated his servants well, making Stookley's violent outburst all the more appalling to witnesses and magistrates alike.

Yet Morley and Pritchard were lucky they survived violent encounters with their servants. Francis and Elizabeth Hall did not. Their indentured servant, Huntington Ayres, "knocked [them] on the head lying in their Bedd in the dead of the night wth a lathing hamer . . . as by the Confession of the said Ayers before us did appeare shewing us the manner." Ayres was later hanged for his offense.[21] Like other servants, Ayres could have been the victim of a "lost" indenture. Without written verification of the expiration of his term of service, the Halls might have kept him in servitude for years, drawing out the legal process of freedom. Or, like other masters, Francis Hall might have beaten his servant mercilessly. Trapped in a system that made long service and physical violence not only possible but acceptable, Ayres struck back and in the process lost his own life. Nevertheless, servants were expected to perform their Christian duty in honoring and obeying their masters. To do otherwise, even in the face of ill treatment, was to upend the social and religious order.

Unhappiness with the state of indentured servitude seems to have been widespread (as the Assembly implied when it passed legislation protecting the basic rights of servants). Servants also were disproportionately more likely to commit suicide: of the nine cases of suicide that required juries of inquest in York County between 1633 and 1670, seven of them were by servants, three women and four men. One servant hanged himself in his master's tobacco shed "with one bridle Reyne of the value of 10 pence."[22] Servants committing suicide and murderers such as Huntington Ayres were said to lack "grace" or "the feare of god" and to have acted at the "instigation of the devil." Yet masters could be pardoned for inflicting mortal injuries on servants. In 1660 Berkeley pardoned Katherine Pannell after the death of her servant Ellinor Cowell (Pannell had struck Cowell in the face with a meat skewer, which "corrupted the Opticke Nerve of the left Eye; & putrifaction thereby had issued into the Braine."[23] Maintaining the social order depended upon maintaining the power of masters or mistresses vis-à-vis their servants.

Troubled relationships between individual planters and their servants were not the only servant problem in Virginia's bowels. Most dangerous to the body politic were challenges of groups of servants not against specific masters but against the power of law and government. Beginning in the 1660s, periodic plots among servants surfaced, convincing planters that indentured servants were indeed a threat to peace and tranquillity. Planters associated a 1661 plot with the leveling tendencies of the English Civil War, and they claimed the servants involved were exiled soldiers from Oliver Cromwell's army. Plotters were arrested for their "seditious words and speeches tending to the mutiny and tumultuous behaviour of divers servants." A few years later, several servants were charged with treason after planning to leave Virginia before the expiration of their indentures. And in 1667 Dutch marauders attempted to undermine the colony by liberating indentured servants in the Tidewater.[24] Indentured servants had to be properly supervised otherwise they constituted a threat to the good order of the colony.

The relationship between planter and indentured servant involved at least some legal boundaries for the acceptability of violence, though unclear and difficult to enforce, but African and Indian slaves had no such legal protection. Anne Dupper had little enough recourse against the "extremity of the correction" her master Watts employed with her; a slave of Watts's, though, would have been entitled to no "Christian-like usage" whatsoever. Burgesses seized ultimate control of African and Indian bodies, essentially allowing masters to beat their own slaves to death without fear of legal prosecution for murder. In October 1669 burgesses passed an act "about the casuall killing of slaves." The burgesses noted that the "obstinacy of many of them [African slaves] by other then [sic] violent meanes supprest" and then absolved masters from murder charges should slaves "by the extremity of the correction . . . chance to die." Their reasoning lay in the ancient definitions of murder in the common law, which required that malice be part of the motivation for a killing, for "it cannot be presumed that prepensed [premeditated] malice (which alone makes murther ffelony) should induce any man to destroy his owne estate."[25] African slaves' only protection came from the legal definition of their bodies as property, which reasonable masters would not willingly destroy because of their own interests, not out of recognition of another human being's bodily integrity. Punishment of slaves, so long as it did not cause death, could presumably be far harsher than that of Christian indentured servants. It also effectively removed "Christian" protections from the people increasingly defined as hereditary heathens. This law was an act of racial definition has well as an act of control. Indentured servants might be "stubborn and incorrigible" but could not be punished out of proportion with their offenses. Slaves were also "obstinate," but their recalcitrance could be punished by death. The law endorsed violence against slaves even as it condemned excessive violence against indentured servants as "unchristian."

The Assembly passed other laws that regulated the conduct of masters and slaves and placed further legal guidelines on servitude. The legislature also clarified who was a servant and who was a slave, using religious definitions to clarify who could own whom, passing in October 1670 an act that "Noe Negroes nor Indians to buy christian servants." On the question of whether Africans and Indians "manumitted, or otherwise free, could be capable of purchasing christian servants," the burgesses answered that "noe negroe or Indian though baptised and enjoyned their owne ffreedome shall be capable of any such purchase of christians."[26] Slaves, though, could be charged with capital crimes (i.e., for killing their masters, even if their masters could not be said to have committed a capital crime for killing their slaves). The Reverend Morgan Godwyn, who ministered in Virginia in the 1660s, described a situation in which casual brutality toward African slaves was the order of the day. Appalled, Godwyn described the "scant allowance of Food" and the "*Negro's* want of provision." He witnessed the beating of slave, who "sustained an hundred Lashes, or more . . . Whereby he was, to the astonishment of the Beholders . . . but one general *Scab*, all over."[27] Such treatment would have been considered "unchristian" when directed at an indentured servant but was acceptable when directed at a non-Christian African slave. The degree of violence masters employed to maintain the social order defined and enacted religious and racial categories.

County magistrates described violence by African and Indian slaves against their masters as "barbarous" and cruell" when those cases came before them. The violent actions of African and Indian slaves were less likely to be prosecuted in the county courts, since by the early 1660s masters were legally empowered to punish those kinds of transgressions on their own authority. Litigants were more likely to involve the courts when slaves violated people or property away from their masters' plantations. In 1675 Thomas Bushrod's slave Luke beat Peter Nash "in a most cruell & barbarous manner" and was sentenced to receive thirty lashes "on his bared shoulders untill the blood come."[28] Peter Nash might have been a free man in his own right or someone else's servant, so Nash (or his master) sued to effect Luke's punishment. Unlike indentured servants convicted of assault, Luke was a slave for life and thus justices could not simply mandate that he serve Bushrod an additional year. Instead, Luke's body paid the price for his barbarous crime.

Thomas Bushrod must have been relieved that Peter Nash did not sue him for monetary damages, for planters sometimes sued one another for damages done by their neighbors' slaves. In 1696 Thomas Nutting sued his neighbor William Wise, alleging that Wise had set a slave named Robin to work near Nutting's property. Wise, Nutting said, "did keep noe Christian overseer to looke after him [Robin] by which means he comitted injurys to severall of the neighbors but especially to him [Nutting]." At the next court, Wise failed to turn up, and the court awarded Nutting two thousand pounds of tobacco for "Wises negro illegal killing & stealing of A hogg . . . & there noe Christian overseer to looke after him." The court later reduced Wise's fine to three hundred pounds of tobacco for abrogating his responsibility to keep a "Christian overseer" to supervise Robin and for Nutting's hog, and Nutting continued the suit. A later court instructed the sheriff to take Robin himself into custody so that Nutting could have full satisfaction for the loss of his animal.[29] What makes the tale interesting is not Nutting's rage over his dead hog, but what he saw as the central problem. Wise was an irresponsible master who did not set "Christian" overseers to look after his slaves. The underlying assumption was that Robin, being heathen, could not be expected to tell right from wrong, and thus not be able to respect Nutting's porcine property. Robin required a Christian overseer to keep his heathenness in check, and Wise had not provided one. Christian servants required protection from their masters, but African and Indian slaves required not protection but rather Christian oversight to mitigate their heathenish behavior. The stability of colonial society depended upon well-governed Christian English households.

Those Anglo-Virginians who placed themselves outside the ecclesiastical polity also posed a potentially disruptive threat to the social order. Though there had been some religious discontent from committed puritans living in Lower Norfolk County in the 1640s, Governor Berkeley had effectively banished most of them to Massachusetts and Bermuda. Members of the Society of Friends, known popularly and pejoratively as Quakers, seemed much more threatening at midcentury than any errant puritans did. Quakers seemed to supplant Spanish Catholics in the Anglo-Virginian imagination as threats. The first Quaker missionaries arrived in Virginia in 1656, bringing with them religious beliefs that even the most radical Protestants found excessive.[30] Quakers rejected the trappings of mainstream English Protestantism, including church buildings, a salaried clergy, the episcopal hierarchy, and conventional church services. For Quakers, divine revelation and prophecy had not ceased, and God was present inside every human in the form of "inner light." Any person, male or female, could be a minister. Quaker religious services appeared disordered and aimless to outsiders; typically Quaker meetings, as they were called, were silent affairs in which members sat in quiet contemplation until one or more of their number felt they should speak. Quakers were also dedicated to the principle of nonviolence, which in the colonial context meant male Quakers refused to muster for militia duty. They had an antagonistic relationship with both the established church and civil authorities—two characteristics that made Anglo-Virginians nervous.

Anglo-Virginians perceived Quakers as having disordered households, which in turn led to a disordered society. This perception was not unique to Virginia; Jamaican legislators noted that Quakers "doe Seduce many women and Some Ignorant men and in Stead of Promoting the Settlement Rather instruct the people and Disturb and Obstruct divers not Onely in their Planting but their Serving in the militia and other Civil Dutyes and Offices contrary to the common goode."[31] Quakers were a threat to the commonwealth. One example of a Quaker household contributing to social and religious chaos was that of Thomas Bushrod, whose disordered household included Luke, the enslaved man who beat Peter Nash. When one of the county's ministers, Justinian Aylmer, encouraged Bushrod to allow his wife Elizabeth to resume attendance at Anglican services, Bushrod chased Aylmer, calling him "a lying Knave an ugly rogue and blind Rogue" and later in the confrontation also called him a "blind Priest" who was the servant of "Episcopal knaves" and "antichrists that precedded from the pope." It was probably extremely provoking to Aylmer to hear himself compared to a Catholic priest. The collective Quaker rejection of Anglican worship and hierarchy, combined with individual belligerent acts of Quaker resistance against Anglican clergy, made Quakers a threat to the colony's religious and social order.[32]

The Quaker presence in Virginia, while not as deadly for its earnest missionaries as it was in New England, was still perilous. Virginians saw the Quaker missionaries and their converts as threats to the peace and stability of the commonwealth and legislated accordingly. In March 1659/

60 the Assembly accused Quakers generally of having "sundry dangerous opinions and tenets" and of terrorizing "the people by maintayning a secrett and strict corresponency among themselves, and in the meane time separating and dividing themselves from the rest of his majesties good and loyall subjects, and from the publique congregations and usuall place of divine service." The Quaker danger, as the burgesses saw it, arose not only from their radically dangerous theological positions but from their voluntary separation from mainstream English society and their rejection of basic participation in civil society by refusing militia duty. Quakers, by "devouring and attempting thereby to destroy religion, lawes, comunities and all bonds of civil societie," would leave the colony in chaos and open to the predations of every "vitious person." Such behavior implied treason and heresy.[33]

County officials quickly followed through with the new Assembly act regarding Quakers. York County magistrates issued a proclamation, claiming that "there are severall dangerous persons now in the County called Quakers who by their frequent private meetings in the nature of Conventicles have seduced & misledd many poor ignorant persons which may be feared will prove the disturbance of the peace." (This proclamation might have been in response to Thomas Bushrod's suggestion that Quakers conference publicly with their Anglican counterparts.)[34] Though it might seem absurd to see pacifist Quakers as a threat for "disturbing the peace," the language the magistrates deployed to describe Quakers indicates just how uneasy they were. Like Roman Catholics, whom Anglo-Virginians also believed they had cause to fear, Quakers "seduced" innocents away from the true religion. Their "Conventicles," as the magistrates called Quaker meetings, represented large unlawful gatherings of people in a place where people congregated usually for court days or for Sunday worship in the Church of England. That large gangs of schismatic nonconformists appeared to be meeting together likely put the magistrates in mind of plots and rebellions.[35] A further proclamation from the York County magistrates denounced "certaine dangerous turbulent seditious persons tearmed Quakers" and authorized sheriffs and constables to break up their "unlawfull meetings . . . [which they] doe frequently Conveene in severall parts of the County which doth apparently tend to the dishonour & disservice of God, the seducing & misleading man the Inhabitants & Disturbance of the Countreyes peace."[36] Quakers, unlike other Anglo-Virginians, dishonored God—a serious transgression—and dishonoring God was intimately connected with disturbing the civil peace.

The law resulted in widespread legal action against Quakers in the late 1650s and early 1660s. One of the imprisoned Quakers, William Robinson, spent at least six months in jail before moving on to New England, where he was eventually executed. William Colbourne was arrested and fined for allowing Quakers to stay in his home; Henry White and Thomas Leatherbury were charged with a similar offense.[37] In 1661 Quakers from around Virginia were tried before the General Court at Jamestown for recusancy; as the judges informed the miscreants, "There is no toleration for wicked consciences."[38] The Virginia Assembly passed legislation criminalizing participation in Quaker meetings in 1661 and 1663. Any ship captains bringing Quaker missionaries or immigrant converts to Virginia would be fined five thousand pounds of tobacco. Anglican parishes received the proceeds from convictions.[39] The legislation, while seeking to limit Quaker access to Virginia, did not prevent the dissident sect from increasing there. By 1673 Virginia Quakers had established a yearly meeting to govern their growing community.[40] In York County, Quakers were routinely presented at county court for non-attendance at the Anglican church. Although Edward Thomas explained to the court in 1682/83 that he was a practicing Quaker and did not attend "out of non conformity to the church hath not resorted to his parish church or chappell ease," the court fined him anyway.[41] Thomas continued to attract the attention of the county's grand jury; a few years later he was prosecuted for allowing traveling Quakers to preach at his house and then fined two hundred pounds of tobacco "for working and mauling of loggs upon Christmas day."[42]

In Surry County, Quakers were routinely fined for nonattendance on militia training days, a transgression other Anglo-Virginians probably found particularly provoking, because that meant that Quakers would not help fend off an Indian raid or a slave rebellion.[43] Quakers also encountered legal troubles because of their refusal to swear oaths, whether that meant oaths of supremacy and allegiance to the crown or simple oaths to attest to the truth of legal testimony. Despite the hassle this caused county courts, in Surry County magistrates seemed increasingly resigned to this difficulty, especially when Quaker widows needed to probate their husbands' estates. After the death of her husband John, Jane Barnes brought his probate inventory to court but refused to swear to its truthfulness. She claimed that Quakers could make a "serious protestation" rather than swear an oath. Surry County magistrates did not think this was the case. Jane Barnes's case dragged out over several months, with the magistrates finally allowing her to find someone else to do the probate inventory and swear to its contents. In this the Surry justices acted with surprising patience, eventually finding a legal way around the Quaker woman's difficulty, and her husband's estate eventually passed to her.[44]

Legislated conformity reinforced an English Protestant identity and affirmed the established Church of England in Virginia as it did in other colonies. In 1663 Bermuda also passed legislation against Quakers, penalizing their "Contempt of Authoritye" and their refusal to testify in court under oath. Bermuda's Friends seem to have been more forceful than Virginia's Friends in their quest for toleration; in 1667 several male and female Quakers were arrested in Bermuda for disturbing a Church of England service by "raysing severall verball noyses & acclamations." The charges alleged that some Quakers "use[d] actuall violence and smiting with the hands" against churchgoers, and another apparently stalked the minister at his home "to the terror & affrightment of his ffamely." For good measure, the Quaker Susana Bayley was accused of "scandalous life," a euphemism for fornication. This active assault on the established church brought home the threat of Quakers against the institution that Bermudians thought enforced the good order of their colony. Quakers, they thought, wanted chaos. To that end, Bermuda legislated further against Quakers, adopting penalties similar to those in Virginia and in addition passed an "Act against disturbers of the Ministers in the Islands." Further legislation in February 1668/69 tainted men who married Quaker women by association; those men were prohibited from holding public office in Bermuda, because Bermudians feared that Quaker women would unduly influence the weak men who married them.[45]

The fear of secret Quakers in positions of authority was not unique to Bermuda. In Lower Norfolk County, Virginia, justices reported to the governor early in 1663 that John Porter, one of the county's burgesses, was at the very least a Quaker sympathizer. (Berkeley wrote to them in June thanking them for their "care of the County & desire you to continue it, & Especially to provide that the abominated seede of the Quakers spread not in your County.")[46] In September 1663 the Assembly ejected Porter from the House of Burgesses because he was "loving to the Quakers and stood well affected towards them, and had been at their meetings, and was so far an anabaptist as to be against the baptising of children." Porter also refused to take the oaths of supremacy and allegiance required of members of the Assembly.[47] It is possible that the specter of having Quakers and Quaker sympathizers such as John Porter prompted the additional legislation against Quakers that session.

The perceived Quaker threat to the colonial political and religious order motivated the vigilante actions of Eastern Shore grandee Edmund Scarburgh in November 1663. Scarburgh led a troop of mounted militia into the border areas between Virginia and Maryland (where it was not at all clear which colonial government ruled). Scarburgh wanted to publicize the recent Acts of Assembly and "to repell that Contempt which I was informed some Quakers & a foole in office had threatened to obtrude." Anglican residents of the region charged that Quakers encouraged rebellion and "Confusion." One Quaker, Scarborough charged, "advised others to Rebellion & to this Day with the Quaker bid defiance to the Government of his Majesties Country of Virginia boasting their insolences & forgeries." Scarburgh arrested other Quakers, including Stephen Horsey, a "man Repugnant to all Government, of all sects yet professedly none, Constant in nothing, but opposing Church Government, his Children at great ages yet uncristened." George Johnson, whom Scarburgh described as "the proteus of heresy . . . notorious for shifting scismaticall pranks . . . A known Drunkard & Reported by the neighbors to be the father of his Negro Wenches bastards" was also arrested. Quakers, Scarburgh charged, were spreading rumors "to the disturbance of the peace and terror of the less knowing which wee are assured doth arise from the Quakers."[48] Like many Anglo-Virginians, he associated the Friends not with peace but with chaos. Scarburgh's Quakers were rumormongers, rebels, and scofflaws who avoided baptizing their children and impregnated their slaves. The Friends were direct threats to the religious and racial order Anglo-Virginians had labored so hard to develop over the previous two generations.

Quakers such as George Johnson or Susana Bayley, who openly flouted boundaries carefully erected against interracial sex, were particular threats to the colony's social order. These threats manifested themselves not just through accusations that Quakers fathered children with enslaved women but also through public demonstrations of Quakers' willingness to preach to and worship with Africans and Indians. As early as 1657, Quaker leader George Fox wrote a brief letter "To Friends beyond the sea, that have Blacks and Indian Slaves." Though not explicitly an abolitionist document, Fox stressed that God "hath made all nations of one blood" and that "the gospel is preached to every creature under heaven; which is the power that giveth liberty and freedom, and is glad tidings to every captivated creature."[49] Though Anglican ministers made similar points about converting Africans and Indians, Fox's letter encouraged Quakers to do so outside the established church. Fox followed up his initial encouragement for Quaker slave owners to do more to convert their slaves with a more explicit indictment issued from Barbados in 1671. In Barbados, Fox had encountered condemnation from planters who disapproved of Quaker conversions. Fox scathingly replied with a few pointed rhetorical questions: "[A]re you not Teachers of *Blacks* and *Taunies* (to wit, *Indians*) as well as of the *Whites*? For, is not the Gospel to be preached to all Creatures? And are not they Creatures? And did not Christ taste Death for every man? And are not they Men?"[50] While still avoiding the question of slavery itself, Fox's attack hit a nerve with Morgan Godwyn, who later wrote that he was inspired to force the issue of baptism for enslaved people in part because of the accusations against Anglicans in Fox's pamphlet.[51]

Other Quakers were less circumspect than Fox on the subject of slavery. One of Fox's missionary companions on the Barbados trip, William Edmundson, visited Rhode Island in 1676 and there openly questioned slavery as an institution, writing that slavery encouraged sin. Edmundson, like Fox, also openly reaffirmed monogenesis and the common descent of all human beings.[52] Fox followed up in 1676 with a pamphlet that Barbadian planters likely found even more inflammatory. Fox reminded Quaker planters that enslaved people were members of their families, and therefore Quakers had a special obligation to bring them to Christianity. Fox also encouraged recognition of marriages among enslaved people, limited terms of enslavement, and education in reading and writing. He concluded the pamphlet by encouraging Quaker planters to set aside time for a slaves' meeting.[53] Fox preached the spiritual inclusion of enslaved people where colonial law required their exclusion. It was a conflict that was sure to result in more trouble for Quakers with Barbadian officials.

New World Quakers were eager to follow through with Fox's recommendations regarding enslaved people in their households. In York County, Virginia, residents reported that "severall Quakers mett . . . in the woods amongst which were Mrs Mary Chisman and 2 or 3 Negroes belonging to hir husband." The Quakers were likely trying to meet somewhere out of sight where they would not attract the attention of authorities or vigilant residents seeking out "unlawfull meetings" where the Quakers discussed "their schismaticall and hereticall doctrines & opinions." The presence of slaves caused the most horror. Although African slaves were increasingly alienated from the Church of England, the Quaker belief in the spiritual equality of all people posed a direct threat to the exclusionary religious order Anglo-Virginians had carefully crafted. The county court ordered Edmund Chisman, Mary's husband, to "restreyne his said Negroes & whole family from repairing to the said unlawfull Assemblyes at his perill." The magistrates appealed to the Christian ideal of household order to encourage Chisman to control his wife and his slaves. Quaker beliefs and teaching negated the natural household order by extending roles in worship to women and to slaves—a dangerous combination.[54] The actual behavior of Quakers such as Mary Chisman undermined the increasingly accepted religious and racial walls between English planters and their African slaves.

This was especially true in Barbados, where Fox and his associates had actively preached the conversion of enslaved people. In 1675 an enslaved woman exposed a slave rebellion days before it was to occur. Several enslaved people were brutally executed for their parts in the planned rebellion (some by beheading and others by burning alive).[55] In the aftermath, Barbadians resisted Quaker efforts to proselytize slaves even more strenuously, seeing gatherings (such as those of the Chismans and their slaves in Virginia) as founts of disorder and rebellion. Barbados governor Jonathan Atkins accused a Quaker missionary of "making the Negroes Christians, and [making] them rebel and cut their Throats." Atkin's accusation struck at the heart of Quaker identity. In Barbados as in other colonies, Quakers refused to participate in the militia. From Atkin's perspective, Quakers were inciting a rebellion, which they would then refuse to defend against, making Quakers de facto allies in any future slave plots. In 1676 Barbados banned Quakers from allowing slaves at meetings and assigned stiff fines to violators, because at such meetings "the fafety of this Island may be much hazarded." For Barbadians, not only was the Quakers' brand of Christianity illegitimate, but its efforts to convert enslaved people constituted a threat to the island. Over the next few years, at least two Quakers were prosecuted for allowing slaves at meeting. In 1671 the island's Church of England ministers petitioned for further suppression of Quakers, who disrupted Anglican services and preached "anti-Christian" doctrine.[56] In Barbados, Quakers and their enslaved coreligionists posed a combined religious and racial threat that made planters even less likely to see their enslaved property as potential Christians.

Quakers also extended opportunities for worship and conversion to Indians. George Fox and other missionaries held regular meetings with Indians on trips to the North American mainland. Quakers enlisted Indians as guides along Indian pathways running from colony to colony; they were as likely to lodge with Indians in their travels as with fellow Quakers, and Indians were welcome at their large public meetings.[57] In 1672, for example, George Fox reported entering Virginia and visiting "an Indian Kings Cabbin about a mile from our Lodginge, where wee mett with severall [Indians], and they was Loveinge."[58] In 1661 the Quaker missionary and Atlantic traveler George Wilson made his way from Massachusetts Bay into Virginia, where he hoped to recruit new converts and to convince Virginia's ruling class to tolerate the presence of Quakers in the colony. Wilson was unsuccessful. The former soldier turned nonviolent Friend found himself in Jamestown jail, "Chained to a post with an Indyan; which they have hanged for killing of an English man, our Legs was made faste upon one boult, and since they have caused me to be put into a dungeon, with four men more, which is arrested for murther."[59] The perverse pairing of the peaceful Friend and the violent Indian suggests that Anglo-Virginians equated each prisoner's level of threat to Virginia's precarious social order. In chaining together the accused Indian murderer and the Quaker who threatened the religious establishment of Virginia, their jailers made an emphatic statement. Perhaps it was intended to be a humorous act, but the result showed the contempt in which Anglo-Virginians held Quakers. By physically binding Wilson with the Indian, their jailers equated their acts—the destruction wrought by Indian violence and the religious destruction threatened by Wilson and other Quaker missionaries. Anglo-Virginians were threatened by Indians from without and by Quakers from within. If Mary Chisman voluntarily associated herself with her slaves, the state could involuntarily associate an active Quaker with another despised group—Indians. Religious outsiders and racial outsiders were profoundly connected in the Anglo-Virginian imagination.

Though Quakers embraced Indians as potential members of their religious community, Anglo-Virginians continued to see Indians as heathens circling the increasingly vulnerable frontiers of their world. Siouan and Iroquoian groups living beyond the fall line were a real and imminent military threat. Though most planters made little effort to distinguish between groups of Indians, many of the remnants of Wahunsonacock's confederation remained allies of the English. Many groups along the fall line and the frontier, though, were increasingly pressed eastward by invading Iroquoian groups coming from the north and west, where they in turn had been squeezed by English and French encroachment. The frontier was a potentially explosive political problem for Governor William Berkeley, who was charged with protecting frontier settlements but at the same time controlled access to the highly lucrative fur trade with the Indians. In a colony suffering from economic difficulties (due in part to the low price of tobacco) and from an increasingly anxious politics, fear on the frontier was the last thing Anglo-Virginians needed. The stability of the colony depended ultimately on the maintenance of its precarious religious and racial order; the Quakers within and the Indians without seemed to undermine Virginia society at every turn.

In February 1675/76 events in New England reminded Governor Berkeley of his earlier characterization of Anglo-Virginians as a "people press'd at our backes with Indians." The "infection of the Indians in New-England has dilated itselfe to the Merilanders and the Northern parts of Virginia, and wee have lost about Forty men Women and Children."[60] Berkeley blamed the Susquehannocks for those deaths, but he feared that Indian groups up and down the eastern seaboard could easily combine to threaten all English people. A month later Berkeley wrote to Charles II that his intelligence indicated "a generall Combination" of Indians, which led him to believe that his only options were "either to establish a firme and lasting peace with them, or to extirpate their whole race."[61] Berkeley's trouble was not simply that Indians seemed to threaten wherever he looked but also that many Anglo-Virginians were leaning toward the second option and favored a wholesale and indiscriminate slaughter of Indians. In September 1675 Nathaniel Bacon, a prominent frontier planter owning around a thousand acres along the fall line of the James River, attacked and kidnapped a group of friendly Appomattuck Indians. Though Bacon had been in the colony for only a little more than a year, he was related to many of the colony's wealthiest and most powerful inhabitants, including the governor, and was already a member of the Governor's Council. Bacon's new political power protected him from serious retaliation by the governor. Although Berkeley reproved him for his rash actions against the Appomattucks, Bacon was undeterred. When Bacon's own overseer was killed during an Indian raid a few months later, Bacon moved to full-scale rebellion against the government of the colony.[62]

Bacon played on the fears of frontiersmen and on the English hatred of Indians to fuel his rebellion. In his "Declaration of the People," Bacon accused Berkeley of having "betrayed and sold His Ma[jesty] Countrie, and the Liberties of his Loyall Subjects to the Barbarous Heathen."[63] Bacon's characterization of Indians as "Barbarous Heathen" stemmed from what seemed to Anglo-Virginian planters to be Indians' unjustified and excessive violence. Anglo-Virginians saw disproportionate violence as a rejection of accepted norms of Christian behavior. Because Bacon and his followers also perceived Indian offensives on the frontier as unjustifiable attacks on innocent settlers, it was natural for them to fall back on their most disparaging description of Indians—that they were barbarous and heathen. Violence on the frontier reawakened the sharp line between the Christian English and the heathen Indians that had emerged after 1622, and Bacon deftly exploited that divide to build his rebel army. According to Bacon, Governor Berkeley's main crime was that he "Protected, favoured, and Emboldned, the Indians against his Ma[jesty's] most Loyall Subjects." Berkeley had abandoned his duty to protect English settlers from Indians, "who immediately prosecuted theire Evil Intentions—Committing horrid Murders and Robberies." Bacon took the traditional position of many seventeenth-century English rebels: he rebelled to protect English lives and liberty when those in power abdicated their responsibilities to do so. That the people's enemies were "Barbarous Heathens" made his cause all the more urgent, for "many of his [the King's] faithfull and Loyall Subjects by Him betrayed in a Barbarous and Shamefull Manner Exposed to the Incursion and murder of the Heathen."[64] In Bacon's emergent rhetoric of English Christians versus Indian heathens, Berkeley had willingly allied himself with the heathen Indians against the interests of the Christian English.

Though Bacon attacked the heathen Indians and their supposed accomplices in the government, other accounts compared Bacon to the "Barbarous Heathen" he claimed to be fighting against. In her *History of Bacon's and Ingram's Rebellion*, Ann Cotton explicitly compared Bacon to the Indians he fought.[65] Cotton sided with Berkeley in her manuscript *History* but did not exonerate the Indians; she described the initial frontier attacks as "most inhumane" murders perpetrated by "ill disarning [discerning] brutish heathens." Cotton wrote, "They dayly commited abundance of ungarded and unrevenged murthers, upon the English which they perpretated [*sic*] in a most barberous and horid maner. . . . For these brutish and inhumane brutes . . . devised a hundred ways to torter [torture] and torment those poore soules with, whose reched [wretched] fate it was to fall in to there unmercyfull hands." Cotton also described Indians skinning victims, tearing out their teeth, fingernails, and toenails, and desecrating English corpses.[66] The Indians' brutality, as Cotton described it, derived from their heathen ways. Cotton went on to argue, though, that the answer to the problems of the frontier was not Nathaniel Bacon, whose followers, according to Cotton, viewed him as a godlike figure of salvation.[67] If indeed the rebels' loyalty to Bacon was such that they saw him as a savior, or that Bacon presented himself as a defender and savior, most English observers would have thought it idolatrous, as Cotton implied. True protection came not from false, rebellious gods, but from the divinely ordained civil government that Berkeley led.

Other anti-Baconians argued that Bacon seduced innocent settlers to follow him, using language reminiscent of magistrates' claims that Quakers misled the innocent and unwary with their blasphemous beliefs. After Bacon's death, royal commissioners sent to assess and remedy the causes of the rebellion offered bounties for those "seduced" by Bacon's promises of safety from the Indians.[68] The metaphor of seduction was one English settlers used to describe what happened to their comrades who fell away from traditional English Christian belief as well as those who rejected the civil order. Bacon seduced men, mostly servants and some slaves, away from their rightful place in Virginia society. Quakers and Catholics seduced English Christians away from the true church into heretical "conventicles." And Anglo-Virginians had feared the seductive power of Indian culture since those initial years of settlement at James-town. The lingering appeal of a heathen lifestyle, especially to those Vir-ginia residents—servants and slaves—who had the least to gain from the emerging plantation system, threatened the civil order. Anti-Baconians like Cotton described the threat also as an attack upon religion, with Bacon and his followers taking on the heathenish characteristics of the Indians they claimed to fight.

Colonel Giles Brent was an ally of Bacon who embodied all the hea-thenish characteristics of Baconians. Cotton wrote that when Brent arrived in Jamestown to engage Berkeley's troops, "he in a most bar-berous maner converts ye whole Towne in to flames, cinders, and ashes not so much as spareing the Church, and the first that ever was in Verginia." The destruction of the town, including its house of worship, was a "Flagitious and sacralidgious action" and an "inn-humane fact."[69] Cotton described Brent's wanton destruction of property much as she described the Indian torture of English settlers. It was barbarous, inhuman, and un-Christian. (After pillaging Jamestown, Brent moved on to Berkeley's estate at Green Spring, slaughtering the governor's animals and cutting down his crops to feed his men.)[70] Another commenter remembered after the rebellion's end that Giles Brent's mother had been the Indian woman Mary Kittamaquund. He supposed that Colonel Brent had inherited his mother's "brutish nature," and that he "dranke of health to the divell."[71] Brent, the son of a Catholic man and an Indian woman, had inherited the unsavory characteristics of both. He behaved as the good English Protestants of Virginia imagined such a person would act, destroying churches and plantations alike. As Catholics and Indians did, he personally worshiped the devil, and that, combined with the immutability of his Indian ancestry, drove him to rebellion and to destruction. Bacon's forces had admitted into their midst the very evil they wanted to defeat.

In addition to destroying the Jamestown church, Bacon purportedly attempted to assert his authority over a captured minister by silencing his theological opinions about the rebellion. The imprisoned minister encouraged Bacon's followers to refuse to take the oaths he required to join his army. Bacon reportedly told the offending minister "that it was his place to Preach in the church, not in the Camp: In the first he might say what he pleased but in the last, he was to saye no more then what should please him [Bacon]."[72] Berkeley accused Bacon in 1676 of "Expressions of Atheisme, tending to take away al religion and lawes."[73] Berkeley ultimately blamed the 1649 execution of Charles I for the problems of the "Universal English Nation," characterizing Bacon's rise to power as an example of "Gods Anger."[74] Bacon's rebellion not only was a threat to the colony's religious order and its civil establishment but was ultimately an act of divine retribution for that definitive act of disorder in the previous generation: the murder of a king. Though ostensibly a movement to protect Anglo-Virginians from heathen Indians, Bacon's rebellion also undermined the precarious racial order by attracting both indentured servants and enslaved Africans to his cause. Bacon's genius lay in his ability to undermine the social order of the colony in his opposition to Governor Berkeley and to dissolve households by attracting slaves and servants to his banner against the Indians. After the rebellion's conclusion, the last group of Baconians to surrender to Berkeley's forces comprised eighty enslaved men and twenty indentured servants.[75] The combination of enslaved people and indentured servants must have chilled the blood of planters who already thought they had but a precarious hold on the colony's social order. After the rebellion's conclusion, Anglo-Virginian planters emphasized whiteness and Christianity as the two bonds that held English people together against Indians who threatened from without and enslaved people who threatened from within.[76]

Bacon's death from disease in 1676 left the rebellion in disarray, and Laurance Ingram took over leadership of the fading movement. When Ingram's lieutenants read his commission to the assembled rebels, Ingram, whom Cotton described as "the Milke-sop," "stoode, with his hatt in his hand, Lookeing as demurely as the grate Turks Muftie, at ye readeing som holy sentance, extracted forth of the Alchron [the Koran]." Cotton's insult was twofold. "Milk sop" connoted a "[a] feeble, timid, or ineffectual person," usually "a man or boy who is indecisive, effeminate, or lacking in courage." Cotton convincingly feminized Ingram with her jibe, insulting his ability to fight and to command.[77] In another calculated barb, she compared Ingram to an infidel Turk and his commission to the holy book of a non-Christian religion. She continued the metaphor of Ingram as a Turk, likening his followers to "Janessarys" (the legendary soldiers who served the sultan of the Ottoman Empire). Ingram was "in imitation of the grat [great] Sultaine, at his election, would have inlarged there [sic] pay, or ells have given them leave to have made Jewes of ye best Christians in the Countrey; but he being more then halfe a jew him self, at present forbad all plunderings, but such as he him selfe should be parsonally at."[78] Bacon's, and now Ingram's, soldiers were in it only for the money, Cotton implied. Her references to Jews suggest greed as well. The seventeenth-century English stereotype of Jewish people involved greed, moneylending, and usurious interest rates. In one sentence, Cotton effectively connected Bacon, Ingram, and their army with two non-Christian religions with unsavory reputations among the English. Cotton adroitly rendered her quarry both effeminate and infidel.

Berkeley rushed to restore order in Virginia, trying, convicting, and executing many of Bacon's followers. One Colonel Hansford defended himself before he was hanged, claiming that he desired that "he dyed a Loyall Subject, and a lover of his Countrey, and that he had never taken up arms, but for the destruction of the Indians, who had murthered so many Christians."[79] Hansford's plea underscored the central tension between the opposing forces of Bacon's Rebellion. Everyone agreed that the Indians were the enemy. Most Anglo-Virginians thought that the Indians were the "barbarous heathen" of Bacon's Declaration. But in defying civil authority and fomenting rebellion, Bacon crossed the line from English Christianity to barbarity and heathenism. Giles Brent, whose Catholic and Indian mother marked him as a brute and as a hereditary heathen, and Ingram, as an exemplar of Ottoman Islam, essentially made Bacon a heathen by behavior and association. Bacon's followers were disaffected English servants and enslaved heathen Africans rebelling against their rightful, divinely ordained masters. Thus Bacon and his motley crew fomented the violence of civil war, and that action itself marked them as "unchristian." Cotton's presentation of Hansford's dying plea, justifying his rebellion as an attempt to avenge the murdered Christian English settlers on the frontier, seems pathetic and muted. Hansford might have wanted to defend Christians, but becoming a heathen to do it was not a solution to the problem.

The presence of the Catholic and half-Indian Giles Brent in Bacon's Rebellion underscored another source of colonial insecurity that re-emerged as a central problem in the 1680s: fear of Catholics and popish conspiracies to extirpate all English Protestants in the New World. Although Catholics had long been objects of suspicion, they did govern Maryland, the colony immediately to Virginia's north, and most Virginians of the planter class had made an effort to remain on good terms with their recusant neighbors. A few Catholic families, most notably the Brents and the Jenifers, held land and some offices in Virginia, but Catholics remained a tiny minority in the colony.[80] Anglo-Virginians' fear of violence and disruption—from chaotic households, indentured servants, religious dissenters, enslaved Africans, Indians, and rebels—recentered on the imagined threat of Roman Catholics in the 1680s. Charles II's Catholic half brother James became king in 1685, prompting fears that he would return England and her colonies to the Roman Catholic religion. In Virginia, a convergence of long-standing concerns about Indians and Catholics redefined what it meant to be Protestant and English in Virginia, and ultimately what it meant to be white.

In 1688 two frontier settlers, known only by their surnames, West and Harris, spread the rumor that a "few Papists in Maryland . . . had Conspired to hyre [hire] the Seneca Indians to ye Cutting off & totall distroying of all the Protestants." As evidence for the plot's existence, West and Harris produced an unnamed Indian who claimed to know all about the

Seneca-Catholic alliance. The two Englishmen had apparently coached the Indian on the story he was to tell. Frontier settlements at the fall lines of the Rappahannock and Potomac Rivers armed themselves and formed "parties upon their defense, and ready to fly in the face of Government, so that matters were very pressingly tending to a Rebellion."[81] The sheer scale of the plot seemed unbelievable and unworkable to the governor and his council in Jamestown, but it played on the fears of the frontier settlers, who remembered the raids that sparked Bacon's rebellion fifteen years earlier. Now the differences were not merely Christian versus heathen but also encompassed the old European feud of Protestant versus Catholic. Catholicism, in alliance with the feared Seneca, was another heathenism the staunch Virginia Protestants were compelled to fight.

Virginia officials decided to verify the plot's existence and sent again for the Indian, in order to question him further about the supposed plot. The Indian, though, was beyond reach, for "these felonious p[er]sons [West and Harris] who sett that Indian at work prevented a delaction [delation] of their villainy by a private destroying of ye Indian." The governor had sent a small party of men to the frontier to fetch the Indian and return him to Jamestown, where Virginia officials intended to interrogate him further about the plot. West and Harris, the "principall Instruments in their wicked machinations," sent the governor's men on ahead, claiming that they and the Indian could not travel as quickly, as they had no horses. West and Harris said "they would bring him [the Indian], but noe such Indian appeared at ye Time and Place appointed, and since found murthered in the Woods." West claimed to find the body, and played well the "Actor of [that] Tragicall Part," but the governor's men were suspicious and brought West and Harris back with them to Jamestown. They uncovered the plot's real goal: the desire of frontier settlers to kill Indians and Catholics alike.[82] The ingenuity and violence of the plot were breathtaking. It took some effort for West and Harris to identify a willing Indian and somehow convince him to spin a tale of murderous alliances between Maryland's Catholics and the Seneca. They then used this as an excuse to muster militias in Stafford and Rappahannock counties and to deceive imperial officials in Jamestown. When suspicious officials there wished to confirm the existence of the plot, West and Harris murdered their Indian conspirator.

County officials on the frontier jailed West and Harris for murdering the Indian. Few Englishmen were ever punished for killing Indians, which suggests that the unnamed victim was not Seneca but rather an allied Pamunkey or Appomattuck. These groups had been all but swallowed by English encroachments on their lands. To maintain peace with Indians who now lived in the midst of English settlements, colonial officials must have felt obliged to attempt to punish West and Harris. In a report to the Board of Trade in London, Governor Thomas Culpepper announced that "a Rescue [was] lately made in Stafford County by a Rabble of ab[ou]t two hundred to [carry?] away three persons from the Custody of the Sherriff Comitted for createing and forgeing the pretended Conspiracy of Papists and Indians against ye Protestants." Rumors claimed the Indian had been "killed by ye Procurement of ye Papists," and it seems that the residents of Stafford County did not believe their neighbors had killed the Indian. The goal, Culpepper reported, was that "the Intrigue would come fully to possess the people with a reall danger from Pap[ists, tear] and Indian Conspiracie, and under that Gloss betake themselves to Armes to plunder and robb." Maryland by that time was a majority-Protestant colony governed by the Calvert family and their Catholic retainers. Protestant Marylanders were keen to proclaim William and Mary but thought the government there would prevent it.[83]

Threats to authority, the possibility of Indian raids along the frontier, and the imagined threats of Catholic Maryland not only spawned West and Harris's convoluted anti-popish plot but also galvanized Anglo-Virginians' support for the Glorious Revolution. The victory of William and Mary meant that Anglo-Virginians had to confront their hostility toward all non-Anglican Virginians. In 1689 Parliament passed "An Act for Exempting their Majestyes Protestant Subjects dissenting from the Church of England from the Penalties of certaine Lawes." Although the law still excluded Catholics and Quakers from the protections of toleration, other Protestant dissenters gained the ability to meet (with unlocked doors) without penalties.[84] The 1689 act meant that colonial legislatures were also obligated to institute protections for Protestant dissenters. Virginia was characteristically slow to act. In 1699 the Assembly officially, if grudgingly, recognized the act by exempting qualified dissenting Protestants from a new blasphemy law.[85] The Glorious Revolution solidified Anglo-Virginia's English, Protestant, Christian identity against threats from within and without—heathen slaves and Indians— in part by neutralizing the threat of Protestant dissenters. Even Catholics seemed less scary; immediately after the Glorious Revolution, a rebellion in Maryland displaced the Catholic Calvert family, and William and Mary acceded to the Protestant Association's request for a Protestant governor. This lessened the threat of a papist plot to Virginia's north, but naturally the Glorious Revolution did not ease Virginia's fears of Indian violence on the frontier. Well into the eighteenth century, settlers wrote to the governor and his council registering their fears of the "violense of ye Haithen" and requested more military assistance from the colonial government.[86]

Anglo-Virginians accepted religious toleration because Christianity was defined as a religion only for whites. The 1705 Act Concerning Servants and Slaves, which gave new and detailed protections to English indentured servants, assumed these servants were white and Christian. The act prohibited the whipping of a "christian white servant naked." This was the first time that Christians were legally and explicitly defined by a physical distinction—skin color—and granted certain privileges based upon color and religious identity. The act also provided for the "christian care and usage of all christian servants" and forbade all "negros, mulattos, or Indians" from owning Christian servants. Christianity was thus strongly equated with whiteness. Fears of Quakers' disordered households, Quaker plots to free enslaved people, and Catholic plots to enlist Indians to slaughter Protestants receded. In 1705 Virginia also removed the legal disabilities from Quakers who wished to testify in court, permitting them at last to "affirm" rather than swear to their truthfulness. Only "popish recusants convict[ed], negroes, mulattoes and Indian servants, and others, not being christians, shall be deemed and taken to be persons incapable in law" (meaning they could not testify in court as a witness). While Catholics remained outside the aegis of those defined as Christians, the laws of 1705 included Quakers as Christians. This scant legal protection became a practical toleration, and race trumped religion as the most important category in an ordered society.[87] Anglo-Virginians focused on the real threats from within, the people they had enslaved and legally defined as incapable of Christianity—their slaves.

CHAPTER SIX

The Children of Israel

In late summer 1723, one or more anonymous enslaved people from Virginia wrote a letter to Edmund Gibson, the newly consecrated bishop of London. The letter writers implored the bishop, who oversaw Anglican affairs in the colonies, for assistance. "[T]here is in this Land of verJennia a Sort of people that is Calld molatters [mulattos] which are Baptised and brouaht [brought] up in the way of the Christian faith and followes the wayes and Rulles of the Chrch of England and sum of them has white fathars and sum white mothers and there is in this Land a Law or act which keeps and makes them and there seed Slaves forever." Had the letter been written a generation earlier, it might have expressed the thoughts and beliefs of people such as William Catillah and Hannah Banks. These enslaved people began their letter by proclaiming their white, Christian, and English ancestry as the basis for their complaint. They sought recognition of their Christianity and their freedom based on English parentage, a strategy used by enslaved people in the seventeenth century. They also proclaimed their allegiance to the Church of England. The letter begged the bishop to "Releese us out of this Cruell Bondegg" and explained that they were commanded to keep the Sabbath holy. They wrote that "wee doo hardly know when it comes for our task mastrs are has hard with us as the Egypttions was with the Chilldann of Issarall [Children of Israel]," a biblical reference that could hardly have been lost on Gibson. It might even be the first instance of enslaved people in the New World referencing the book of Exodus and the Israelites' struggle for freedom from the Egyptians, a trope later popular in the antebellum United States. The letter writer also noted that slaves were kept from attending church and from Christian marriage, and that in freedom they wished to see their "childarn may be broatt up in the way of the Christian faith . . . and wee desire that our childarn be putt to Scool and and [*sic*] Larnd to Reed through the Bybell." The plea established their own Christian credentials and pressed their desire to raise their children as Christians, which planters thwarted. The letter writer ended by claiming "wee dare nott Subscribe any mans name to this for feare of our masters for if they knew that wee have Sent home to your honour wee Should goo neare to Swing upon the gallass [gallows] tree."[1]

It was a clever letter, and it opens a window into the world of enslaved people that historians are seldom able to glimpse, since there are few first-person accounts from the eighteenth century. The letter suggests that enslaved people challenged their status from within the institution of slavery and that Christianity shaped their understanding of race and freedom. These letter writers understood what was at stake in getting their masters to recognize their Christianity—their freedom. They even knew to whom they should write their letter; Gibson, as bishop of London, oversaw Church of England affairs in all British colonies. They had written straight to the top, bypassing hostile planters and Anglican ministers who were at the mercy of planter-dominated vestries and antagonistic colonial legislatures. The letter, written on probably pilfered scraps of good paper with faded homemade ink, made its way across the Atlantic to London, possibly in the hold of a tobacco ship. For centuries it was misfiled with the bishop of London's Jamaica papers; there is no evidence that Gibson took any action based upon the letter.

The letter writers were victims of the ideology of hereditary heathenism, which by 1700 was fully entrenched in Britain's American colonies. Planters and their colonial allies had successfully defined Indians and blacks as essentially unable to become Christian, a belief that both justified and bolstered the legal underpinnings of slavery. Even the letter writers, who claimed visible English ancestry and Anglican Christianity (the letter's scribe claimed "my selfe I am my brothers Slave but my name is Secrett"), were excluded from the Christian community.[2] It was easy for planters to discount the beliefs and claims of black Christians. White colonial Americans had successfully dismantled older ideas about the unity of mankind in favor of a racial ideology in which they harnessed Christianity to racialize human difference. Christianity had become strongly equated with whiteness—at least among the planter class. The brave letter writers illustrate that enslaved people themselves were among the forces working to undermine hereditary heathenism in the eighteenth century.

The connection between hereditary enslavement and heathenism was a site for constant conflict and negotiation among planters, missionaries, and enslaved people. Anglican clergy and imperial appointees challenged planter ideology by insisting upon conversion schemes for Indians and blacks. To engage planters on this question, Anglican ministers and missionaries had to strike a deal with the devil and concede a critical point: they upheld slavery as legally and morally right regardless of Christian conversion. Underneath the public and full-throated debate between planters and ministers, a quieter change was taking shape. Enslaved people were absorbing Christianity, and without regard for the intellectual and theological debates among whites, enslaved people were reshaping Christianity to serve them. Like the letter writers, these people continued to cherish the belief that Christian conversion entitled them to the freedoms enjoyed by white Christians. For them, Christianity created a space for both spiritual and temporal equality. It mattered very little that most colonial legislatures had passed legislation separating baptism from freedom (as Virginia had done in 1667) because planters continued to assert that Christian conversion endangered their interest in their human property. To the Anglican hierarchy and imperial officials, enslaved people were commodities and real property but also potential converts whose souls required care. Successive bishops of London were increasingly affected by the formation of groups dedicated to conversion, such as the Society for the Propagation of the Gospel, and so they strongly urged that Indians and blacks be converted to Christianity. Planters great and small disliked this idea intensely, resulting in a number of small-scale conflicts between ministers and slave-owning parishioners and large-scale conflicts between wealthy and politically powerful planters and royally appointed governors who were ordered to effect conversion as part of their appointments. The result was a long argument between imperial authorities and colonial planters, who for the most part strenuously resisted the conversion of blacks and Indians.

Anglo-Virginians had more or less abandoned any efforts to convert Indian people in the wake of the devastating Anglo-Indian violence between 1622 and 1644. Though some royal governors gently inquired after the state of Indians' souls in the later part of the seventeenth century, few imperial officials were willing to risk antagonizing both planters and frontier settlers on the subject of Indian conversion. It took a fifty-four-hundred-pound bequest from the estate of the famous English natural philosopher Robert Boyle, which endowed the Indian College at the newly founded College of William and Mary, to revive interest in Indian conversion in 1697. Boyle had been an outspoken advocate and financial supporter of Christian conversion, funding Turkish and Lithuanian translations of the New Testament and serving as the governor of the New England Company, an organization dedicated exclusively to the conversion of Indians to Christianity. No doubt Boyle was familiar with the Indian College at Harvard. Boyle might also have been aware of the earlier experiment in Indian conversion and education at the College of Henrico in the 1610s.[3] The Indian College at William and Mary was remarkably similar to that at Harvard; Indian parents would bring their boys to the Indian College at the age of seven or eight—when they were old enough to learn to read, but not yet old enough to have been permanently corrupted by Indian ways. (The Indian College at Harvard had been founded in the 1650s, although there is no evidence that Indian boys studied there before 1660, and only four are recorded in the decade between 1660 and 1670. Boyle did receive letters from Indian students as well as copies of a catechism and the Bible, translated by John Eliot into Wampanoag. Harvard's Indian College buildings were demolished in 1698, just as William and Mary's college was getting its start.)[4] Anglican leaders, like their Massachusetts counterparts, especially wanted to acquire the children of Indian leaders, who when they returned to their families would be committed Christians, and who could in their turn evangelize other Indians. The curriculum included reading, writing, "all other arts & sciences" and instruction in the mysterious ways of the "great Almighty God."[5]

Initially Indian attendance at the college was spotty and often forced. Lieutenant Governor Alexander Spotswood, who took an active interest in Indian College affairs after his arrival in Virginia in 1710, noted that asking "Tributary Indians" to send their children to the College had "been judged a matter so impracticable that the Governors of the College have thought it in vain to attempt it, and have chosen rather to be at a great expence for buying Indians of remote nations taken in war to be educated in pursuance of a donation left for that purpose by Mr. Boyle." The idea that enslavement was a necessary vehicle for conversion was an old one, yet in the British Empire it had seldom been used as a way of converting Indians. Spotswood thought it would be cheaper and less ethically dubious to work with the children of nearby Indians with whom Virginia had a relationship, rather than relying upon Indians enslaved in wars in the interior.[6] To that end, Spotswood pressed the Assembly for more funds. The Assembly refused to cooperate, but Spotswood reported to the bishop of London that he went ahead with his plans to bring Indian children "from our Neighbouring Nations" into the college. By 1712, he counted twenty students. Spotswood continually decried the Assembly's refusal to fund Indian conversion efforts, because "the Revenue of the College settled by Mr. Boyle for that Service is insufficient to support so great a charge."[7] Spotswood begged for financial assistance from the bishop of London, the archbishop of Canterbury, and the Society for the Propagation of the Gospel in Foreign Parts. Though the society did elect Spotswood to membership in its ranks, no money besides Boyle's was forthcoming from London (much to Spotswood's disgust).[8]

Spotswood also financed an Indian school at the trading post Fort Christanna from his own pocket (the Assembly also refused to pay for that), modeled on the school at William and Mary. Spotswood agreed to pay the teacher's salary of fifty pounds per year and reported to the bishop of London in 1715 that the school had seventy children.[9] Members of the House of Burgesses were not inclined to view Spotswood's efforts favorably, however. In September 1715, in an angry address to that House, Spotswood pointed out that burgesses had referred a bill for "Discouraging the Propagation of the Gospel amongst the Indians, as if the Preaching [of] the Gospel to the Heathen were a Crime which ought to be Restrain'd by Law," to the house for its consideration (surely a direct rebuke of Spotswood's efforts). The House of Burgesses had earlier debated a bill "Suppressing that Society [for the Propagation of the Gospel], one of the main ends of the whole Institution is, to promote Christianity among the Indians." Spotswood's rage failed to cow the unrepentant burgesses, and powerful planters remained skeptical of any efforts to convert Indians or enslaved people.[10] By 1717 the burgesses had succeeded in shutting the Fort Christanna Indian school down.[11]

Conflicts like these between governors and the Virginia Assembly reflected a fundamental ambivalence toward Indians among Virginians. Virginia residents who were born in England tended to have a more positive view of Indians and their ability to become Christian. Hugh Jones, an English-born and Oxford-trained minister who also served as professor of mathematics at the College of William and Mary, wrote in 1724 that Indians must be "some of the posterity of Shem, driven thither by providence." Jones's appeal to the unity of mankind echoed William Strachey's claims from the early seventeenth century, but instead of connecting Indians with Ham, the cursed (and blackened) son of Noah, Jones assigned Indians a much nobler pedigree—descent from an uncursed Noachic line. Jones added that Indians had been "separated from the rest of mankind, and . . . debarred [from] the light of grace, and kept in their barbarous ignorance," but that God had protected the Indians and sent Europeans to assist in their redemption to the true religion.[12] Jones thus appealed to Indians' commonality with the English and other Europeans, rather than a hereditary difference, and advocated education for Indians. Education, Jones and Spotswood both thought, would lead to conversion. Other observers still strained to connect Indians with the lost tribes of Israel; on several occasions the Reverend Francis Le Jau chased rumors in South Carolina of an Indian tribe that practiced circumcision, and he also recalled a long conversation with an elder that indicated to him some familiarity with the Flood and Noah's Ark.[13] Other Englishmen in Virginia echoed John Smith's 1612 contention that Indians were actually white; John Fontaine wrote that Indians' darker skin color came from the bear's grease they rubbed on themselves and the smoke from their fires.[14] The Indians, noted one French Huguenot traveler to Virginia, were "a far better breed" than African slaves.[15]

Yet colonials remained steadfastly suspicious of Indian conversion. As Spotswood reported to the bishop of London in 1715, "Among ye Indian Children . . . there are several that can read and write tolerably well, can repeat the Church Chatechism, and know how to make their responses in ye Church, both the parents and the boys themselves, have shewn a great desire they should be admitted to Baptizm." He was eager to show results from his Indian College project, but Virginia's Anglican ministers (possibly acting under the influence of planters in their parishes) reiterated one of the arguments for hereditary heathenism: "[I] found them [members of the clergy] divided in their opinions, some agreeing [that] they might, but the greater Part that, (not being born of Christian Parents,) they could not be baptiz'd till they were capable of giving an Acc't of their Faith." The ministers also expressed their concern that Indian children would live far from their (presumably British) godparents. The critical point was the Indians' lack of Christian parentage. Indian culture and lineage remained suspect, despite some inclination to trace their origins to untainted Noachic lines. Spotswood requested guidance from the bishop of London on the question of under what circumstances Indian baptisms might be performed (the bishop declined to take on the issue).[16] In South Carolina, Francis Le Jau dealt with similar issues regarding Indian conversion. Le Jau was an enthusiastic advocate for missionaries among the Creeks and Yamasees; he invited several Indians and their children, to live with him and study Christianity. "[I] wou'd Cloath them but they will not consent to it, nor part with their Children tho' they lead miserable poor lives." Without the support of a college or a colonial governor, Le Jau found it difficult to pursue Indian conversion and, by the end of his life in 1717, had spent far more time and energy on the conversion of enslaved blacks in his district.[17]

Despite the destruction of the Fort Christanna Indian school, the Indian College at William and Mary persisted, though its funds were successfully cannibalized by other interests in the college. Anglican missionaries continued to take an interest in Indian education and conversion; in 1740 the Society for the Propagation of the Gospel sent copies of Bishop Thomas Wilson's tract *An Essay towards an Instruction for the Indians* to Virginia, presumably to assist in furthering the work of the Indian College (now called, Boyle's bequest notwithstanding, the Brafferton School, after an English estate whose proceeds helped fund the building in which the school was housed). Though it is not clear how many Indian students attended school there between 1720 and 1750, the numbers evidently declined, even as the college's finances and ability to teach and house Indian students improved. In the 1750s Indians students at the school included Cherokees and Delawares, and Virginians also approached the Catawbas about providing students. Nevertheless, numbers dwindled, with only eight students attending between 1753 and 1755. By the Revolution, the Indian College had sputtered to a close.[18]

It was odd that the Indian College had to wander so far afield to find Indian students willing to partake in its missionizing proclivities, because there were plenty of tributary groups in the Chesapeake that could have provided students. In Virginia, as in other parts of the early eighteenth-century British Empire, Indians remained on the edges of white colonial society. In 1745 the Reverend Thomas Bacon (no relation to Nathaniel Bacon), an Anglican minister born and educated in England and who had lived in Ireland, reproved his Maryland flock's failure to convert Indians, by either effort or example. Bacon had abandoned a lucrative career as an imperial customs agent to take holy orders and minister to colonial Christians, but his published sermons betray his shock at the spiritual state of his parishioners' Indian servants and neighbors. He questioned why "the christian religion hath been no farther propagated among its ancient heathen inhabitants, many of which dwell in the midst of us, yet remain as much Heathens as if the sun of righteousness had not as yet risen upon it. I have not so much as heard of a single Indian in this whole province, who is converted to, and lives in the profession of the christian faith."[19] Admonitions and shame from the metropole were all very well, but unless colonial governments were willing to finance and coordinate efforts to convert Indians, the venture was unlikely to have much success. As it was, most of the moneys supporting the Indian College venture came from Great Britain, and the Revolution put an end to that flow of cash. Indian education and conversion were defeated by planters deeply attached to the ideology of hereditary heathenism.

There were even fewer resources for managing conversion schemes for enslaved blacks. After all, enslaved people were unlikely to be offered admission to the College of William and Mary, even for missionary purposes, and no governor dared show interest in schools for slaves. The population of enslaved people of African descent in the British Empire exploded, increasing from around 86,000 in 1680 to about 550,000 by 1750. In 1680 there were about 4,000 enslaved blacks in the Chesapeake, and by 1750 there were 150,000 slaves of African descent. By 1780, there were 220,000 African American slaves in Virginia; from the late seventeenth century onward, Virginia was a slave society. Enslaved people in Virginia began to reproduce their population by the mid-1710s, successfully producing a creole population that grew faster than the population of new arrivals from Africa, thus rendering the colony's slave population a mix of native-born and African-born slaves, with the former always outnumbering the latter.[20] This burgeoning population of enslaved people posed a vexing problem for Anglican missionaries: how could these people be brought into the community of Christians? Planters had an answer for that: enslaved people were hereditary heathens incapable of Christian conversion. For Anglican officialdom, though, the demography of enslavement indicated that increasing numbers of enslaved children were being born in British territory and no effort was being made to reach them. By the late seventeenth century, the Anglican hierarchy and a small but growing coterie of missionaries began to challenge the planters' assumptions about race, slavery, and Christian conversion.

The growth of the enslaved population coincided with the Church of England's renewed efforts to assert administrative control over its ministers and parishes in the colonies. To better administer colonial churches, the bishop of London appointed commissaries in each colony to act as his personal representatives. James Blair, a Scottish cleric born and educated in Edinburgh, held this position in Virginia from 1689 until his death in 1743. During his extraordinary tenure of more than half a century, Blair oversaw all aspects of the established Church of England in Virginia (and theoretically Bermuda as well, although he often protested that he could not be expected to exert any influence over so distant a colony), duties that ranged from setting the religious curriculum at the College of William and Mary to overseeing ministerial posts and salaries, and to converting enslaved blacks to Christianity. Blair arrived in 1685 and within two years had concluded an advantageous marriage to Sarah Harrison, the daughter of a prominent planter. Blair also pursued property, acquiring land and thus endearing himself to Virginia's plantocracy. Marriage and property provided Blair with a secular as well as an ecclesiastical base of power. Blair was also the rector of Bruton Parish Church in Williamsburg, the sometime head of the College of William and Mary, an occasional holder of a variety of imperial patronage posts, including acting governor, and a permanent member of the Virginia Council, as well as the bishop of London's commissary. Known to contemporaries as stubborn, irascible, and a tenacious political enemy, Blair so staunchly represented the interests of the king's church in Virginia that he often pitted himself politically against governors he thought showed little respect for his position as commissary of the church. His complaints resulted in the removal of two governors, Edmond Andros and Francis Nicholson, and contributed to the ouster of Indian conversion advocate Alexander Spotswood.[21]

While Blair was in London arranging for Andros's removal in the late 1690s, he collaborated with two other Virginians to write an assessment of the colony for the Board of Trade. Blair undoubtedly contributed the most to the sections describing religion and the state of the church. Blair's portion of *The Present State of Virginia, and the College* shows that in 1697 the commissary was more concerned with the support of his ministers and the specter of lay power in the parishes than with the legions of heathen Indians and Africans who also lived in the colony. Blair worried that ministers' glebes were insufficient to support them and their families and that lay influence exceeded that of ministers, complaining that "the Minister is dismiss'd or retain'd again at the Vestries Pleasure." Church governance, and not the spiritual needs of the people, captured his attention.[22] Yet in a treatise Blair wrote for John Locke to present to the Board of Trade in 1699, he complained about familiar themes from his writings two years previously, but he also fumed, "Little Care is taken to instruct the Indians and Negroes in the Christian ffaith." To remedy his last grievance, Blair suggested that all enslaved people attend church, that baptism and catechism for enslaved people be mandated through legislation, and that Indians attend William and Mary to evangelize their own people. It was a tripartite solution focused mostly on education of the rising generations of African slaves and Indians, one that did not deviate significantly from earlier plans for evangelization, which since the 1610s had focused on converting children and instructing them in Christian beliefs and morals.[23]

Blair also noted that the "Conversion, and Instruction of Negroes and Indians is a work of such importance and difficulty that it would require a Treatise of it self."[24] Yet Blair, the Church of England's titular head in Virginia, who was arguably the person best positioned to successfully advocate for conversion at home and in London, never wrote such a treatise. In September 1699 he followed up his recommendations to Locke and the Board of Trade with a lengthier missive on attracting more clergy and providing them with adequate salaries, to which he also appended "A Proposition for encouraging the Christian Education of Indian, Negroe and Mulatto Children." In this short addendum, Blair repeated his threefold plan for evangelization through baptism and education, aimed at enslaved children ("the old ones that are imported into the Countrey, by reason of their not understanding the Language, being much more indocile"). He wisely added a significant financial incentive to his plan to encourage planters to allow their slaves to receive religious instruction. Under Blair's plan, masters or mistresses whose slave children were baptized, attended church regularly, and could give a public account of their faith would not have to pay taxes on those children until they reached the age of eighteen. Planters who did not allow their young slaves to be catechized would still have to pay levies.[25]

Blair's enthusiasm for conversion schemes might have reflected his exposure to activists in Great Britain who were committed to converting enslaved people and Indians. In the first decade of the eighteenth century, proposals abounded for legislation governing the conversion problem. One such proposed bill protected "any Persons who shall be appointed to Instruct their Negroes," from interference, surely a response to the hostility missionaries and clerics such as Morgan Godwyn faced in the colonies. This bill also prevented planters from forcing their slaves to work on Sundays and encouraged funding for more "Catechists and Ministers both in Africa itself, and her Majesties [*sic*] Plantations particularly in Barbados and Jamaica to Instruct the Heathen." Most importantly, the draft bill emphasized long-standing colonial practice regarding baptism and emancipation, that "no Negro professing ye Christian Religion, and Baptized thereunto, shall be thereby freed from that Property his Master might have in him previously to his being Baptized."[26]

This was a critical point for Blair or any other imperial official or missionary working on slave conversions in the colonies. In order to protect their ability to minister to the enslaved population, missionaries had to agree to the proposition that converted Christians could still be held in slavery. In 1711 the archbishop of Canterbury was apparently involved in drafting new legislation to deal with the problem of baptism and manumission. "For better avoiding of any disputes that may arise concerning such negros as are or may be baptised at the Plantations" (a phrase later crossed out) was the draft bill's stated purpose, and it reiterated that Christian baptism could not "be Construed to be any Manumission of such Negro or Servant."[27] The Society for the Propagation of the Gospel also tried repeatedly to convince Parliament to amend slave trade bills with clauses officially divorcing baptism from emancipation, but without success.[28] With no parliamentary legislation ratifying colonial law on the subject of baptism and freedom, planters tended to look on conversion schemes as a metropolitan plot to deprive them of their enslaved property.

Blair's grandiose schemes had little chance of success among colonial slave owners. Planters, as another minister dedicated to the conversion of Indians and Africans noted, "disapprove of it [conversion]; because they say it often makes them [enslaved people] proud, and not so good servants."[29] And many planters still feared, legislation to the contrary notwithstanding, that Christian conversion and baptism would somehow emancipate their enslaved human property. Planters preferred to keep their slaves ignorant of Christianity, even though Blair dangled the tempting possibility of tax breaks for baptisms. Planters repeatedly stymied efforts to encourage conversion. In 1715 Burgesses "at first sight" refused a bill for encouraging the conversion of enslaved people to Christianity; in 1720, the burgesses rejected a petition from Middlesex County to provide a catechism for enslaved people. A few years later, William Todd presented a petition to the House of Burgesses suggesting that a law be passed requiring planter efforts "to bring up Negro Children born in this country in the Christian Religion." The burgesses rejected the suggestions as "being at present impracticable."[30] Virginia's planters were determined to block any effort to proselytize among enslaved people, no matter who was pushing that agenda. Hereditary heathenism was sustained by the power of the great planters and their political allies.

Blair, as crusty and as irritable as he was powerful and influential, became as attached to the interests of the great landowners of Virginia as any Virginia-born gentleman. Although upon his arrival in Virginia Blair was inclined to tout the bishop of London's request that the commissary and his ministers encourage the conversion of Indians and African slaves, by the 1720s he no longer considered conversion a laudable goal. Blair's brief interest in conversion waned as he tackled what he probably viewed as larger problems in Virginia's church—underpaid ministers and power-hungry vestries packed with planters who were hostile to conversion. Blair's efforts focused on the institutional church and the needs of those who were already in it and ignored those whom metropolitan officials increasingly believed needed to be brought into the church. Without Blair's advocacy, conversion of Africans and Indians would be difficult to push in a colony where slaveholding planters controlled wealth, power, and political influence.

At Blair's death in 1743 at the age of eighty-seven, Lieutenant Governor Sir William Gooch reported to his brother the bishop of Norwich that after Blair's death "there were found, in a Cock-loft over his Kitchen, a great number of Books, spoilt by the Catts and Rats that were sent him by the Bp. [Bishop] of London or the Society to be dispersed, which he never reported to anyone."[31] Gooch often complained in his private correspondence that James Blair was less than sympathetic to the cause of baptizing and catechizing Indians and African slaves, which had not been the case early in Blair's career. Gooch thought it a final insult that tracts printed and sent to Blair by the Society for the Propagation of the Gospel for the express purpose of catechizing the slaves were found fouled by cat urine and rat's teeth, hidden in Blair's attic. (Gooch was a newly elected member of that organization, and took its goals very seriously.) Blair had been transformed, in his fifty-four years in Virginia, from Scottish outsider and conversion advocate to Virginia insider and conversion detractor. Virginia planters and their interests co-opted Blair's initial intentions in the Chesapeake. Possibly resistance from planters sapped the aging commissary of the energy required to make even a little headway on the conversion question. Blair's early enthusiasm and his later impotence personified the power of hereditary heathenism.

Eighteenth-century planters' opinions on enslaved people's fitness for baptism and participation in Christian ritual varied little from their seventeenth-century ancestors' opinions. Francis Le Jau reported that one woman asked him if "any of my slaves could go to Heaven, & must I see them there?" Another young man reported that he would not accept Communion as long as "slaves are Recd [received] there."[32] Both interlocutors were clearly uneasy about the implications and repercussions of including enslaved people in the community of believers. Le Jau's South Carolina flock irritated him in other ways as well. They forced enslaved people to work on Sundays, and as Le Jau noted, "the Generality of the Masters oppose that they [enslaved people] should know anything of Christianity."[33] South Carolina planters' more particular objections to converting slaves matched those of their Virginia counterparts. As Le Jau lamented, "Masters Seem very much Averse to my Design. Some of them [slave owners] will not give them [enslaved people] Leave to come to Church to learn how to Pray to God & to Serve him, I cannot find any reason for this New Opposition but the Old pretext that Baptism makes the Slaves proud and Undutifull."[34] A minister in Virginia lamented that there "is no law of the Colony obliging their Masters or Owners to instruct them in the principle of Christianity and so they are hardly to be persuaded by the Minister to take so much pains with them, by which means the poor Creatures generally live and die without it."[35] Although the Reverend Hugh Jones remarked that "baptizing wild Indians and new Negroes [i.e., newly arrived from Africa]" might be "a prostitution of a thing so sacred," he did advocate for the conversion of "the children of Negroes and Indians, that are to live among Christians." Jones commented further that for those individuals, "it is not out of the power of their masters to take care that they have a Christian education, learn their prayers and catechism, and go to church," implying that planters were currently ignoring that obligation.[36] These ministers' comments are likely indicative of the massive resistance they encountered from planters in their parishes and vestries when they broached the topic of conversion. Despite nearly a century of effort, imperial officials were no closer than they were in the early seventeenth century to bringing Christian conversion to Indians and Africans in the colonies.

The gulf between planters and royal officials had never been wider. In 1723 Virginia's burgesses enacted a law preventing any "free negro, mullatto, or indian" from voting in any election in the colony. The law itself governed the criminal trials of slaves, regulated the times when slaves could be off their masters' plantations, declared the death of a slave at the hands of a slave owner to be manslaughter rather than murder, dictated which free African Americans, mulattoes, and Indians could own guns, and also promised the "better government of Negros, Mulattos, and Indians, bond or free." Virginia was reeling from the recent revelation of a slave conspiracy in its midst; another act passed the same session provided for the sale of a slave named Dick and other unnamed slaves, possibly the conspirators whose planned rebellion inspired the legislation, to plantations in the Caribbean.[37] Like other colonial laws, this law had to be approved by the Board of Trade and Parliament. The board inquired why former slaves and their descendants could not vote in provincial elections, "as it carries an Appearance of Hardship towards certain Freemen, meerly upon Account of their Complection, who would otherways enjoy every Priviledge belonging to Freemen."[38] The board was concerned about black former slaves as well as mulatto former slaves, the children of English planters and black slaves. These "certain Freemen," both black and mulatto, would have had the rights of free Englishmen had they lived in England. The board was understandably troubled by the manner in which Anglo-Virginians had limited the rights of free Afro-Virginians on account of their complexion.

Virginia's Governor Gooch responded to the board's questions, telling them of the abortive slave rebellion that prompted the law, and explaining why former slaves were also penalized, by emphasizing the lack of suffrage as a mark or a brand, more legal evidence that former slaves and their descendants were not fit for civil society as the English knew it: "[Y]et such was the Insolence of the Free Negros at that time, that the next Assembly thought it necessary . . . to fix a perpetual Brand upon Free Negros & Mulattos by excluding them from that great Priviledge of a Freeman, well knowing they always did, and ever will, adhere to and favour the Slaves." Former slaves and their descendants were, in Gooch's mind, a dangerous constituency whose power and influence had to be limited, even into posterity, as an everlasting mark of slavery and slave descent. The offenders' skin was already marked with the badge of implied slavery, but Gooch went on to explain that the law proved to freed slaves that "a distinction ought to be made between their Offspring and the Descendants of an Englishman, with whom they were never to be Accounted Equal." Gooch assured the Board of Trade that such shocking and severe laws were necessary, because manumitted slaves had the temerity to consider themselves as good as their Anglo-Virginian neighbors. Free mulattoes did have some English ancestry, but Gooch wrote that these people were proud and therefore as dangerous as any other freed slaves, making it reasonable to "preserve a decent Distinction between them and their Betters." Gooch concluded by noting that the burgesses would no doubt revisit the issue in the future, in order to determine to what "Degree of Descent this Incapacity shall extend."

Gooch's arguments apparently persuaded the Board of Trade of the inherent utility of the Assembly's 1723 law; the board made no reply to Gooch's explanation. There the matter rested.[39]

The board's inquiry and Gooch's response demonstrate the dissonance between the imperial officials' cultural understanding of slavery and the daily realities planters faced as precarious grandees in a world of labor-intensive cash crops and a burgeoning slave population. For the Board of Trade, slavery and freedom were absolute conditions; one could not be free and still retain some of the legal detriments of slavery. In the colonies, freedom for blacks and mulattoes was a condition to be minimized and whose pernicious and prideful effects were to be mitigated, as Gooch eventually came to understand. While imperial officials accepted Gooch's explanations on this "mark of difference" imposed by Virginia, on other issues London was less likely to accept the planter desire to relegate free blacks and Indians to a permanently inferior status.

In 1727 Bishop of London Edmund Gibson decided to up the ante with two public letters, one to colonial planters and one to Anglican ministers serving in the colonies. In his letter to planters, Gibson effectively demolished arguments against conversion because of age and language difficulties, and he addressed perennial planter fears that "*Baptizing* them when instructed, would destroy . . . the Property which the Masters have in them." Gibson went on to note that "embracing of the Gospel, does not make the least Alteration in Civil Property, or in any of the Duties which belong to Civil Relations."[40] A planter from the Leeward Islands responded predictably in a pamphlet published in 1730; the anonymous writer noted that if a baptized enslaved person attempted manumission based on baptism, "the *Sugar*-Planters would either refuse to buy them at the same Rates as before, or buy no more of them at all, and then what would become of the Nation's Trade to *Guinea* and the *Sugar-Colonies*?" Gibson's colonial opponent also used the excuse of hereditary heathenism to decline proselytizing among enslaved people: "*Polygamy* . . . and *Divorce* upon any Occasion, are connived at in all the Slaves, and in their Descendents," implying that enslaved people, regardless of where they were born, were morally degenerate. In any case, the pamphleteer concluded, "I never knew a Negro-Slave (and I have talk'd with Hundreds on the Subject) shew the least Curiosity to know what our Religion is."[41]

If we take the anonymous planter-pamphleteer at his word, then Gibson's reassurances and encouragements meant little in the colonies. What was required was a definitive statement from London on the legal question of baptism and emancipation. Missionaries and their British supporters also realized that settling the legal question at home rather than in the colonies might be a smart move as well, and in 1729 they got their wish in the form of what was known as the Yorke-Talbot opinion. The opinion, promulgated by Attorney General Philip Yorke and Solicitor General Charles Talbot, unequivocally stated, "Baptism doth not bestow Freedom on him [an enslaved person], nor make any alteration in his temporal Condition in these Kingdoms." Though the opinion was not the product of a court case (a more traditional method for clarifying the common law), it was intended to assist missionaries in their quest to convert more enslaved people.[42] It also was unequivocally proslavery: the opinion tied evangelization and the continuation of the legal institution of slavery in precise terms. This opinion in hand, Anglican missionaries could proceed to the colonies and pursue their goal of transforming the British Empire into an empire of Christian slaves. Virginia's burgesses reacted favorably to the Yorke-Talbot opinion. In May 1730 they reversed course and voted "to encourage the Conversion of Negros and Indians to the Christian Religion," though they were not forthcoming on how such encouragement was to be achieved.[43]

The May 1730 vote was not the end of controversy about baptizing enslaved people, but perhaps it paved the way for Anglican ministers to officially pursue converting enslaved people without having to worry about planters looking over their shoulders. In response to Gibson's queries (about, among other things, the conversion of Indians and Africans) of Virginia clergy in 1724, almost a third of the twenty-nine respondents reported making no effort at all to teach enslaved people about Christianity. Eleven ministers reported outright obstructionism from masters on the subject of converting slaves or at least had to receive permission before catechizing enslaved people. Only two reported baptizing large numbers of enslaved people: in Accomack County, William Black claimed to have baptized 200 enslaved people; and in Richmond County, John Garzia sent in a list of enslaved people he baptized between 1725 and 1732 totaling 354 people.[44] These zealous missionaries were definitely outliers, though. John Worden of Lawns Creek Parish put it succinctly when he informed Bishop Gibson that some masters allowed baptism, and some did not.[45] The question after 1730 for Anglican ministers was how to proceed with Gibson's directives for converting enslaved people without incurring the wrath of the planters who were responsible for their salaries. Ministers such as William Willie, a Scottish transplant who spent his half-century ministerial career in a Virginia parish, slowly but surely worked against the Anglo-Virginian mindset, eventually convincing planters to accept slave baptism as a matter of course.

The Albemarle Parish Register that Willie kept is a particularly good source for an inquiry about slave baptism and conversion in the eighteenth century. The parish clung to the southwestern edge of Surry County, and when Sussex County was formed in 1753, it incorporated portions of that frontier county as well. Albemarle included lands long settled and lands newly settled and had a mix of large planters with many slaves, small planters with a few slaves, and yeoman farmers with no slaves at all. The parish records also indicate a small community of free blacks that grew over the course of the eighteenth century. Willie served the parish from its formation in 1739 until his death in 1775, during which time he was a meticulous record-keeper, recording births, baptisms, godparents, marriages, and deaths among the parish's Anglo-Virginian and enslaved populations (excluding slave marriages, which, if he celebrated them, he did not seem to have recorded). Willie segregated white and black records, placing free black births and baptisms among the slave records (free blacks are apparent only because Willie left the "owner" column blank). In long neat columns he recorded the name and sex of the slave, the owner's name, who brought the information to the minister (usually the owner, but sometimes a manager or the executor of a recently deceased planter's estate), the slave's birthday, and the date of baptism if there was one. Willie adhered strictly to a law of 1713 that required ministers to keep vital records of all people—slave and free—in their parishes.[46] Willie required planters to come to him with new vital statistics of slave births and deaths on a quarterly basis. That Reverend Willie had a column for the baptismal date in his section for slave births, though it would sometimes run empty for pages at a time, shows he was interested in baptizing his parish's slaves and in making them parishioners along with their masters.

Willie set out to be a good example for his parish. Willie owned several slaves (whether they belonged to him personally or to the parish glebe land is unclear). Between 1753 and 1774, fourteen slaves were born in Willie's household, and he baptized all of them within a few months of birth. The only slave listed in his register who was not baptized was a boy named Cato, born in 1748, whom Willie had bought from another planter in the late 1760s. (Cato joined several other slaves in the Willie household named for heroes of Greek and Roman mythology or well-known figures from classical antiquity.) By owning slaves, Willie was in the mainstream of the Church of England, which approved of slavery on the grounds that it could lead to the conversion of more heathen peoples, and by baptizing them he furthered the goal of baptizing all slaves owned by Anglicans in the colony. It would be anachronistic to look to William Willie or any other Anglican minister of his time and place as an advocate of emancipation and the abolition of slavery. Even before slave children were born in his own household, Willie encouraged his parishioners to baptize their slaves by his own actions: in December 1742 he stood as a godfather to one of Captain James Gee's infant slaves, a boy named Sam. Captain Gee did not participate in the ceremony; Robert and Mary Nichols, who do not otherwise appear in the register, stood with Willie as sureties. In owning and baptizing his own slaves, and standing as a godfather to Captain Gee's slave, Reverend Willie probably intended to prove to his Anglo-Virginian parishioners that baptism would not result in freedom, that slaves were capable of being baptized, and that doing so would not have adverse effects on the slave's fitness for servitude. No doubt Willie hoped that as Sam grew and was instructed in the Christian faith, he would show that slaves too were able to be good Christians, thus neutralizing through the act of baptizing an infant slave the main objections planters advanced against it.

The infant Sam was not the only African American slave to have Anglo-Virginians serving as godparents. In the spring of 1742, John Weaver brought his youngest slave, an infant nine months old, to his parish church to be baptized. The tiny boy, named Printer, was christened on 5 May, with John, his wife Mary, and their daughter Elizabeth standing as godparents for the youngster. And in the autumn of 1743, Jean, an infant boy belonging to Richard Pepper, was also baptized with godparents, including Pepper's daughter Eliza (although Pepper himself was not involved in the ceremony). But of the 913 slaves William Willie baptized during his tenure, only these 3 enslaved infants, were baptized with godparents, white or black, representing only about .003 percent of the total baptisms. Why were these children and not others baptized with godparents? The infants might have been the blood relations of their masters, either their own illegitimate children or the children of the planters' male relatives. Mulatto status, combined with a verifiable and acknowledged blood relationship with Anglo-Virginians, provided some incentive for planters to allow baptism, to stand as godparents, and to provide other protections. Another plausible explanation is that

these particular infants were born to slaves who directly served planters in their households. Their parents or even their grandparents were
likely American-born, and therefore fluent in English, conversant with
Anglo-Virginian culture, and possibly even baptized Christians themselves. Anglo-Virginians recognized cultural differences between African-born slaves and those born in Virginia and might have rewarded
those they regarded as faithful creoles with baptism and a godparentage
relationship. It is also possible that the parents of these enslaved infants
requested their children to be baptized and their masters or members
of their masters' families to serve as godparents. Yet planters were likely
reluctant to stand as godparents in most circumstances. Francis Le Jau
lamented "the difficulties of prevailing upon the white People to be so
charitable [as to serve as sureties]."[47] Adam Dickie, a Virginia minister,
did not accept "Christian slaves" as godparents but asked the bishop of
London what to do "since masters are reluctant to stand surety."[48] There
was a moment, early in the 1740s, when Reverend Willie attempted to
convince his Anglo-Virginian parishioners, by his own example, that
baptizing one's slaves and standing as their godparents was a good idea.
John Weaver, Richard Pepper, and James Gee either allowed or participated in these baptisms, but the very idea of it went against everything
Anglo-Virginians believed about the appropriateness of fictive kinship
ties between slaves and masters. The idea did not catch on.[49]

Early in Willie's tenure as Albemarle Parish minister, few planters
consented to have their slaves baptized. John Weaver, whose infant slave
Printer was baptized and had godparents, did not baptize any more of
the five slave children born in his household between 1743 and 1751.
Captain James Gee, who apparently consented to Sam's baptism in 1742,
reported the births of twenty-five slaves to William Willie in the two decades between 1739 and 1759, but of these twenty-five infants, only Sam
was baptized. During the 1740s, only a few planters allowed their slaves
to be baptized. Among those who allowed baptism was Sylvanus Stokes,
a planter who reported the births of twelve slaves between 1742 and
1757. Of these twelve, Stokes allowed the baptism of ten (only Solomon,
born in 1741, and Peter, born in 1743, were not baptized). Willie might
have persuaded Stokes that baptizing his slaves was a good idea; four of
his slaves who had been born before 1746 were baptized on 6 January
1745/46, suggesting that Stokes had made a decision to baptize some of
his young slaves en masse. His son, Sylvanus Stokes Jr., who reported
the births of eight slaves between 1747 and 1765, seems to have followed

closely in his father's footsteps; four of those eight children were baptized. It would be interesting to know why Stokes allowed the baptism of some slave children and not others. Did enslaved parents have to request baptism for their children? Did Stokes himself make decisions based on the catechism and readily apparent Christian faith of the parents? Perhaps Stokes used his own unique moral calculus to decide fitness for baptism.

Some slave owners allowed baptisms among their slaves, using criteria not apparent in the extant sources to determine who would be baptized. William Pettway (sometimes written Pothway) seems to have converted to Reverend Willie's point of view; he began allowing his slaves to be baptized after 1755. Pettway reported nineteen slaves born between 1740 and 1774, of whom fifteen were baptized, all after 1755. (Tom, who was born in 1740, was finally baptized at the age of seventeen in 1757; it would be interesting to know if Pettway encouraged him to take instruction or if Tom pursued baptism on his own.) The last slave listed under Pettway's name was actually born after his death in 1773; Franky was born in 1774 and baptized a few months later. Perhaps Pettway's will required slaves born to his estate to be baptized, or enslaved African Americans in his household now considered baptism to be part of their own religious traditions and saw to it that Franky was baptized.

Pettway was representative of the trend in Albemarle Parish. During the course of the thirty-six years that Willie served the parish, more and more planters began baptizing at least some of their slaves. In 1740, immediately after his arrival, planters reported 48 slave births, and Willie recorded performing only 2 baptisms. The year before his death, in 1774, planters also reported 48 slave births, but Willie performed 38 baptisms that year. In 1740 Willie baptized only 4.9 percent of newborn slaves, but in 1774 he baptized 79.2 percent. In fact, the decade of the 1740s was a slow one for slave baptisms; from 1740 through 1749, planters reported 412 births, and Willie baptized only 36 infant slaves, or 8.7 percent. In the 1750s, though, Willie began to have more success in convincing planters to baptize their slaves; planters reported 502 slave births, and Willie baptized 125 of them, or just over 25 percent. In 1751, for example, Willie succeeded in baptizing exactly a quarter of enslaved infants—the first time he had baptized so many. Viewed from this perspective, the 1760s were an even better decade, with planters reporting 559 slave births and Willie recording baptisms for 396 of them, or 70.8 percent. The 1770s, had they not been interrupted by revolution and the minister's death, would have been an excellent decade by Willie's standards. Even in the first four and a half years of the decade, Willie recorded 290 births and baptized 252 enslaved African American babies, or 86.9 percent. In the closing years of his life, Willie's Anglican message of inclusion had gotten through to planters, who were overwhelmingly allowing their young enslaved property to be initiated as Christians. Yet unlike Pettway and the other planters who followed Reverend Willie's lead, some planters never allowed their slaves to be baptized. The planter James Chappel, a vestryman of Albemarle Parish, reported 24 slave births between 1739 and his death in 1773, but none of those enslaved children were ever baptized. Willie reached out to the slave owners in his parish and convinced most of them that their slaves could and should be made Christians, yet a steadfast Anglican churchgoer and member of the parish vestry continued to resist the message.

Growing planter acceptance of slave baptisms meant that ultimately planters were rethinking the place of Christianity in their racial ideology. Ministers like William Willie had successfully pressed their point; Africans and their descendants, though slaves, could be Christians without risking their status as property. With that impediment removed from the equation, planters were more likely to take seriously a religious obligation to convert enslaved people. Albemarle Parish's experience indicates a generational shift among planters, suggesting that rising generations of planters were more willing to support baptism. Planters were less likely to view baptism as a threat to their enslaved property and might even have thought of baptism and the conversion it implied as a form of social control. Some planters, encouraged by ministers such as Le Jau and Willie, clearly believed that conversion would result in more docile slaves who accepted their life of perpetual servitude. Le Jau certainly saw Christian conversion as an opportunity to refashion the lives of enslaved people to suit himself. Le Jau recruited baptized slaves, whom he described as "Religious zealous, honest, they can read well" and then tasked them with informing him "when there is any disorder among their fellows slaves that it may be remedied. I discountenance the changing of wives as much as it lyes in my power and I hope the Danceings upon Sundays are quite over in this Neighbourhood."[50]

Other planters, including James Chappel, apparently rejected the idea that baptism would encourage docility or good behavior, and thus made no effort to convert enslaved people. Planter motivations in regards to baptism were varied, and they had a disturbing tendency to view slave conversions as incomplete, illegitimate, or merely opportunistic. The Tidewater grandee Landon Carter noted that even his supposedly Christian slaves were "ungratefully neglectfull" and frequent inebriation among enslaved people was a "strong instance against the pretended honesty of a slave founded on Religious Principles."[51] Continued bad behavior on the part of an enslaved person was, for planters, obvious evidence of a spurious conversion. As Carter also noted, "I give leave to all to go to Church who are so inclined; those who are not so inclined will do less injury to religion if they are kept at work at home."[52] It is also possible that the swing in planter favor toward Anglican baptism after about 1750 was symptomatic of anxiety about an increasing dissenter presence in Virginia. By 1750, enslaved people were beginning to discover evangelical Protestantism as well. Presbyterians and Baptists, and even later some Methodists, espoused a Christianity that was somewhat different from and more inclusive than Anglicanism. Primed by their familiarity with Anglicanism, enslaved people took the opportunities afforded by evangelical preachers to explore Christianity in other forms.

Samuel Davies, a Presbyterian minister from New Jersey, lived and preached in Virginia starting in 1748. Although Anglican ministers watched the itinerant Davies's efforts with a wary eye, they did seem genuinely interested in his progress. Davies maintained an extensive correspondence about his efforts to convert enslaved people. In 1757 he reported, "I have baptized in all 150 Adults [black slaves]. And at the last Sacramental Occasion I had the Honour (for so I esteem it) of sitting down at the [communion] Table of the Lord with about 60 of them. I have now a few more Catechumens for Baptism under Instruction." Davies was a firm believer in education and catechism prior to baptism and took special care to teach his slaves to read English prior to their baptism. Though he thought that some slaves requested baptism as a way of gaining additional privileges and not for reasons of faith, he waxed optimistic about their prospects: "Some [come] from a pious Thirst after christian Knowledge some from Curiosity & some from Ambition. But whatever be the present principle I hope many happy Effects will follow from this acquisition as it will render them more capable of being their own Instructors & of receiving Instruction from others." Davies believed that success with a few slaves would make Christianity self-sustaining among slave populations, for slaves could teach one another and their offspring. Davies denied, as planters were wont to claim, that slaves were not intelligent enough to learn Christianity: "Their natural genius is not discouraging & when they set about learning in good Earnest, it is astonishing what progress some of them make tho' with little Leisure or Assistance."[53]

Davies, like William Willie, owned slaves and, like Willie, thought of his slaves as examples for Anglo-Virginians. He wrote extensively about one of his own slaves: "[He] was about 40 when he entred into my Service, a very stupid lubberly Fellow in appearance & but very indifferently acquainted with our Language. . . . He can give but a very broken account of his Religion in Words, but when I look to his Life there I can see the Christian, he is a faithful Servant & generally inoffensive to all. He has sometimes been overheard in secret Prayer when it has been past Midnight & he suppos'd the rest of the Family were in their Beds." Davies's unnamed slave's lack of proper English indicates he might have been African-born, the very type of slave most Virginia planters would have supposed could not be taught to read, let alone be taught about Christianity. Davies intended to prove otherwise in his persistence in teaching the "lubberly fellow." That he could give an "account of his Religion in Words" and was a good servant were two points Davies very much wanted to spread. A Christian slave, Davies implied, was a better slave than a heathen one. It was an argument that ministers and missionaries alike were at pains to make. If planters could be made to believe that converting slaves not only was the proper Christian thing to do but also improved their labor force, they would be more open to conversion generally speaking. Davies ended his letter with a not-so-veiled jibe at Anglo-Virginian planters: "There is however a Number of them who I have not the least doubt are the genuine Children of Abraham by Faith, & some of them seem to have made a greater Progress in experimental Religion than many sincere Christians of a fairer Colour."[54]

Planters thought evangelical conversions were spurious. Landon Carter described one of his enslaved people, a carpenter named Tony, as a "hypocrite of the vilest kind." Carter complained that "[Tony's] first religion that broke out upon him was new light and I believe it is from some inculcated doctrine of those rascals that the slaves in this Colony are grown so much worse." Carter's refusal to recognize any genuine faith in Tony's conversion had seventeenth-century roots. Yet faced with growing numbers of enslaved black Christians, Carter and other planters focused on the supposedly un-Christian aspects of their slaves' lives (in Tony's case, drunkenness and shoddy workmanship on a garden fence) as evidence of their "vile" nature and the insincerity of their conversions.

Also troubling to Carter was the influence of New Light, dissenting Protestant ministers on Tony. Dissenters threatened the social order (as Quakers once had) by undermining Anglican authority and encouraging what planters thought of as insincere conversions. For Carter, this meant he had to pay more attention to the spiritual lives of his enslaved people. "Mine," he wrote, "shall be brought to their [p]iety though with as little severity as [possible]." Carter was clearly uncomfortable with any version of Christianity among enslaved people that did not conform to his own expectations. Indeed, Carter's promise in his diary to "do what I can" for the souls of his enslaved people is belied by the rest of his journal: Carter made little if any effort to convert his slaves to the Church of England besides allowing some to attend church.[55]

Planter acceptance of baptism and the fixation on the supposedly un-Christian behavior of baptized slaves suggests that planters and ministers alike had a very particular and rather parochial definition of what conversion meant. For adult enslaved people, only a strong dose of catechism covering basic doctrine and prayers, followed by a sincere baptism, could achieve conversion. Following baptism, only those who behaved in accepted Christian ways would be considered sincere. Planters might have supposed that baptizing enslaved infants and children was merely a way of placating missionaries and ministers; it required no effort on planters' parts. By downplaying the significance and sincerity of slave baptism, planters were still able to hold themselves up as the "real Christians" in the colonies. Allowing slave baptism did not require planters to make any serious changes to the lines they had drawn connecting their religion to their unfolding definition of race.

While planter attitudes about slave conversions can be extrapolated from records such as William Willie's and from the letters and diaries of planters themselves, the thoughts and beliefs about Christianity among the enslaved population in Reverend Willie's parish and other places is much more difficult to divine. No enslaved people wrote anything that survives about Christian conversion from Willie's tenure. Yet the small amount of available evidence suggests that, whereas planters saw conversion as an absolute change in belief, morals, and behavior, enslaved people approached Christianity and Christian conversion from a much more inclusive perspective. The presumption of slave insouciance stands only if we accept the restrictive definition of conversion offered by planters and ministers. Though enslaved people themselves generated far fewer sources than planters on the subject of what Christian conversion meant to them, those that do survive suggest that enslaved people fashioned Christianity in their hearts and minds into forms that suited them.[56] For enslaved people, Christianity became, over the course of the eighteenth century, a way of articulating both their spirituality and their rejection of slavery.

Enslaved people born in Africa were likely to have some passing familiarity with Christianity and might even have been practicing Christians before their capture. Le Jau noted several examples of enslaved converts to Anglicanism who had previously been practicing Catholics, including enslaved people who "were born and baptised among the Portuguese."[57] Perhaps practicing Catholics found Anglicanism comfortingly familiar, or perhaps these people knew that in Iberian traditions of slaveholding, conversion to Catholic Christianity conferred certain privileges and made gaining freedom easier. Enslaved people also had experience reconciling African and Catholic beliefs by focusing on similar articulations of the afterlife, prophetic revelation, divination, and possession.[58] Exposure to Christianity began in Africa, with either Afro-Catholicism or the growing number of Protestant missionaries who worked to convert those enslaved people who were embarking for the New World. Slaves arriving in the Americas were armed with some knowledge. Le Jau's Catholic slaves, perhaps like the enslaved people in William Willie's parish, absorbed the Anglo-American religious culture and assimilated those aspects of Christianity that they deemed useful and attractive. Though African cosmologies were different from European ones, on American plantations various African beliefs mixed freely with European Christianities to produce creole understandings of Christianity and freedom that were neither purely African nor instantly recognizable as Christian. In Virginia this was especially true because the creole population consistently outnumbered new African arrivals. An inclusive and varying religious worldview that included aspects of Anglican Christianity was probably broadly understood among Virginia's enslaved people. After all, a plantation that included the anonymous mulatto letter writers of 1723 and African-born slaves probably had a fascinating and vibrant mix of religious cultures and beliefs.

Enslaved people like Le Jau's Catholics and the letter writers of 1723 developed strategic knowledge of Anglicanism in order to protect their interests vis-à-vis their masters.[59] By attempting to force their masters to recognize their common Christianity, and therefore their spiritual equality, enslaved people were advancing an agenda that denied the position of

Anglican missionaries in support of the enslavement of black Christians. In effect, they were articulating a Christian antislavery position. Some enslaved people, like the letter writers of 1723, were able to speak about their Christianity in ways that planters would recognize. The anonymous letter writers coded their missive with the language of Anglican piety: they were baptized, followed "the wayes and Rulles of the Church of England," wished to keep the Sabbath and marry in the church, knew the Lord's Prayer, the Apostles' Creed, and the Ten Commandments, and wanted their children's Christian knowledge "Every Lord's Day att Church before the Curatt to bee Exammond." Their beliefs and goals, in other words, were indistinguishable from those of their masters. They also built biblical references into their letter. They were like the enslaved Israelites in Egypt and claimed they must "seeke first the kingdome of god and all things shall be addid un to us."[60] Their biblical knowledge and thorough understanding of Anglican piety was carefully calculated to win the bishop of London's attention and support. The letter writers had picked the strongest arguments for their plea for freedom, or at least freedom to worship, that they could.

Like the anonymous letter writers, Williamsburg slave Mary Aggie knew what actions to take to attempt to gain her freedom. Instead of writing to the bishop of London, Mary used the legal system to sue her mistress for her freedom, testifying before the General Court and Governor Gooch that she had been baptized. She answered all their questions, giving a "tolerable account" of her faith, but the court invoked the 1667 and 1705 laws that divorced baptism from freedom, and Mary Aggie remained a slave.[61] Yet evidently slaves had not accepted that baptism and Christian conversion did not put them on an equal spiritual footing with their masters. Mary Aggie was ready, over half a century after the 1667 law, to invoke the bonds of spiritual kinship and Christian community that the planters and Anglican missionaries rejected. Though Mary Aggie's testimony of faith might have made little impression on most of the judges in her case, she moved Governor Gooch, and he remembered her a few years later when she came before the General Court again, this time guilty of the theft of some sheets from her mistress. Ordinarily such a crime was a capital offense (when committed by a slave), but Gooch, remembering Aggie's earlier Christian protestations, convinced the court to allow her to be sold out of the colony instead (Aggie probably was sold to slave traders serving Barbados or another sugar island). Having saved Aggie's life, Gooch then pressed the burgesses to extend benefit of clergy to slaves. Benefit of clergy was an ancient provision of the common law that allowed a person accused of a capital offense in England to prove he was a member of the clergy by reading a portion of the Bible, usually a Psalm. (The benefit the accused gained was a transfer of his case to a more lenient ecclesiastical court.) As benefit of clergy evolved, it came to be basically a second-chance rule in a world without an incarceration system. When accused of a crime such as theft or even manslaughter, anyone could claim benefit of clergy once, be branded, and get a second chance at life—anyone, that is, except slaves. After 1730 slaves in Virginia could claim benefit of clergy as Englishmen could, thanks to Mary Aggie.[62]

The letter writers identified themselves as mulattoes, which probably improved their access to knowledge about Christianity. Mary Aggie was almost certainly American born; she had both a surname and a Christian name, and thus had probably had some education in Christianity from her childhood. Yet the connection between Christianity and freedom was more widespread among enslaved people than just the letter writers and Aggie. In September 1730 enslaved people plotted an insurrection using the argument that baptism should result in freedom for converted blacks. Lieutenant Governor Gooch wrote to the Board of Trade in London that there were "many Meetings & Consultations of the Negroes in several Parts of the Country in order to obtain their Freedom." The plot was somewhat looser than planters and officials had initially believed, for as Gooch also noted, "no discovery made of any formed Design of their Rising, only some Loose discourses that His Majesty had sent Orders for setting them free as soon as they were Christians, and that these Orders were Suppressed, a Notion generally Entertained amongst them, but I have not been able to learn who was the Author of it." The "Notion generally Entertained amongst them" held that King George II had decreed that all baptized slaves would be freed and that Virginia's slave owners had intentionally disobeyed the order. George II never issued any such order; it was the formal policy of the Church of England to encourage slave baptism but to recognize that baptism was not an accepted legal basis for a claim of freedom. Yet black slaves understood enough about the British government and Anglicanism to suppose that such a declaration might be forthcoming. The news alarmed Virginia; Gooch also wrote to the Board of Trade that he had mustered the colonial militia to apprehend all slaves found off their masters' plantations.[63]

The plot did not end quietly. In a subsequent letter, Gooch informed the Board of Trade that preventive actions by the militia had not prohibited more illicit meetings of enslaved people throughout the autumn of 1730. "[T]he negros in the Countys of Norfolk & Princess Anne," Gooch opined, "had the boldness to Assemble on a Sunday while the People were at church, and to Chuse from amongst themselves Officers to comand them in their intended Insurrection." Slaves took advantage of the fact that their masters would be busy with their own religious observance, an obligation planters denied their slaves, to plan a potentially bloody rebellion. Enslaved rebels melted into the swamps and forests of Norfolk and Princess Anne, where Anglo-Virginians and their allies surrounded them, eventually hanging twenty-four of them. One later chronicler averred that as many as three hundred enslaved people escaped during the rebellion, after committing "many outrages against the Christians." Anglo-Virginians did not recognize the Christian basis for the plot. In the wake of the rebellion, planters saw fit to resume the moribund practice of bringing their weapons to church—in earlier decades, armed churchgoing protected against a cleverly timed Indian attack. Now, it protected slave owners against their property, enslaved people whose Christianity they denied.[64]

The planned insurrection centered on baptism, Christianity, and freedom. Like the anonymous letter writers and Mary Aggie, these rebellious slaves thought about Christian conversion in the context of rights and privileges Anglo-Virginian planters denied them. Perhaps the slaves gathering and claiming a proclamation connecting Christian baptism and freedom preserved a historical memory of the earlier route to freedom via Christian conversion in the tradition of people such as John Graweere and Mihill Gowen, later colonial laws to the contrary notwithstanding. Or perhaps, like the enslaved people involved in South Carolina's Stono Rebellion in 1739, these enslaved Virginians were drawing upon Kongolese strains of Catholicism brought with them from Africa. Though it is impossible to trace the origins of the enslaved people involved in the 1730 rebellion, it is possible that unrest in the kingdom of Kongo brought more enslaved people from that region to Virginia in the late 1720s and early 1730s. These people would have brought with them military training, knowledge of firearms, and knowledge of an Afro-Portuguese Catholicism that suggested a link between baptism and freedom. Though the exact date of the start of the 1730 uprising is unknown, that it began in late summer or early autumn also suggests a connection with traditional Kongolese celebrations of Mary's nativity. Perhaps a homegrown black Christianity and Kongolese Christianity melded together on Virginia's plantations, mutually reinforcing a belief in the right of baptized Christians to both spiritual and temporal freedom. In any case, the 1730 rebellion was a powerful if violent assertion of enslaved people's Christianity in the face of planters' unwillingness to recognize that Christianity.[65]

Evidence suggests that the suppression of royal orders emancipating baptized slaves remained a feature of black Christianity and continued to spur rebellion. In 1775, on the eve of the American Revolution, a concerned Georgia planter reported to the local Committee of Safety a grave threat to local security. Enslaved people were gathering at "Nocturnal Meetings . . . under the Sanction of Religion." Believing a slave rebellion was imminent, planters investigated and discovered that a white evangelical preacher named John Burnet had told enslaved people that "they were equally intitled to the Good things of this Life in common with the Whites." Additionally, an enslaved man named George preached that "the old King [George II] had reced [received] a Book from our Lord by which he was to Alter the World (meaning to set the Negroes free) but for his not doing so, was now gone to Hell, & in Punishmt That the Young King [George III], meaning our Present One, came up with the Book, & was about to alter the World, & set the Negroes Free." George's story was remarkably similar to the tale Gooch reported around the 1730 rebellion. More than half a century later, this belief in the connection between Christianity and freedom reappeared, though it was no longer attached to Anglican interests but rather to evangelical ones. At least one enslaved man was hanged, and the preacher John Burnet was expelled from the colony.[66] Around the Atlantic world, enslaved people hatched at least twenty plots involving rumors of intercepted or ignored decrees for freedom.[67]

These incidents—the anonymous slaves' letter, Mary Aggie's suit for freedom, and the planned insurrection—all show enslaved people who had an understanding of their Christianity that was radically different from that of their masters. Although some imperial officials, such as Governor Gooch, might have been sympathetic to these slaves' efforts, no planters thought that conversion required freedom. Yet slaves retained an older, radical view of Christian conversion. To them, their religious status gave them rights to freedom and respect, for which they were willing to fight—in courtrooms, in letters to imperial officials, and, as a last resort, in rebellions. When the letter writers of 1723 described themselves as the "Childann of Issarall," they fundamentally challenged hereditary heathenism. They embraced the famous and easily recognizable biblical story of the Israelites' flight from slavery in Egypt, positioning themselves metaphorically as the oppressed but faithful enslaved. The metaphor was subversive in another way as well: it attached enslaved Christians to an older understanding of Christian lineage, in which all people were the descendants of Adam and Noah and all were equally entitled to claim the benefits of Christian conversion. In becoming advocates for their own Christianity, and in embracing Christianity at its most radical and egalitarian, enslaved people defied their status and their masters' religious and racial ideology. Yet slave appropriation of Christianity did not undo slavery itself. Anglican and evangelical missionaries successfully convinced enough planters that baptized slaves were no threat to the institution or to the racial ideology that supported slavery. Planters made reluctant room for enslaved Christians in their worldviews and then began defining a proslavery Christianity that was in active opposition to the beliefs espoused by the letter writers of 1723. Yet these very arguments about the nature of slavery and the nature of Christianity also opened the door for Christian abolitionism—the idea that slavery and Christianity were fundamentally opposed for both slave owners and enslaved people alike.[68] By the end of the eighteenth century, the idea that enslaved people could become Christian, and the fact that enslaved people were Christians, fundamentally altered the mutually supportive relationship between religion and race. By 1800, black and white Christians were poised to challenge slavery and, indeed, to challenge the concept of race in new and profound ways.

Epilogue

Christian Abolitionism and Proslavery Christianity

In 1770 an anonymous Englishman who had traveled in Virginia published a tract admonishing his colonial planter friend's refusal to baptize his slaves. "What a reproach, what an Infamy and Disgrace is it to Christians to suffer Thousands of Heathens and Idolators to swell among them, and even to make a Part of their Houshold and Family, without attempting their Conversion!" opined the pamphleteer.[1] The anonymous writer's words echoed Morgan Godwyn's complaints from a century before about the perfidy of planters who withheld Christianity (and its benefits) from their enslaved property. Godwyn, of course, encountered this world while it was in the process of forming. In the seventeenth century, Godwyn wanted to counter the pernicious effects of hereditary heathenism. A century later, hereditary heathenism was a constitutive part of planter culture, though aspects of the ideology were besieged by missionaries, imperial officials, and enslaved people themselves. The pamphlet also showed the gulf between British and American views of the potential Christianity of blacks and Indians. The split between British and American opinion about enslaved people presaged the fissure among American Christians in the nineteenth century over issues of race, religion, and slavery.

Perhaps the pamphleteer's bold words were met with rolled eyes and a shrug among Virginia's planters—even those who did allow the baptism of their slaves. And perhaps Church of England ministers and officials applauded those words. Yet how successful would any assault upon hereditary heathenism be? By the time of the American Revolution, some planters seem to have agreed that baptism for enslaved people in the Church of England was acceptable. Yet the anger and disbelief of the traveler's dialogue with the planter and his final reproach suggest that most planters did not take the baptism of slaves terribly seriously. The two-pronged attack on hereditary heathenism, though, did succeed in transforming the way planters, enslaved people, and a growing number of abolitionists used Christianity to both support and undermine ideologies of race and slavery. As enslaved African Americans overwhelmingly adopted evangelical Christianity in the first decades of the nineteenth century, arguments citing the biblical endorsement of slavery and the Christian basis for racial hierarchy competed with the growing Christian abolitionist clamor against slavery and racial prejudice.

The British pamphleteer's concerns about his American friend's curious attitudes, though, would have been wholly unfamiliar to the English settlers in the Atlantic world of the late sixteenth and early seventeenth centuries. In that moment, the identities of Europeans, Indians, and Africans were fluid, and any person could cross religious boundaries—often with more ease than the English would have liked. In identifying Indians as potential Christians, the English embraced the common view of the universality of Christianity. To these colonizers, anyone could become Christian. Observed religious differences between Christians and non-Christians were surmountable—even though the English predicted a scenario in which everyone would become Christian. In Virginia, the English experienced the universality of heathenism as well, finding that the harsh uncertainties of life there drove some English Christians to embrace heathenism.

Over the course of the seventeenth century, English people in the New World redefined Christianity and came to view Africans and Indians as hereditary heathens. Anglo-Virginians restricted Africans' and Indians' access to marriage, baptism, and other rituals governed by the English church. Anglo-Virginians used the regulation of licit and illicit sex among Anglo-Virginians and Africans and Indians, as well as the redefinition of the rights that baptized people received vis-à-vis unbaptized people, to define Indians and Africans as hereditary heathens. Faced with the political ructions of the late seventeenth century and an influx of Protestant dissenters, Anglo-Virginians ultimately adopted a pragmatic religious toleration in which race was more important than religious affiliation. In the process, Anglo-Virginians created an understanding of what it meant to be "white." By the beginning of the eighteenth century, the idea that Christianity was a religion almost exclusively for white people was a conceit commonly held among Virginia's planter class.

This story is one of transformation, from an early seventeenth-century understanding of Christianity that stressed its universality to a mid-eighteenth-century understanding that stressed its exclusivity. This was not an instantaneous transformation; it occurred in county courthouse battles, in legislation, in households, and among individuals who were enslaved, indentured, and free. English people struggled to explain the differences they observed between themselves and Africans and Indians, and they saw religion as a way of articulating and explaining those differences. The qualities they assigned to themselves as Christians, as well as the rights and freedoms they believed derived from their Christianity, divided them from Indians and Africans. Indians and Africans resisted this tortuous process by struggling to force Anglo-Virginians to recognize their Christianity. Imperial officials and Anglican ministers trained in Great Britain also struggled to overcome the idea of hereditary heathenism by pressing for the conversion of Indians and Africans whenever they could, though they did not challenge slavery as an institution.

Among those who challenged hereditary heathenism, the universality of Christianity reemerged as a potent weapon. In a late eighteenth-century antislavery manuscript, the Congregationalist minister Lemuel Haynes attacked not only slavery but also the idea that undergirded it—that blacks were hereditarily inferior to whites and therefore ought to be enslaved. He began with the same verses Morgan Godwyn used in his attack upon Virginia planters: "It hath pleased god to *make of one Blood all nations of men, for to dwell upon the face of the Earth*. Acts 17, 26." In reaffirming the common descent of all human beings, Haynes went further than Godwyn and proclaimed that the laws of nature applied to all people. "Therefore we may reasonably Conclude, that Liberty is Equally as pre[c]ious to a *Black man*, as it is to a *white one*, and Bondage Equally as intollarable to the one as it is to the other."[2] Haynes went on to negate various justifications for slavery, including the Curse of Ham and defenses of slavery taken from the letters of Saint Paul. Haynes, the son of a white mother and a black father who grew up an indentured servant in Massachusetts, forcefully challenged the biblical exegesis that sustained both race and slavery. There is no evidence, however, that his manuscript was circulated or that it was even delivered as a sermon.

Enslaved people also embraced the American Revolution's rhetoric of liberty and pointed out inconsistencies between Christianity and slavery in petitions for freedom in the 1770s. One such from Massachusetts in 1777 was written in the "bowels of a free and Christian country" and requested the freedom and equality guaranteed by "that great Parent of the Universe."[3] In the aftermath of Revolution, some Americans realized that their newfound commitment to political liberty should extend to enslaved people. As Quaker antislavery activist Anthony Benezet asked in 1783, "Why ought a Negro be less free than the subjects of Britain, or a white face in America? Have we not all one Father? Hath not one God created us?"[4] In 1787 Philadelphians formed the Pennsylvania Society for Promoting the Abolition of Slavery and recruited Benjamin Franklin as the society's first president. In February 1790 Franklin drafted an antislavery petition for Congress, stating that "mankind are all formed by the same Almighty Being, alike objects of his Care, and equally designed for the Enjoyment of Happiness the Christian Religion teaches us to believe."[5] Franklin and the society, like Benezet, explicitly reaffirmed monogenesis and the common descent of mankind in their attack against slavery, using arguments that would have been familiar to late sixteenth-century Englishmen.

Yet the pernicious biblical arguments that defined race and supported slavery over the long seventeenth century persisted in the post-Revolutionary era, and indeed they gained new life. While enslaved people in Massachusetts petitioned for their freedom, Virginia's slave owners reengaged biblical justifications for slavery in a series of petitions in the 1780s protesting the state's trend toward manumission. One petition from Brunswick County resurrected the Curse of Ham as a justification for slavery, as well as rehearsing the story of Abraham and Hagar and the laws of Leviticus as reasons for "one Nation to buy and keep slaves of another Nation."[6] Similar petitions from Amelia County and Halifax County also cited Old Testament law, especially Leviticus 25:44: "Thy bonde servant also, and thy bonde maid, which thou shalt have, shal be of the heathen that are rounde about you."[7] The Virginia petitioners' use of the Curse of Ham and Leviticus stressed what they saw as the unbridgeable divide between Christian and heathen at the root of race and slavery.

To the increasing numbers of enslaved Virginians who adopted Christianity and learned to read, planters' tortured explanations for slavery made less and less sense. In 1800 an enslaved man named Gabriel led a rebellion in Richmond in which the rebels' Christianity almost certainly played a critical role. Gabriel and his coconspirators read the Bible, used it in their planning, and ultimately thought of themselves as God's chosen people. They also agreed among themselves that slavery was not biblically sanctioned. While he attempted to evade capture after his plot had been uncovered, Gabriel used the name Daniel to hide his identity, suggesting the trials of the biblical Daniel, who was saved from the lions' jaws by an angel.[8] In the end, Gabriel and several other enslaved people were hanged. The role of Christianity was even more explicit in Nat Turner's rebellion in 1831. Turner was also a Baptist preacher, who later described prophetic experiences as part of his inspiration for rebellion. He recalled that, a few years before his rebellion, "I saw white spirits and black spirits engaged in battle, and the sun was darkened—the thunder rolled in the Heavens, and blood flowed in the streams." Turner's rebellion put Virginia's Baptist churches on the defensive and resulted in legislation that forbade slave owners to teach their slaves to read. Further legislation also required the presence of a white minister at black religious gatherings.[9]

As a response to the challenges posed to slavery by enslaved people such as Gabriel and Nat Turner, as well as northern abolitionists, southern planters developed a thoroughly proslavery Christianity. They utilized biblical accounts of slavery and complex exegesis to defend the idea that blacks were racially inferior. Some southern proslavery intellectuals resurrected and expanded upon old polygenist ideas to reject the common descent of blacks and whites.[10] While some slavery apologists avoided polygenist explanations for race because they were extrabiblical, planters remained attracted to biblical explanations of racial difference. One commentator wrote in 1852 that "Japheth [was] a blue eyed white man, and Ham a woolly headed black eyed black man" and went on to explain that Ham's "whole character and nature" were deficient, which led to the hereditary curse of bondage.[11]

Hereditary heathenism remained a powerful ideology that meshed too neatly with the goals of slave societies for planters to agree to overturn it; instead, planters harnessed Christianity as a tool of separation, oppression, and defined inferiority for Indians and Africans. Yet Christianity retained its extraordinary explanatory power for Christian abolitionists and proslavery Christians alike. Even as Christianity buttressed the emergence of multiple ideas of race, it also undermined racial ideologies with its universalizing appeal and suggestion of common descent. Christianity also provided a path of resistance for enslaved people, couched in language their masters could not ignore. The story of race as it unfolded in seventeenth- and eighteenth-century English North America shows that race was not a predictable product of colonization; it was carefully invented and reinvented, and religious belief was a critical part of constructing and defining human difference. The remarkable part of the story is how hard colonial planters had to work to undermine the idea of potential Christianity and to construct hereditary heathenism. The framework they devised, though, fueled the proslavery arguments of the antebellum era and dovetailed with the emerging pseudoscientific understandings of race in the nineteenth century.

The world of racialized religion did not end with the nineteenth century. Despite the assault of Christian theologians in the twentieth century against polygenist attitudes and the use of Christian theology to buttress ideas about race, southern white Christians used biblically based ideas about race to defend segregation.[12] In 1957 a South Carolina Baptist church issued a statement on desegregation, using Acts 17:26 as its reference point. "1) God made men of different races and ordained the basic difference between races; 2) Race has a purpose in the Divine plan, each race having a unique purpose and a distinctive mission in God's plan; 3) God meant for people of different races to maintain their race purity and racial identity and seek the highest development of their racial group. God has determined 'the bounds of their habitation.'"[13] The same verse that Morgan Godwyn used to uphold the unity of mankind and that Lemuel Haynes used to attack slavery was repurposed to reaffirm race and American apartheid in the wake of *Brown v. Board of Education*. The link between Christianity and race has ebbed and flowed; Christianity has been deployed to both make and unmake race. Christianity has been used to define whiteness and blackness, and it has been used to attempt to make those categories meaningless. Religious and racial categories continue to matter today, though they are no longer rendered in their seventeenth-century form. Yet Christianity is still used (and abused) to create race and difference in ways that should profoundly disturb the modern world.

NOTES

ABBREVIATIONS

ACCR   Accomack County Court Records, Library of Virginia Microfilm

AM   William Hand Browne, ed., *Archives of Maryland* (Annapolis: Maryland Historical Society, 1883–1972, 1990–)

BP   Warren M. Billings, ed., *The Papers of Sir William Berkeley, 1605–1677* (Richmond: Library of Virginia, 2007)

CWCJS Philip L. Barbour, ed., *The Complete Works of Captain John Smith*, 3 vols. (Chapel Hill: University of North Carolina Press, 1986)

FP   The Ferrar Papers, Magdalene College, Cambridge (available online at www.amedu.com/Collections/Virginia-Company-Archives.aspx)

Hening William Waller Hening, ed., *The Statutes at Large, being a Collection of all the laws of Virginia* (New York: R. & W. & G. Bartow, 1819–23)

JHB   H. R. McIlwaine, ed., *Journals of the House of Burgesses of Virginia* (Richmond: Colonial Press, E. Waddey Co., 1914–20)

Lefroy J. H. Lefroy, ed., *Memorials of the Discovery and Early Settlement of the Bermudas Somer Islands*, 2 vols. (London: Longmans, Greene, 1877)

LJCCV H. R. McIlwaine, ed., *Legislative Journals of the Council of Colonial Virginia*, 3 vols. (Richmond: Colonial Press, E. Waddey Co., 1818–19)

MCGC H. R. McIlwaine, ed., *Minutes of the Council and General Court of Virginia* (Richmond: privately printed, 1924)

NCCR   Northampton County Court Records, Library of Virginia Microfilm

RVCL Susan Myra Kingsbury, ed., *Records of the Virginia Company of London*, 4 vols. (Washington, DC: Government Printing Office, 1906–34)

SCCR   Surry County Court Records, Library of Virginia Microfilm

YCCR   York County Court Records, Colonial Williamsburg Foundation

INTRODUCTION

1. Morgan Godwyn, *The Negro's and Indians Advocate, Suing for their Admission into the Church* (London, 1681), 37–38. For Godwyn's biography, see Alden T. Vaughan, "Slaveholders' 'Hellish Principles': A Seventeenth-Century

Critique," in *Roots of American Racism: Essays on the Colonial Experience* (New York: Oxford University Press, 1995), 55–81.

2. Godwyn, *The Negro's and Indians Advocate*, 36 (emphasis in original).

3. Ibid., 14, 15. Godwyn also noted that some planters insisted that enslaved blacks were of "a *flock* different from *Adam's*" or perhaps also were the descendants not of Ham but rather of Cain.

4. On the general absence of race from discourse in the ancient world, see Frank M. Snowden Jr., *Before Color Prejudice: The Ancient View of Blacks* (Cambridge, MA: Harvard University Press, 1983), and Ivan Hannaford, *Race: The History of an Idea in the West* (Baltimore: Johns Hopkins University Press, 1996). For a counterview, see Benjamin Isaac, *The Invention of Racism in Classical Antiquity* (Princeton: Princeton University Press, 2004). For medieval and early modern Europe, see George M. Fredrickson, *Racism: A Short History* (Princeton: Princeton University Press, 2002); David Brion Davis, *The Problem of Slavery in Western Culture* (New York: Oxford University Press, 1966); Davis, *In the Image of God: Religion, Moral Values, and Our Heritage of Slavery* (New Haven: Yale University Press, 2001). For race and religion in the New World, see Davis, *Inhuman Bondage: The Rise and Fall of Slavery in the New World* (New York: Oxford University Press, 2008); Colin Kidd, *The Forging of Races: Race and Scripture in the Protestant Atlantic World, 1600–2000* (Cambridge: Cambridge University Press, 2006); Winthrop Jordan, *White over Black: American Attitudes toward the Negro, 1550–1812* (Chapel Hill: University of North Carolina Press, 1968); Edmund S. Morgan, *American Slavery, American Freedom: The Ordeal of Colonial Virginia* (New York: Norton, 1975).

5. Godwyn, *The Negro's and Indians Advocate*, 18 (emphasis in original). The full verse reads "And hathe made of one blood all mankinde, to dwell on all the face of the earth, and hathe assigned the times which were ordeined before, and the boundes of their habitation."

6. Though the scholarship on race in the early American South is fairly well developed, most work does not explicitly engage Christianity as a causal factor. See, for example, Kathleen M. Brown, *Good Wives, Nasty Wenches, and Anxious Patriarchs: Gender, Race, and Power in Colonial Virginia* (Chapel Hill: University of North Carolina Press, 1996); Kirsten Fischer, *Suspect Relations: Sex, Race, and Resistance in Colonial North Carolina* (Ithaca: Cornell University Press, 2001); Anthony S. Parent, *Foul Means: The Formation of a Slave Society in Virginia, 1660–1740* (Chapel Hill: University of North Carolina Press, 2003). There is an interesting historiography on race and religion in the modern South. See, for example, Paul Harvey, *Freedom's Coming: Religious Culture and the Shaping of the South from the Civil War through the Civil Rights Era* (Chapel Hill: University of North Carolina Press, 2005).

7. For the importance of Anglican religiosity to the colonial project, see esp. John F. Woolverton, *Colonial Anglicanism in North America* (Detroit: Wayne State University Press, 1984), and Edward Bond, *Damned Souls in a Tobacco Colony: Religion in Seventeenth-Century Virginia* (Macon, GA: Mercer Univer-

sity Press, 2000). For the eighteenth century, see Lauren Winner, *A Cheerful and Comfortable Faith: Anglican Religious Practice in the Elite Households of Eighteenth-Century Virginia* (New Haven: Yale University Press, 2010), and Travis Glasson, *Mastering Christianity: Missionary Anglicanism and Slavery in the Atlantic World* (New York: Oxford University Press, 2012).

8. See Bond, *Damned Souls*; James Horn, *Adapting to a New World: English Society in the Seventeenth-Century Chesapeake* (Chapel Hill: University of North Carolina Press, 1994), esp. chap. 9, "Inner World: Religion and Popular Belief."

9. Philip D. Morgan, "Religious Diversity in Colonial Virginia: Red, Black, and White," in Paul Rasor and Richard E. Bond, eds., *From Jamestown to Jefferson: The Evolution of Religious Freedom in Virginia* (Charlottesville: University of Virginia Press, 2011), 74–107.

10. For the eighteenth-century emergence of race, see esp. Hannaford, *Race*, and Roxanne Wheeler, *The Complexion of Race: Categories of Difference in Eighteenth-Century British Culture* (Philadelphia: University of Pennsylvania Press, 2004). For scholars who see an earlier emergence of race, see esp. Joyce E. Chaplin, *Subject Matter: Technology, the Body, and Science on the Anglo-American Frontier, 1500–1676* (Cambridge, MA: Harvard University Press, 2001), and the essays on "Constructing Race: A Reflection" in the January 1997 issue of the *William and Mary Quarterly*, 3rd series.

11. Adam Serwer, "Bachmann's Views on Slavery Are Worse Than You Thought," American Prospect, http://prospect.org/csnc/blogs/adam_serwer_archive?month=08&year=2011&base_name=bachmanns_views_on_slavery_are.

12. http://abcnews.go.com/WN/franklin-graham-president-obama-born-muslim-pew-poll/story?id=11446462.

CHAPTER ONE: *English Christians among the Blackest Nations*

1. S. G. Culliford, *William Strachey, 1572–1621* (Charlottesville: University of Virginia Press, 1965).

2. William Strachey, *For the colony in Virginea Britannia: Lawes Divine Morall and Martiall, &c* (London, 1612), [A1]r. "Mores" [moors] was often used to mean heathen or pagan.

3. Eamon Duffy, *The Stripping of the Altars: Traditional Religion in England, c. 1400–c. 1580* (New Haven: Yale University Press, 1992), 4.

4. John Guy, *Tudor England* (Oxford: Oxford University Press, 1988), 238.

5. John E. Booty, ed., *The Book of Common Prayer 1559: The Elizabethan Prayer Book* (Charlottesville: University of Virginia Press, 1976), 16, 35–47.

6. Diarmaid MacCulloch, *The Reformation: A History* (New York: Penguin Books, 2003), 588, 295.

7. Ibid., 392.

8. *The Geneva Bible*, ed. Lloyd E. Berry (Madison: University of Wisconsin Press, 1969; facsimile of 1560 edition), iiii.

9. See Colin Kidd, *British Identities before Nationalism: Ethnicity and Na-*

tionhood in the Atlantic World, 1600–1800 (Cambridge: Cambridge University Press, 1999), and also Kidd's *The Forging of Races: Race and Scripture in the Protestant Atlantic World, 1600–2000* (Cambridge: Cambridge University Press, 2006). For the view that prominent theorists of empire such as Richard Hakluyt did not see England as the elect nation in the late sixteenth and early seventeenth centuries, see David Armitage, *The Ideological Origins of the British Empire* (Cambridge: Cambridge University Press, 2000), 61–90.

10. Edward L. Bond, *Damned Souls in a Tobacco Colony: Religion in Seventeenth-Century Virginia* (Macon, GA: Mercer University Press, 2000), 1–35, esp. 3–5.

11. Winthrop D. Jordan, *White over Black: American Attitudes toward the Negro, 1550–1812* (Chapel Hill: University of North Carolina Press, 1968), 49–50.

12. Meredith Hanmer, *The Baptizing of a Turk, A Sermon Preached at the Hospitall of St Katherin* . . . (London, 1587), 3–5.

13. David Beers Quinn, "Turks, Moors, Blacks, and Others in Drake's West Indian Voyage," *Terrae Incognitae* 14 (1982): 97–104.

14. Edmund S. Morgan, *American Slavery, American Freedom: The Ordeal of Colonial Virginia* (New York: Norton, 1975), 20–21; Jane Ohlmeyer, "'Civilizinge of those Rude Partes': Colonization within Britain and Ireland, 1580s–1640s," in Nicholas Canny, ed., *The Oxford History of the British Empire*, vol. 1: *The Origins of Empire* (Oxford: Oxford University Press, 1998), 134–35, and Ohlmeyer, "A Laboratory for Empire? Early Modern Ireland and English Imperialism," in Kevin Kenny, ed., *Ireland and the British Empire* (Oxford: Oxford University Press, 2004), 34–35.

15. Thomas Churchyard, *A Generall rehearsal of warres and joyned to the same some tragedies and epitaphes* (London, 1579), quoted in Nicholas P. Canny, "The Ideology of English Colonization: From Ireland to America," *William and Mary Quarterly* 30, no. 4 (October 1973): 582.

16. On the colonial farce at Roanoke, see esp. Michael Leroy Oberg, *The Head in Edward Nugent's Hand: Roanoke's Forgotten Indians* (Philadelphia: University of Pennsylvania Press, 2008).

17. John Smith, "The True Travels, Adventures, and Observations of Captaine John Smith in Europe, Asia, Affrica, and America, from Anno Domini 1593 to 1629," *CWCJS*, III, 211.

18. "A Justification for Planting Virginia [before 1609]," *RVCL*, III, 1–3; "A Courte Held for Virginia the Last of May 1620," *RVCL*, I, 367.

19. George Abbot, *The Reasons which Doctour Hill hath brought for the upholding of Papistry, which is falselie termed the Catholike Religion, Unmasked and shewed to be very weake* . . . (Oxford, 1604), 25. On Abbot's impeccable anti-Catholic credentials, see *Oxford Dictionary of National Biography Online*, s.v. "Abbot, George (1562–1633)" (by Kenneth Fincham). Abbot eventually became Archbishop of Canterbury.

20. William Strachey, *The Historie of Travell into Virginia Britania* (1612), ed. Louis B. Wright and Virginia Freund (London: Hakluyt Society, 1953), 54–55.

21. Kidd, *The Forging of Races*, 57.

22. Isaac La Peyrère, *A Theological Systeme upon the Presupposition that Men were Before Adam* (London, 1655); La Peyrère, *Man Before Adam* (London, 1656). On Isaac La Peyrère, see Richard H. Popkin, *Isaac La Peyrère (1596–1676): His Life, Work, and Influence* (New York: E. J. Brill, 1987). There were earlier pre-Adamite and multiple creation theories; see David Abulafia, *The Discovery of Mankind: Atlantic Encounters in the Age of Columbus* (New Haven: Yale University Press, 2008), 3–9.

23. William Crashaw, *A Sermon Preached in London before the right honorable the Lord Lawarre, Lord Governour and Captaine Generall of Virginea, and others of his Maiesties Counsell for that Kingdome, and the rest of the Adventurers in that Plantation* . . . (London, 1610), C3r.

24. Ibid., [C4]v.

25. The full verse reads, "And thei that be wise, shal shine, as the brightnes of the firmament: & they that turne many to righteousnes, shal shine as the starres, for ever and ever."

26. Thomas Hariot, *A Briefe and True Report of the New Found Land of Virginia* (London, 1590; repr., New York: Dover, 1972), 25.

27. Ibid., 25, 26.

28. On the importance of chronology in understanding humanity and human history, see Arno Borst, "Computus: Zeit und Zahl im Mittelalter," *Deutsches Archiv* 44, no. 1 (1988): 1–82.

29. Hariot, *A Breife and True Report*, 27.

30. Strachey, *Historie*, 101–2.

31. Ibid., 55; on Acosta, see Anthony Pagden, *The Fall of Natural Man: The American Indians and the Origins of Comparative Ethnology* (Cambridge: Cambridge University Press, 1982), 193–95, and Pagden, "Dispossessing the Barbarian: The Language of Spanish Thomism and the Debate over the Property Rights of the American Indians," in Pagden, ed., *The Languages of Political Theory in Early Modern Europe* (Cambridge: Cambridge University Press, 1987), 79–98. Acosta's work appeared in English, translated by Edward Grimeston as *The Naturall and Morall Historie of the East and West Indies* (London, 1604). On Spanish debates regarding the origins and status of Indians, see also Abulafia, *The Discovery of Mankind*, 28–99.

32. Strachey, *Historie*, 54.

33. Benjamin Braude, "The Sons of Noah and the Construction of Ethnic and Geographical Identities in the Medieval and Early Modern Periods," *William and Mary Quarterly*, 3rd ser., 54, no. 1 (January 1997): 103–42. Braude notes that before the middle of the seventeenth century, Ham's descendants were more likely to be associated with Asia than with Africa.

34. Strachey, *Historie*, 54.

35. Genesis 9:20–27. Part of what makes the verse so opaque is its reference to Ham's transgression in mocking his father and Noah's subsequent curse not of Ham but his son Canaan. Theologians were bothered by the notion that

Ham had sinned and Canaan's descendants suffered because of it. What became known as the "Curse of Ham" was originally Canaan's curse; early Christian biblical exegesis was probably responsible for the confusion in proper labeling of the curse. See David M. Goldenberg, *The Curse of Ham: Race and Slavery in Early Judaism, Christianity, and Islam* (Princeton: Princeton University Press, 2003), 157–67.

36. Jordan, *White over Black*, 35–37, 54, 56; Goldenberg, *The Curse of Ham*, 168.

37. Braude, "The Sons of Noah," 128, 133.

38. Goldenberg, *The Curse of Ham*, 169–70.

39. George Best, *A True Discourse of the Late Voyages of Discoverie* . . . (London, 1578), 31, 32.

40. Richard Jobson, *The Golden Trade, or A Discovery of the River Gambra, and the Golden Trade of the Aethiopians* (London, 1623), 52, 62.

41. Winthrop Jordan argued forcefully for the early racialization of Africans in *White over Black*; more recent scholarship suggests opinions like Best's were not widely held. See Jonathan Schorsch, *Jews and Blacks in the Early Modern World* (Cambridge: Cambridge University Press, 2004), 151–65.

42. Samuel Purchas, *Purchas his Pilgrimage* (London, 1613), 545–46.

43. Strachey, *Historie*, 54–55.

44. Ibid., 53–55.

45. Alexander Whitaker, *Good Newes from Virginia Sent to the Counsell and Company of Virginia* (London, 1613), 27. On Whitaker's life and theology, see Harry Culverwell Porter, "Alexander Whitaker: Cambridge Apostle to Virginia," *William and Mary Quarterly*, 3rd ser., 14, no. 3 (July 1957): 317–43.

46. Father Andrew White, "A Briefe Relation of the Voyage unto Maryland, 1634," in Clayton Colman Hall, ed., *Narratives of Early Maryland, 1633–1684* (New York: Charles Scribner's Sons, 1910), 45.

47. Hariot, *A Breife and True Report*, 26. Hariot also described incidents in which Indians had been raised Lazarus-like, from the dead.

48. [Gabriel Archer], "A Breife Discription of the People," in Philip L. Barbour, ed., *The Jamestown Voyages under the First Charter, 1606–1609* (Cambridge: Cambridge University Press, 1969), I, 104.

49. John Smith, *A Map of Virginia*, CWCJS, I, 172. Strachey echoed Smith's comments, agreeing that only religious practitioners lived after death and that their souls lived to the west over the mountains.

50. On accounts of the Powhatan afterlife, see Helen C. Rountree, *The Powhatan Indians of Virginia: Their Traditional Culture* (Norman: University of Oklahoma Press, 1989), 139. Rountree writes that late seventeenth-century accounts of Powhatan afterlife show evidence of a distinctive heaven and hell, reserved for souls on the basis of deeds during lifetime, but that these could be wishful thinking among the English or perhaps some adoption of English religious ways by the Powhatan. That does not explain Hariot's observations which, while they might be a case of optimistic presentation, do indicate that the Eng-

lish were willing to read Indian beliefs about the immortality of the soul as corruptions of past Judeo-Christian belief.

51. Strachey, *Historie*, 100.

52. Ibid., [6]. The standard early modern abbreviation for "res publica" is "respub." Strachey has pluralized both words. The plural of "res publica" is "rei publicae," abbreviated as "Reipub."

53. See Karen Ordahl Kupperman, "Angells in America," in Philip D. Beidler and Gary Taylor, eds., *Writing Race across the Atlantic World Medieval to Modern* (New York: Palgrave Macmillan, 2005), 28.

54. Strachey, *Historie*, 60.

55. Whitaker, *Good Newes*, 26, 27.

56. Ibid., 25, 24.

57. [Archer], "A Breife Discription," 104. Barbour comments in the footnotes that "witty" means here "clever"—but "not necessarily in the favorable sense." Late sixteenth- and early seventeenth-century meanings of "witty" (intelligent, capable, ingenious, and clever, having good intellectual ability) and "ingenious" (having high intellectual capacity, able, talented, possessed of genius) seem to make more sense in Archer's narrative. See *Oxford English Dictionary Online*, s.v. "witty" and "ingenious."

58. [Archer], "A Breife Discription," 103; Smith, *A Map of Virginia*, 160; Strachey, *Historie*, 70.

CHAPTER TWO: *The Rise and Fall of the Anglo-Indian Christian Commonwealth*

1. "Letters patent to Sir Thomas Gates and others 10 April 1606," in Philip L. Barbour, ed., *The Jamestown Voyages under the First Charter, 1606–1609* (Cambridge: Cambridge University Press, 1969), I, 25.

2. Patricia Seed, "Taking Possession and Reading Texts: Establishing the Authority of Overseas Empires," *William and Mary Quarterly*, 3rd ser., 49, no. 2 (April 1992): 183–209, esp. 188.

3. "Instructions for Government, 20 November 1606," in Barbour, *Jamestown Voyages*, I, 43.

4. "Instructions given by way of Advice, November or December 1606," in ibid., I, 51.

5. Karen Ordahl Kupperman, *Indians and English: Facing Off in Early America* (Ithaca: Cornell University Press, 2000). Nicholas Canny makes a similar argument regarding the Elizabethan conquest of Ireland. Canny, "The Ideology of English Colonization: From Ireland to America," *William and Mary Quarterly*, 3rd ser., 30, no. 4 (October 1973): 575–98.

6. William Crashaw, *A Sermon Preached in London before the right honorable the Lord Lawarre, Lord Governour and Captaine Generall of Virginea, and others of his Maiesties Counsell for that Kingdome, and the rest of the Adventurers in that Plantation* ... (London, 1610), G3r–[G4]v. William Strachey made a similar claim in 1612. See William Strachey, *The Historie of Travell into Virginia*

Britania, ed. Louis B. Wright and Virginia Freund (London: Hakluyt Society, 1953), 25–26.

7. "Dispensation for Richard Hakluyt and Robert Hunt, 24 November 1606," in Barbour, *Jamestown Voyages*, I, 63.

8. Edward Maria Wingfield, "Discourse, after 21 May 1608," in ibid., I, 233.

9. John Smith, *A Map of Virginia*, CWCJS, I, 204.

10. On Hunt's troubles in England, see Benjamin Woolley, *Savage Kingdom: Virginia and the Founding of English America* (London: Harper, 2006), 35–36.

11. George Percy, *Discourse* [1608], in Barbour, *Jamestown Voyages*, I, 135.

12. On the Spanish Jesuit mission, see Clifford M. Lewis and Albert J. Loomie, eds., *The Spanish Jesuit Mission in Virginia, 1570–1572* (Chapel Hill: University of North Carolina Press, 1953); Charlotte M. Gradie, "The Powhatans in the Context of the Spanish Empire," in Helen C. Rountree, ed., *Powhatan Foreign Relations, 1500–1722* (Charlottesville: University of Virginia Press, 1995), 154–72.

13. Helen C. Rountree, *Pocahontas, Powhatan, Opechancanough: Three Indian Lives Changed by Jamestown* (Charlottesville: University of Virginia Press, 2005), 8, 39–46.

14. Gabriel Archer, "A relatyon of the Discovery of our River, from James Forte into the Maine: made by Captain Christofer Newport: and sincerely written and observed by a gent. of ye Colony," 21 May–21 June 1607, in Barbour, *Jamestown Voyages*, I, 88. On the authorship of "A relayton . . . ," see *Dictionary of Virginia Biography*, s.v. "Gabriel Archer" (by David B. Quinn).

15. Percy, *Discourse*, in Barbour, *Jamestown Voyages*, I, 141.

16. [Gabriel Archer], "A Breife Discription of the People," in ibid., I, 103–4.

17. Percy, *Discourse*, in ibid., I, 145, 143.

18. William White, "Fragments" [1608, published 1614], in ibid., I, 148–50.

19. [Archer], "A Breife Discription," in ibid., I, 104.

20. Carville V. Earle, "Environment, Disease, and Mortality in Early Virginia," in Thad W. Tate and David L. Ammerman, eds., *The Chesapeake in the Seventeenth Century: Essays on Anglo-American Society* (Chapel Hill: University of North Carolina Press, 1979), 96–125.

21. Percy, *Discourse*, in Barbour, *Jamestown Voyages*, I, 144. John Smith took a similar line in describing the famine and death at Jamestown. "God (being angrie with us) plagued us with such famin and sicknes, that the living were scarce able to bury the dead." Smith also noted that "shortly after it pleased God (in our extremity) to move the Indians to bring us Corne . . . when we rather expected when they would destroy us." Smith, *A True Relation*, CWCJS, I, 33, 35. It is easy to ignore these characterizations of God's actions (both punishment of English transgressions and Indian changes of heart) as formulaic explanations for frightening events, but that dismisses the sincere belief among the English that both the famine and the relief of suffering at Jamestown were attributable to divine intervention.

22. Percy, *Discourse*, in Barbour, *Jamestown Voyages*, I, 144–45.

23. Michael A. Lacombe, "'A Continuall and Dayly Table for Gentlemen of Fashion': Humanism, Food, and Authority at Jamestown, 1607–1609," *American Historical Review* 115, no. 3 (June 2010): 669–87.

24. Smith, *A True Relation, CWCJS*, I, 37, 43.

25. Ibid., 47.

26. Smith was initially impressed with this display of Wahunsonacock's power and wealth. In *A True Relation* (1608), he wrote that Wahunsonacock had "such a grave and Majesticall countenance, as drave me into admiration to see such state in a naked Salvage." Smith, *A True Relation, CWCJS*, I, 53. In a later retelling of his first audience with Wahunsonacock in the *Generall Historie* (1624), Smith omitted his "admiration" and referred to the young women who were likely Wahunsonacock's wives pejoratively. See the *Generall Historie, CWCJS*, II, 150–52.

27. Smith, *A True Relation, CWCJS*, I, 57.

28. There are many scholarly refutations of the old story that Pocahontas saved Smith from certain death; the most succinct discussion of the evidence is Camilla Townsend, *Pocahontas and the Powhatan Dilemma* (New York: Hill and Wang, 2004), 52–56.

29. Smith, *A True Relation, CWCJS*, I, 65.

30. George Percy, "A Trewe Relacyon (1625)," *Tyler's Quarterly Historical and Genealogical Magazine* 3, no. 4 (April 1922): 263, 266.

31. Ibid., 272–73.

32. J. Frederick Fausz, "An 'Abundance of Blood Shed on Both Sides': England's First Indian War, 1609–1614," *Virginia Magazine of History and Biography* 98, no. 1 (January 1990): 3–56, 33; Frederic W. Gleach, *Powhatan's World and Colonial Virginia: A Conflict of Cultures* (Lincoln: University of Nebraska Press, 1997), 97–98.

33. The French Jesuits noted the possibility of European reversion to heathenism as well. See James Axtell, *The Invasion Within: The Contest of Cultures in Colonial North America* (Oxford: Oxford University Press, 1985), 71–90.

34. Smith, *Generall Historie, CWCJS*, II, 232–33. Historians occasionally dispute the veracity of the English cannibalism story, noting that Smith did not include it in his earlier treatise *A Map of Virginia* (1612) and that other eyewitness accounts make no mention of cannibalistic misdeeds among the English. Many early accounts, though, were written for public circulation specifically at the request of the Virginia Company, which would have had every reason to hide such misbehavior among its colonists. Smith must have had an informant who told him the story of the Jamestown cannibalism (he was not present at the time but rather a prisoner of Powhatan's upriver at Werowocomoco). George Percy also wrote about the cannibalism episode in more detail in 1625 in an effort to correct what he saw as errors in Smith's *Generall Historie* (1624). Percy gave more ghastly details; the man in question "Ripped the childe outt of her woambe and threwe itt into the River and after Chopped the Mother in pieces and salted her for his foode." Percy claimed he was the one who "Ajudged him to be executed

the acknoledmt of the dede beinge inforced from him by torture haveinge hunge by the Thumbes with weightes att his feete A quarter of An howere before he wolde Confesse the same." Percy, "A Trewe Relacyon," 267. Since Percy was in charge of the struggling settlement at that point during Smith's enforced absence and the illness and death of other potential leaders, it seems plausible to me that he had interrogated and ordered the execution of the unnamed perpetrator. Smith and Percy were rivals when it came to accounts of early Jamestown; that Percy corroborated Smith's account of cannibalism indicates that he was not Smith's informant and that he was willing to confirm Smith's account because he knew it to be true (he challenged Smith on other points but not that one). This makes it likely that something of a cannibalistic nature did indeed happen at Jamestown. On the date of Percy's second manuscript and his conflict with Smith, see Philip L. Barbour, "The Honorable George Percy: Premier Chronicler of the First Virginia Voyage," *Early American Literature* 6 (Spring 1971): 13; John W. Shirley, "George Percy at Jamestown, 1607–1612," *Virginia Magazine of History and Biography* 57, no. 3 (1949): 227–43, 236.

35. Smith, *Generall Historie, CWCJS*, II, 232; Percy, "A Trewe Relacyon," 267.

36. Helen C. Rountree, *The Powhatan Indians of Virginia: Their Traditional Culture* (Norman: University of Oklahoma Press, 1989), 142; James Horn, *A Land as God Made It: Jamestown and the Birth of America* (New York: Basic Books, 2005), 59; Bernard Sheehan, *Savagism and Civility: Indians and Englishmen in Colonial Virginia* (Cambridge: Cambridge University Press, 1980), 60–63.

37. Ralph Hamor, *A True Discourse on the Present State of Virginia, and the Successe of Affaires there till the 18 of June, 1614* (London, 1615), 44.

38. Smith, *Generall Historie, CWCJS*, II, 213; Trudy Eden, "Food, Assimilation, and the Malleability of the Human Body in Early Virginia," in Janet Moore Lindman and Michele Lise Tarter, eds., *A Centre of Wonders: The Body in Early America* (Ithaca: Cornell University Press, 2001), 29–42, esp. 30. Food and political authority went hand in hand in Jamestown. See Lacombe, "Humanism, Food, and Authority," 670–71.

39. Percy, "A Trewe Relacyon," 265.

40. Francis Mangel, *Relation of the First Voyage and the Beginnings of the Jamestown Colony*, in Barbour, *Jamestown Voyages*, I, 151–57, quotation from 156. On Kendall's identity, see Philip L. Barbour, "Captain George Kendall: Mutineer or Intelligencer?" *Virginia Magazine of History and Biography* 70, no. 3 (July 1962): 297–313.

41. William M. Kelso, *Jamestown: The Buried Truth* (Charlottesville: University of Virginia Press, 2006), 187–88.

42. Percy, "A Trewe Relacyon," 269.

43. Ibid., 277.

44. Reverend Alexander Whitaker to Reverend William Crashaw, 9 August 1611, in Alexander Brown, ed., *The Genesis of the United States* (New York: Russell & Russell, 1898; repr., 1964), I, 498–99. Brown supposes that the sound the

Englishmen heard was that of an owl. It is also possible that the English had somehow imbibed jimsonweed (*Datura stramonium*), which can cause hallucinations. See Ivor Noël Hume, *The Virginia Adventure: Roanoke to James Towne: An Archaeological and Historical Odyssey* (New York: Alfred A. Knopf, 1994), 302. On English settlers' belief in magic and the supernatural, see Edward L. Bond, "Lived Religion in Colonial Virginia," in Paul Rasor and Richard E. Bond, eds., *From Jamestown to Jefferson: The Evolution of Religious Freedom in Virginia* (Charlottesville: University of Virginia Press, 2011), 43–73.

45. William M. Kelso, J. Eric Deetz, Seth W. Mallios, and Beverly A. Straube, eds., *Jamestown Rediscovery VII* (Richmond: Association for the Preservation of Virginia Antiquities, 2001), 19–20. Witch's bottles dating from the seventeenth to the nineteenth century have been found extensively in East Anglia; there the bottle of choice was not glass but stoneware and was generally filled with nails, bent pins, thorns, or other sharp objects. The intended victim then urinated into the bottle and buried it under a hearth or doorway. The witch would track her victim to the urine in the bottle and then be pricked by the pins. On the origins and permutations of witch repellants, see Keith Thomas, *Religion and the Decline of Magic: Studies in Popular Beliefs in Sixteenth and Seventeenth Century England* (London: Weidenfeld and Nicolson, 1971), 543–44, and Ralph Merrifield, *The Archaeology of Ritual and Magic* (New York: New Amsterdam Books, 1987), 163–75. Camilla Townsend also points out that the witch bottle would have protected the English from Indians entering the fort for legitimate purposes as well, such as trade and diplomacy. See Townsend, *Pocahontas*, 68, and Ivor Noël Hume, "Witchcraft and Evil Spirits," in *Something from the Cellar: More of This & That* (N.p.: Colonial Williamsburg Foundation, 2003), 91.

46. "The Second Charter to the Treasurer and Company, for Virginia, erecting them into a Corporation and Body Politic . . . 23 May 1609," in Hening, I, 97. Subsequent instructions from the Virginia Company to settlers insisted that conversion be attempted: "You shall, with all [pro]penses and diligence, endeavour the conversion of the natives to the knowledge and worship of the true god and their redeemer Christ Jesus, as the most pious and noble end of this plantacon." See "Instruccions Orders and constitucons to Sr Thomas Gates Knight Governor of Virginia, May 1609," *RVCL*, III, 14.

47. William Symonds, *A Sermon Preached at White-Chappel, in the presence of many, Honourable and Worshipfull the Adventurers and Planters for Virginia, 25 April 1609* (London, 1609), 9, 28, 54 (emphasis in the original).

48. Crashaw, *A Sermon*, F3r–[F4]v, I3r.

49. [Robert Gray], *A Good Speed to Virginia* (London, 1609), C2r, C3v, [D4]v. Gray's sermon also contained a well-developed justification for colonization based on English overpopulation, though he was at pains to refute arguments for completely dispossessing Indians solely on the grounds that the English had more people and therefore required more land. Company investor Robert Johnson echoed Gray's claims; see [Robert Johnson], *Nova Britannia Offering most excellent fruites by planting in Virginia* (London, 1609), C[1]v.

50. Crashaw, *A Sermon*, L[1]r.

51. Thomas Dale to the Earl of Salisbury, 17 August 1611, in Brown, *Genesis*, I, 506–7.

52. Virginia Council, "Instruccions Orders and constitucons," *RVCL*, III, 14.

53. William Strachey, *For the colony in Virginea Britannia: Lawes Divine Morall and Martiall, &c* (London, 1612), 12, 3, 16, [A3]v. The *Lawes* listed forty-nine capital crimes. Dale expanded the *Lawes* in 1611, and they were published under William Strachey's name in London in 1612.

54. Edward L. Bond, *Damned Souls in a Tobacco Colony: Religion in Seventeenth-Century Virginia* (Macon, GA: Mercer University Press, 2000), 88–90.

55. Crashaw, *A Sermon*, L[1]r.

56. Edmund S. Morgan has argued that the *Lawes* did not "even contemplate that the Indians would become a part of the English settlement." See Morgan, *American Slavery, American Freedom: The Ordeal of Colonial Virginia* (New York: Norton, 1975), 80. The text of the *Lawes*, and their context, strongly suggests the opposite interpretation, which I have adopted here.

57. Strachey, *Lawes*, 37, 20, 15, 99.

58. John Smith, *The Proceedings of the English Colony in Virginia*, CWCJS, I, 261, 263, 265; Smith, *Generall Historie*, CWCJS, II, 210, 212, 214; Rountree, *Pocahontas, Powhatan, Opechancanough*, 137.

59. Strachey, *Historie*, 61–62.

60. "A Letter of Sir Thomas Dale, from James Towne in Virginia," 18 June 1614, in Samuel Purchas, ed., *Hakluytus Posthumus or Purchas his Pilgrimes, Contayning a History of the World in Sea Voyages and Lande Travills by Englishmen and Others*, vol. XIX (Glasgow, 1906; repr. from 1625 ed.), 102.

61. Richard Hakluyt, *Virginia richly valued* (London, 1609), A[4]v.

62. Like all Algonkians who survived childhood, the woman most Americans know as Pocahontas had many names during her lifetime. Her birth name was Amonute; as a child "Pocahontas" was probably her nickname. At puberty or perhaps at her first marriage, Amonute took the name Metoaka. The English persisted in calling her Pocahontas, though, until she took her baptismal name Rebecca. I have chosen to refer to her by her adult Algonkian name, Metoaka.

63. Strachey, *Historie*, 72.

64. Ibid., 62. On the possibility of a child from Metoaka's first marriage to Kocoom, see Townsend, *Pocahontas*, 87, and Rountree, *Powhatan, Pocahontas, Opechancanough*, 143.

65. Hamor, *A True Discourse*, 6.

66. Ibid., 6–7.

67. Thomas Dale to D.M., 18 June 1614, republished in Hamor, *A True Discourse*, 55.

68. John Rolfe to Thomas Dale, undated manuscript [late 1613 or early 1614], Bodleian Class Ashmole MSS 830, Virginia Colonial Records Project Microfilm, X9 07244, 119v.

69. Symonds, *Sermon*, 35.

70. Rolfe to Dale, 119v.

71. Rolfe to Dale, 119r. The verse is Daniel 12:3, which Crashaw had also used in his 1609 sermon.

72. Rolfe to Dale, 119r. The manuscript version differs from the version published by Ralph Hamor as part of *A True Discourse* in 1615 in that the manuscript includes the gloss from Calvin. It is not clear why Hamor left Calvin's opinion out of his printed version. The biblical verse is 1 Corinthians 7:12-14. Rolfe had correctly cited Calvin. See John Calvin, *Institutes of the Christian Religion*, ed. John T. McNeill (Philadelphia: Westminster Press, 1960), II, 1329.

73. On this point, see in particular, Townsend, *Pocahontas*, 118-20.

74. John Smith noted in 1608 that "Powhatan hath three brethren [brothers], and two sisters, each of his bretheren succeeded other. For the Crowne, their heyres inherit not, but the first heyres of the Sisters, and so successively the weomens heires." Smith, *A True Relation*, *CWCJS*, I, 59, 61. Strachey noted also that "his kingdome descendeth not to his sonnes, nor Children, but first to his breathren ... and after their deceasse to his sisters ... and after them to the heires male and Feemale of the eldest sisters, but never to the heires of the male." Strachey, *Historie*, 77.

75. Rolfe to Dale, 118r. The verse is Psalm 118:23.

76. See "College for Indian Youth," in Edward Duffield Neill, ed., *Virginia Vetusta, During the Reign of James the First containing Letters and Documents Never Before Printed* (Albany, NY: Joel Munsell and Sons, 1885), 167.

77. *RVCL*, III, 116-17.

78. Samuel Purchas, *Purchas his Pilgrimage* (London, 1613), 631.

79. Purchas, *Purchas his Pilgrimes*, 118.

80. Townsend, *Pocahontas*, 137.

81. Purchas, *Purchas his Pilgrimes*, 118.

82. Warrant, 10 March 1616/17, FP, 72/1611.2. For more details on the award of money, see David R. Ransome, "Pocahontas and the Mission to the Indians," *Virginia Magazine of History and Biography* 99, no. 1 (January 1991): 81-94.

83. John Rolf[e] to Sir Edwin Sandys, 8 June 1617, *RVCL*, III, 70-72.

84. A Court for Virginia, 9 June 1619, *RVCL*, I, 226; A Court for Virginia, 14 June 1619, *RVCL*, I, 230, 231; A Court for Virginia, 24 June 1619, *RVCL*, I, 234; A Court for Virginia, 3 November 1619, *RVCL*, I, 256-57. For a useful narrative of events regarding the foundation of the college, see Robert Hunt Land, "Henrico and Its College," *William and Mary Quarterly*, 2nd ser., 18, no. 4 (October 1938): 453-98.

85. On the donations, see A Court for Virginia, 2 February 1619, *RVCL*, I, 307-8, and A Court for Virginia, 16 February 1619, *RVCL*, I, 310-11. Edward Waterhouse wrote that Dust and Ashes' donation was £550 in gold; Waterhouse, *A Declaration of the State of the Colony and Affaires in Virginia* ... (London, 1622), 52. Nicholas Ferrar's bequest was recorded at A Court for Virginia, 17 May 1620, *RVCL*, I, 354. The books were donated at A Court for Virginia, 15 November 1620, *RVCL*, I, 421-22; Waterhouse, *A Declaration*, 53. Other donors gave

money for church buildings and furnishings. In 1619 Mary Robinson gave two hundred pounds to build a church in Virginia, and two anonymous donors gave Communion plates, cups, "a linnen damaske Table-Cloth," and other rich objects for churches and the college. See the list in Waterhouse, *A Declaration*, 51.

86. Dust and Ashes to Sir Edwin Sandys, 2 February 1620/21, *RVCL*, I, 307–8; Dust and Ashes to the Company, 28 January 1621/22, *RVCL*, I, 585–88. The name "Dust and Ashes" might refer to Job's repentence: Job 42:6.

87. *RVCL*, I, 588.

88. John Rolf[e] to Edwin Sandys, 8 June 1617, *RVCL*, III, 71.

89. Sir George Yeardley to Sir Edwin Sandys, 1619, *RVCL*, III, 128.

90. Court for Virginia, 2 March 1619, *RVCL*, I, 319.

91. George Thorpe to Sir Edwin Sandys, 15 and 16 May 1621, *RVCL*, III, 446–47.

92. Council of Virginia to Virginia Company of London, January 1621/22, *RVCL*, III, 584.

93. Council of Virginia to Virginia Company of London, 20 January 1622/23, *RVCL*, IV, 11.

94. Population and Livestock Census, March 1619/20, FP, 159/1597a; William Thorndale, "The Virginia Census of 1619," *Magazine of Virginia Genealogy* 33 (1995): 155–70; Martha W. McCartney, "An Early Virginia Census Reprised," *Quarterly Bulletin of the Virginia Archaeological Society* 54 (1999): 178–96.

95. Population and Livestock Census, March 1619/20, FP, 159/1597a.

96. John Rolfe to Edwin Sandys, January 1619/1620, *RVCL*, III, 243. The earliest date for enslaved Africans in Virginia is a controversial topic, but I share Michael J. Guasco's position on the matter. See Guasco, " 'Free from the Tyrannous Spanyard': Englishmen and Africans in Spain's Atlantic World," *Slavery and Abolition* 29, no. 1 (March 2008): 1–22, 15fn10.

97. Waterhouse, *A Declaration*, 17.

98. Ibid., 21–22, 12–13, 21–26.

99. Ibid., 33, 34, 24.

100. Waterhouse, *A Declaration*, 14.

101. A Council and Assembly for Virginia, Laws and Orders, 5 March 1623/24, *RVCL*, IV, 580–85.

102. Council in Virginia to the Virginia Company of London, 30 January 1623/24, *RVCL*, IV, 450.

103. See Rebecca Anne Goetz, "Indian Enslavement and the Anglo-French Conquest of St. Christopher," unpublished seminar paper, 19 May 2011.

104. [John White], *The Planters' Plea* (London, 1630), 53–57; Michael J. Guasco, "Settling with Slavery: Human Bondage in the Early Anglo-Atlantic World," in Robert Appelbaum and John Wood Sweet, eds., *Envisioning an English Empire: Jamestown and the Making of the North Atlantic World* (Philadelphia: University of Pennsylvania Press, 2005), 252.

105. A Court Held for Virginia, 7 May 1623, *RVCL*, II, 395.

106. Ibid., 397.

CHAPTER THREE: *Faith in the Blood*

1. Robert Beverly, *The History and Present State of Virginia*, ed. Louis B. Wright (Chapel Hill: University of North Carolina Press, 1947), 31, 39–44, quotations from 31 and 41–42 (emphasis in original). For Smith's original letter, see John Smith, *Generall Historie, CWCJS*, II, 259–60.

2. Beverly, *History*, 44 (emphasis in original).

3. Students of the origin of race as a concept have long understood that European ideas about lineage were involved in the process. Though seventeenth-century Europeans did not have a biological understanding of how characteristics were (and were not) passed from generation to generation, their legal systems recognized legitimacy as the way property and privilege passed from parents to children. See Joyce E. Chaplin, "Race," in David Armitage and Michael J. Braddick, eds., *The British Atlantic World, 1500–1800* (Basingstoke: Palgrave Macmillan, 2002),154–72, but esp. 155–58; Ivan Hannaford, *Race: The History of an Idea in the West* (Baltimore: Johns Hopkins University Press, 1996), 125–26. Hannaford notes the flexibility of a concept like "lineage" but shows that, in the early modern period, purity of blood became more important for religious affiliation. Keith Thomas points out that English people had a well-developed sense of lineage and of the heritability and desirability of certain characteristics in animals; see Thomas, *Man and the Natural World: Changing Attitudes in England, 1500–1800* (London: Allen Lane, 1983), 58–62.

4. John Rolfe to Thomas Dale, undated manuscript [late 1613 or early 1614], Bodleian Class Ashmole MSS 830, Virginia Colonial Records Project Microfilm, X9 07244, 119r.

5. Kathleen M. Brown, *Good Wives, Nasty Wenches, and Anxious Patriarchs: Gender, Race, and Power in Colonial Virginia* (Chapel Hill: University of North Carolina Press, 1996), 198–99.

6. Kathleen Brown (ibid.) traces the complex relationship among sex, gender, reproduction, and race; see also Kirsten Fischer, *Suspect Relations: Sex, Race, and Resistance in Colonial North Carolina* (Ithaca: Cornell University Press, 2002), and Anthony Fletcher, *Gender, Sex, and Subordination in England, 1500–1800* (New Haven: Yale University Press, 1995). For marriage as a vital part of the colonial project, see Ann Marie Plane, *Colonial Intimacies: Indian Marriage in Early New England* (Ithaca: Cornell University Press, 2000).

7. Thomas Blake, *The Birth Priviledge, or, Covenant-Holinesse of Beleevers and their Issue in the time of the Gospel Together With the Right of Infants to Baptisme* (London, 1644), 5–6, 13. On Blake, see *Dictionary of National Biography Online*, s.v. "Blake, Thomas" (by William Lamont). See also Holly Brewer, *By Birth or Consent: Children, Law, and the Anglo-American Revolution in Authority* (Chapel Hill: University of North Carolina Press, 2005), 70–74.

8. Increase Mather, *Pray for the Rising Generation: A Sermon Wherein Godly Parents are Encouraged to Pray and Believe for their Children . . .* (Cambridge, 1678), 12.

9. Richard Baxter, *The catechizing of families a teacher of housholders how to teach their housholds: useful also to school-masters and tutors of youth: for those that are past the common small chatechisms, and would grow to a more rooted faith, and to the fuller understanding of all that is commonly needful to a safe, holy comfortable and profitable life* (London, 1683), 407.

10. William Strachey, *The Historie of Travell into Virginia Britania* (1612), ed. Louis B. Wright and Virginia Freund (London: Hakluyt Society, 1953), 112–13.

11. Brown, *Good Wives*, 42–74.

12. Strachey, *Historie*, 113, 116.

13. John Smith, *A Map of Virginia, CWCJS*, I, 174; Strachey noted matrilinity among the Indians as well. Strachey, *Historie*, 77.

14. Letter of Don Pedro de Zúñiga, in Alexander Brown, ed., *The Genesis of the United States* (Boston: Houghton, Mifflin, 1890), II, 632–33.

15. On the archaeological evidence, see Judith Reynolds, "Marriage between the English and the Indians in Seventeenth-Century Virginia," *Quarterly Bulletin of the Archaeological Society of Virginia* 17, no. 2 (December 1962): 19–25; William M. Kelso, *Jamestown: The Buried Truth* (Charlottesville: University of Virginia Press, 2006), 111–14. Any children born to Indian women and fathered by English men likely would have remained with their mothers. No English chroniclers wrote of many Indian women at Jamestown, which some historians have used to dismiss Zúñiga's claims. However, there would have been little incentive for settlers to advertise their vulnerability and reliance on Indian women to Virginia Company leaders in London, which might bridge the gap between the English records' silence on the subject and the archaeological evidence suggesting the presence of Indian men and women. For an opposing view, see Richard Godbeer, *The Sexual Revolution in Early America* (Baltimore: Johns Hopkins University Press, 2002), 160–61.

16. William Strachey, *For the colony in Virginea Britannia: Lawes Divine Morall and Martiall, &c* (London, 1612), B3r. The same section also mandated the death penalty for sodomy and adultery.

17. *Oxford English Dictionary 3rd Edition Online*, s.v. "maid."

18. *RVCL*, I, 485, 496; on the conversion, naming, and provisioning of the women, see David R. Ransome, "Pocahontas and the Mission to the Indians," *Virginia Magazine of History and Biography* 99, no. 1 (January 1991): 88–90.

19. Virginia Bernhard, *Slaves and Slaveholders in Bermuda, 1616-1782* (Columbia: University of Missouri Press, 1999), 11.

20. 3 November 1619, *RVCL*, I, 256.

21. "A Note of the Shipping, Men, and Provisions, Sent to Virginia," 7 July 1620, *RVCL*, III, 115; "His Majesties Council for Virginia," 22 June 1620, 313; "A Court," 7 July 1620, *RVCL*, I, 391.

22. Company to the Governor and Council of Virginia, 11 September 1621, *RVCL*, III, 505; "A Note of the Shipping, Men, and Provisions Sent and Provided for Virginia," May 1622, *RVCL*, III, 640.

23. "John Pory's Report," July–August 1619, *RVCL*, III, 173–74; "Charges against Sir Thomas Smyth," April 1623, *RVCL*, IV, 82; "Law against Implied Contract of Marriage," 24 June 1624, *RVCL*, IV, 487; "Notes Taken from the Letters Which Came from Virginia," 19 June 1623, *RVCL*, IV, 232.

24. For a genealogy of the Bass family (the only record of this marriage), see Albert D. Bell, *Bass Families of the South* (Rocky Mount, NC: privately printed, 1961), 12. See also Helen C. Rountree and E. Randolph Turner III, *Before and After Jamestown: Virginia's Powhatans and Their Predecessors* (Gainesville: University Press of Florida, 2002), 152, for a digital image of the page describing the marriage. The descendants of John and Keziah Bass constitute most of the present day Nansemond tribe in Virginia; see Jay Hansford C. Vest, "From Nansemond to Monacan: The Legacy of the Pochick-Nansemond among the Bear Mountain Monacan," *American Indian Quarterly* 27, nos. 3–4 (Summer–Fall 2003): 781–806, esp. 786–89.

25. On Mary Kittomaquund, see Lois Green Carr, *Margaret Brent: A Brief History*, Maryland State Archives, www.msa.md.gov/msa/speccol/sc3500/sc3520/002100/002177/html/mbrent2.html.

26. Martin Ingram, *Church Courts, Sex, and Marriage in England, 1570–1640* (Cambridge: Cambridge University Press, 1987), 3.

27. "Proceedings of the Virginia Assembly, 1619," in Lyon Gardiner Tyler, ed., *Narratives of Early Virginia, 1606–1625* (New York: Barnes and Noble, 1907), 271–72.

28. Brown, *Good Wives*, 189–90.

29. Susie M. Ames, ed., *County Court Records of Accomack-Northampton, Virginia, 1632–1640* (Washington, DC: American Historical Association Publications, 1954), 26 November 1638, 138; 23 September 1639, 151.

30. Susie M. Ames, ed., *County Court Records of Accomack-Northampton, Virginia, 1641–1645* (Charlottesville: University Press of Virginia, 1973), 13 September 1641, 117.

31. NCCR, III, 11 November 1646, fol. 103.

32. Brown, *Good Wives*, 190.

33. Hening, I, 146.

34. *MCGC*, 17 October 1640, 477. Robert Sweat's partner might have been Margaret Cornish, a free black woman from Surry County he might have later married. The available records are unclear about the substance of the connection between Sweat and Cornish.

35. Leeward Islands MSS, National Archives at Kew CO 154/17/55–56.

36. Bernhard, *Slaves and Slaveholders*, 52–53.

37. Lefroy, II, 103.

38. NCCR, III, November 1646, fol. 48.

39. NCCR, III, February 1646/47, fol. 66.

40. *Oxford English Dictionary 3rd Edition Online*, s.v. "pipkin."

41. NCCR, III, February 1646/47, fol. 62.

42. NCCR, III, February 1646/47, fol. 66.

43. NCCR, III, February 1646/47, fol. 62.

44. *AM*, IV, 2 March 1643/44, 258. (No outcome was recorded in the case.)

45. NCCR, V, 7 May 1655, fol. 134.

46. Will Watts and Mary, in James Horn, *Adapting to a New World: English Society in the Seventeenth-Century Chesapeake* (Chapel Hill: University of North Carolina Press, 1994), 173.

47. NCCR, VII, 4 November 1654, fol. 21.

48. YCCR, III, 26 October 1657, fol. 2.

49. YCCR, III, 10 March 1661/62, fol. 151; YCCR, III, 10 March 1661/62, fol. 160.

50. YCCR, III, 26 August 1661, fol. 125.

51. Hening, II, 170.

52. YCCR, III, 25 August 1662, fol. 169.

53. Lefroy, II, 190.

54. Lefroy, II, 314–15.

55. *AM*, I, September 1664, 527, 533–34. The only extant Maryland statute punishing fornication prior to the Glorious Revolution does not mention interracial couples. It prescribed that "offenders shall be publickly whipped or otherwise pay such fine to some publique use" and that adulterers should have a "more painfull whipping or grevious fine," but the only interracial interactions the Maryland Council was concerned about were marital. See *AM*, I, March 1638/39, 53.

56. YCCR, III–VI.

57. YCCR, VI, 25 June 1683, fol. 498; YCCR, VI, 24 October 1682, fol. 432.

58. ACCR, IX, January 1671/72, fol. 52. John Pagan also notes that the case's results benefited Lang's master, since he gained both Lang's labor for three years and her infant son's labor until he reached the age of twenty-four. See John Ruston Pagan, *Anne Orthwood's Bastard: Sex and Law in Early Virginia* (New York: Oxford University Press, 2003), 108–9.

59. Hening, III, 86–88.

60. YCCR, X, 24 August 1694, fols. 28–29.

61. Hening, III, 87.

62. *LJCCV*, I, 11 May 1699, 262; *JHB*, 1695–96, 1686–97, 1698, 1699, 1700–1702, 8 May 1699, 148.

63. ACCR, X, 5 December 1704, fol. 37a.

64. Hening, III, 447–50, 453–54.

65. On *Mungo Ingles v. Rachell Wood*, see YCCR, XIII, 24 June 1707, fol. 72; YCCR, XIII, 24 February 1707/8, fol. 115; YCCR, XIII, 24 May 1708, fol. 137; YCCR, XIII, 24 May 1709, fol. 216; YCCR, XIII, 24 June 1709, fol. 228; YCCR, XIII, 25 July 1709, fol. 235; YCCR, XIII, 24 January 1709/10, fol. 263. On Rebecca Stephens, the only woman the records show as conclusively sold under the 1705 law in York County between 1705 and 1710, see YCCR, XIII, 26 September 1706, fol. 19. She was ordered sold for "15£ current money of Va for the use of the s[ai]d parish according to the late law in that case made & provided

entituled an act concerning servants & slaves." See also a similar case in Acomack County, which carried on over the course of four years and ended only when the English servant woman, Jane Salmond, disappeared. ACCR, IX, 4 February 1701/2, fol. 126a. Salmond could not be found at that point but a year later pled guilty to fornication and bastardy, alleging that "Peter Negro" was the father of her child. She was sentenced to be sold according to the terms of the 1691 law. ACCR, IX, 2 March 1702/3, fol. 140a; ACCR, X, 4 October 1704, fol. 35a. Jane Salmond did have a problem with recidivism, though. In 1705 her master Francis Makemie reported the birth of another mulatto child, ACCR, IX, 5 December 1705, fol. 55. The case continued without resolution through two more court sessions in 1706, ACCR, X, 2 April 1706, fol. 66; ACCR, X, 5 June 1706, fol. 72. In 1708 Jane Salmond had yet another mulatto child, ACCR, X, 3 February 1707/8, fol. 107a; ACCR, X, 4 May 1708. Her last appearance in the county court records indicates that she fled the county, ACCR, X, 2 July 1708, fol. 118. Like Rachell Wood, Jane Salmond should have been legally sold but managed to avoid this fate not through legal machinations but by running away. What happened to Peter Negro and her children went unrecorded in the court records.

66. ACCR, X, 3 June 1707, fol. 94; ACCR, X, 5 May 1708, fol. 114a; ACCR, X, 10 October 1708, fol. 135.

CHAPTER FOUR: *Baptism and the Birth of Race*

1. Hening, II, 260 (emphasis in original).

2. Treatments of the 1667 law generally integrate it into a suite of other laws enacted between 1660 and 1705. Historians' treatment of the baptism law thus fits into an existing narrative about the parallel developments of slavery and freedom, but this approach to the 1667 law subsumes it into a context that distorts its unique place in the history of Christianity and in the construction of race. Oscar Handlin and Mary Handlin, "Origins of the Southern Labor System," *William and Mary Quarterly*, 3rd ser., 7, no. 2 (April 1950): 211–12. Edmund Morgan argued in 1975 that the 1667 law seemed to encourage slave owners to instruct their slaves in Christianity but actually removed all incentive for slaves to express interest in English religion. See Edmund S. Morgan, *American Slavery, American Freedom: The Ordeal of Colonial Virginia* (New York: Norton, 1975), 331–32. Other historians have also discussed the baptism law in this context, discussing it as part of the problem of slavery and freedom, and attributing its passage to fears generated among Virginia's gentry about changing demographic patterns: in other words, as African slaves became a greater percentage of the population, the English imagined the threat of more free, baptized blacks. Warren M. Billings, "The Cases of Fernando and Elizabeth Key: A Note on the Status of Blacks in Seventeenth-Century Virginia," *William and Mary Quarterly*, 3rd ser., 30, no. 3 (July 1973): 467–74; Edward L. Bond, *Damned Souls in a Tobacco Colony: Religion in Seventeenth-Century Virginia* (Macon, GA: Mercer University Press, 2000), 196–203. This demographic explanation, though, is unconvincing, because the real explosion of African slaves did not occur until

after 1680; in 1667 there were only about two thousand Africans and as many as thirty-eight thousand English settlers in Virginia. When Anglo-Virginians shut the door on Christian baptism as a route to freedom, they still lived in a society with slaves, not a slave society fully dependent on bondage for economic stability, rendering the historical argument that the English were threatened by legions of free Christian Africans premature and irrelevant to the circumstances in 1667. Lorena Walsh notes that Virginia's lawmakers were also Virginia's top planters and slave owners, and as such were invested in the legal institutionalization of slavery from around the mid-1630s. Walsh, *Motives of Honor, Pleasure, and Profit: Plantation Management in the Colonial Chesapeake, 1607-1763* (Chapel Hill: University of North Carolina Press, 2010), 141–42. See also John C. Coombs, "Building 'the Machine': The Development of Slavery and Slave Society in Early Colonial Virginia" (Ph.D. diss., College of William and Mary, 2004), and his "The Phases of Conversion: A New Chronology for the Rise of Slavery in Early Virginia," *William and Mary Quarterly*, 3rd ser., 68, no. 3 (July 2011): 332–60.

3. John D. Krugler, *English and Catholic: The Lords Baltimore in the Seventeenth Century* (Baltimore: Johns Hopkins University Press, 2004), 13. Krugler goes on to argue that the fact that the Lords Baltimore, the English Catholic founders of Maryland, were able to openly profess their Catholicism and still be in the service of the crown indicates that the Protestant English suspicion of Catholics was not absolute. Nevertheless, it is fair to say that Catholics with less wealth and influence than the Calvert family would not have had an easy time of it.

4. David Cressy, *Birth, Marriage, and Death: Ritual, Religion, and the Life-Cycle in Tudor and Stuart England* (New York: Oxford University Press, 1997), 101.

5. 27th Article of the Faith, *Book of Common Prayer* (London, 1687), n.p.

6. Cressy, *Birth*, 108.

7. Hening, II, 165–66.

8. NCCR, IX, 6 September 1665, fol. 11.

9. SCCR, IV, 7 January 1690/91, fols. 776–77.

10. SCCR, III, 5 November 1672, fol. 14.

11. Susie Ames, ed., *County Court Records of Accomack-Northampton, Virginia, 1632-1640* (Washington, DC: American Historical Association Publications, 1954), 28 April 1639, 144.

12. YCCR, II, 25 July 1646, fol. 160.

13. For John Foster, see YCCR, II, 24 August 1648, fol. 400; for Elizabeth Lang, see NCCR, X, 28 January 1677/78, fol. 225; for Hannah Harlow, see NCCR, X, 28 January 1677/78, fols. 225–26; for Jarrett and Anne Hawthorne, see YCCR, V, 26 February 1671/72, fol. 8.

14. Lorena Walsh first noted this practice in Maryland. Walsh, "'Till Death Do Us Part': Marriage and Family in Seventeenth-Century Maryland," in Thad W.

Tate and David L. Ammerman, eds., *The Chesapeake in the Seventeenth Century: Essays on Anglo-American Society* (New York: Norton, 1979), 147.

15. William P. Palmer, ed., *Calendar of Virginia State Papers and Other Manuscripts*, 11 vols. (New York: Kraus Reprint Corporation, 1875–93; repr., 1968), I, 31.

16. Annie Lash Jester and Martha Woodroof Hiden, eds. (1956; 2nd ed., 1964), Virginia M. Meyer and John Frederick Dorman, eds. (3rd ed., 1987), John Frederick Dorman, ed. (4th ed., 2004), *Adventurers of Purse and Person in Virginia, 1607–1624/25* (Baltimore: Genealogical Publishing Company, 2004), 51, 62.

17. *RCVL*, III, 117.

18. *MCGC*, 31 March 1641, 477–78.

19. Hening, I, 395.

20. Hening, I, 455–56.

21. Lefroy, II, 54–55. In 1661 ministers were ordered to continue catechizing these Indians and "all other the Negroes, and to endeavour to bring them to the knowledge of the true God and the way of Salvation by Je: Christ." Lefroy, II, 154–55.

22. Francis Yeardley to John Ferrar, 8 May 1654, in Alexander S. Salley Jr., ed., *Narratives of Early Carolina, 1650–1708* (New York: Charles Scribner's Sons, 1911), 26, 28. See also Bond, *Damned Souls*, 170.

23. ACCR, II, 1, 6 August 1667, fols. 33b and 35a; 25 October 1667, fol. 35a; 25 October 1667, fols. 40b–41a; 17 December 1667, fols. 44a–44b. See also 17 August 1668, fol. 62b, for another case that looks similar to the 1667 renamings.

24. See, for example, ACCR, VII, 1 January 1683/84, fol. 28a; 6 August 1684, fol. 47; 2 December 1684, fol. 53a.

25. "Angelo a Negro Woman in the *Treasuror*" (no date), "Mary a Negro Woman in the *Margrett & John* 1622," and "John Pedro a Negar aged 30 in the *Swan* 1623," in *Adventurers of Purse and Person in Virginia, 1607–1624/25*, 31, 48, 64.

26. Ibid., 51.

27. Ira Berlin, *Many Thousands Gone: The First Two Centuries of Slavery in North America* (Cambridge, MA: Belknap Press of Harvard University Press, 1998), 17. Berlin has called people like Antoney and Isabell "Atlantic Creoles." James W. Sweet agrees that those Africans in Virginia before 1630 had been exposed to Christianity and that allowed them to be more fully "integrated into the day-to-day affairs of English colonial life," but he questions the validity of the category of Atlantic Creoles. Sweet, "African Identity and Slave Resistance in the Portuguese Atlantic," in Peter C. Mancall, ed., *The Atlantic World and Virginia, 1550–1624* (Chapel Hill: University of North Carolina Press, 2007), 246–47.

28. *MCGC*, November 1624, 33.

29. On the early African population of Virginia, see Engel Sluiter, "New Light on the '20. and Odd Negroes' Arriving in Virginia, August 1619," *William and Mary Quarterly*, 3rd ser., 54, no. 2 (April 1997): 395–98; John Thornton, "The

African Experience of the '20. and Odd Negroes' Arriving in Virginia in 1619," *William and Mary Quarterly*, 3rd ser., 55, no. 3 (July 1998): 421–34.

30. T. H. Breen and Stephen Innes, *"Myne Owne Ground": Race and Freedom on Virginia's Eastern Shore, 1640–1676* (New York: Oxford University Press, 1980), 8–10; Berlin, *Many Thousands Gone*, 29–31.

31. NCCR, IX, 29 September 1673, fols. 220–21.

32. NCCR, X, 11 March 1678/79, fol. 247.

33. NCCR, III, 22 March 1644/45, fol. 82.

34. *Dictionary of Virginia Biography*, IV, s.v. "Emanuel Driggus" (by Rebecca A. Goetz, forthcoming).

35. Breen and Innes, *Myne Owne Ground*, 68.

36. Richard Ligon, *A True & Exact History of the Island of Barbados* (London, 1657), 50, 54, 82; Katharine Gerbner, "The Ultimate Sin: Christianising Slaves in Barbados in the Seventeenth Century," *Slavery and Abolition* 31, no. 1 (March 2010): 57–73.

37. William Golding, *Servants on Horse-back, or, A free-people bestrided in their persons and liberties, by worthlesse men being a representation of the dejected state of the inhabitants of Summer Islands . . .* (London, 1648), 13.

38. *AM*, I, 526, September 1664.

39. *AM*, II, March–April 1670/71, 272.

40. Hening, II, 260.

41. *MCGC*, 31 March 1641, 477.

42. YCCR, III, 26 January 1657/58, fol. 16.

43. Warren M. Billings, ed., *The Old Dominion in the Seventeenth Century: A Documentary History of Virginia* (Chapel Hill: University of North Carolina Press, 1975), 165–69. In 1654 Virginia did not yet have a law that explicitly made slave status hereditary through maternal lines (that law passed in 1662). Thus the question of Elizabeth Key's parentage would have been critical to the outcome.

44. Petition of William Whittacre to the Honourable Sir Wm. Berkeley Kinght Governor &c. And the Honourable Council of Virginia, ca. 24 October 1666, Randolph MSS, Virginia Historical Society. For a printed version of the petition, see *BP*, 297–98.

45. SCCR, I, 2 July 1659, fol. 137.

46. Hening, II, 155. Surry County, writes Kevin Kelly, "was tobacco's child." See Kelly, "Economic and Social Development of Seventeenth-Century Surry County, Virginia" (Ph.D. diss., University of Washington, 1972), 210.

47. Lower Norfolk County Order Book, 1666–75, fol. 17.

48. Hening, II, 260. I am grateful to Chris Morris for suggesting that "more carefully" as used here might be plausibly interpreted to mean "more discerningly."

49. *Oxford English Dictionary 3rd Edition online*, s.v. "capability."

50. "Instructions for the Council of Foreign Plantations, 1 December 1660," in *BP*, 142–44. Though similar instructions had been drawn up during the Com-

monwealth, the clause relating to spreading Christianity and working for the conversion of Africans and Indians was added in the 1660 version quoted in the text. Charles McLean Andrews, *British Committees, Commissions, and Councils of Trade and Plantations, 1622–1675* (Baltimore: Johns Hopkins Press, 1908), 70.

51. From the Council for Foreign Plantations, 17 February 1660/61, *BP*, 149.

52. Bodleian Library Class Tanner MSS 447, Virginia Colonial Records Project, reel 635. The VCRP record dates this document to 1619, but after examining the original I have concluded that this is almost certainly a Restoration-era document, probably from the early 1660s.

53. John Evelyn, *The Diary of John Evelyn in three volumes*, ed. Austin Dobson (London: Macmillan, 1906), III, 178. I am grateful to Noah McCormack for noting Evelyn's reference to the baptism controversy. James's later plea for a "magna Charta for Conscience" included an interesting line suggesting royal opposition to any kind of persecution based on skin color: "[S]uppose said he [James II] there should be a law made that all black men should be imprisoned, twould be unreasonable and we had as little reason to quarell with other men for being of different opinions as for being of different Complexions." While it is not clear that James was here referring to African people as opposed to dark-complected Englishmen, and it is also not clear that this remark was a condemnation of slavery, that James tied liberty of conscience to physical differences so starkly is deeply interesting and suggests his earlier condemnation of planters was genuine. Scott Sowerby, "Of Different Complexions: Religious Diversity and National Identity in James II's Toleration Campaign," *English Historical Review* 124, no. 506 (February 2009): 29–52, quotation from 32.

54. Morgan Godwyn, *A Supplement to the Negro's and Indians Advocate* (London, 1681), 10.

55. Morgan Godwyn, *The Negro's and Indians Advocate, Suing for their Admission into the Church* (London, 1680), 38.

56. Morgan Godwyn, "A Brief Account of Religion, in the Plantations . . . ," in Francis Brokesby, *Some Proposals towards Propagating of the Gospel in Our American Plantations* (London, 1708), 3. (Godwyn's piece was probably written, along with his other missives, in the early 1680s.) For more on Godwyn's biography, see Alden T. Vaughan, "Slaveholders' 'Hellish Principles': A Seventeenth-Century Critique," in *Roots of American Racism: Essays on the Colonial Experience* (Oxford: Oxford University Press, 1995), 55–81. Charles Irons argues that Godwyn "inadvertently helped engender a powerful proslavery argument" in his pamphlets. While later proslavery Christians would make arguments similar to Godwyn's regarding the docile behavior of enslaved Christians, it is important to note that Godwyn's quarrel was not with slavery per se; for him the moral outrage was denying access to Christianity. There were no members of the Church of England or any other religious group who were advancing antislavery or abolitionist arguments in the seventeenth century. Charles F. Irons, *The Origins of*

Proslavery Christianity: White and Black Evangelicals in Colonial and Antebellum Virginia (Chapel Hill: University of North Carolina Press, 2008), 29.

57. Godwyn, *Negro's and Indians Advocate*, 53, 15.

58. Vaughan writes, "It is barely possible that Godwyn's insistence on baptizing blacks spurred the Virginia legislature to clarify the heretofore uncertain relationship between slavery and Christianity." Vaughan, "Slaveholders' 'Hellish Principles,'" 59.

59. Godwyn, *Negro's and Indians Advocate*, 107.

60. Quoted in Vaughan, "Slaveholders' 'Hellish Principles,'" 74. Vaughan notes that after 1673, Baxter's new editions of the *Christian Directory* ceased to mention slavery.

61. Philotheos Physiologus [Thomas Tryon], *Friendly Advice to the Gentlemen-planters of the East and West Indies* (London, 1684), 122–39. For more on Tryon's position and arguments, see David Brion Davis, *The Problem of Slavery in Western Culture* (New York: Oxford University Press, 1966), 371–74; *Oxford Dictionary of National Biography*, s.v. "Thomas Tryon."

62. Tryon, *Friendly Advice*, 115–16.

63. YCCR, X, 6 April 1695 fol. 138; YCCR, X, 24 May 1695, fol. 153.

64. YCCR, VI, 24 June 1683, fol. 498; YCCR, XII, 24 November 1702, fol. 67; YCCR, XII, 24 February 1703/4, fol. 181.

65. YCCR, XII, 24 May 1703, fol. 136.

66. YCCR, XIII, 25 February 1706/7, fol. 51.

67. YCCR, XI, 24 December 1700, fols. 401–2.

68. *Ancient Journals of the House of Assembly of Bermuda* (Hamilton, Bermuda: G. V. Lee, 1890), IV, 16, 18.

69. Hening, III, 447–48.

CHAPTER FIVE: *Becoming Christian, Becoming White*

1. The Governor and Council of Virginia to Charles II and the Privy Council, ca. 24 June 1667, *BP*, 321–22.

2. Sir Robert Filmer, *Patriarcha, or the Natural Power of Kings* (New York: Hafner Publishing Company, 1947 [1653]), esp. 251–63. On the Filmerian family and state as a method for understanding the early American family, see Mary Beth Norton, *Founding Mothers and Fathers: Gendered Power and the Forming of American Society* (New York: Knopf, 1996), esp. 8–10.

3. Terri L. Snyder, *Brabbling Women: Disorderly Speech and the Law in Early Virginia* (Ithaca: Cornell University Press, 2003), 93–94. Brown argues that female servants and slaves were in more danger of beatings from their mistresses than their masters, suggesting a gendered component to household violence. Kathleen M. Brown, *Good Wives, Nasty Wenches, and Anxious Patriarchs: Gender, Race, and Power in Colonial Virginia* (Chapel Hill: University of North Carolina Press, 1996), 305–6. Mary Beth Norton argues that servants and other dependents in the Chesapeake were more likely to have to sue in civil courts for protection from dangerously abusive household situations; the Chesapeake and

the Caribbean had fewer laws regulating family governance than did New England. Virginia laws were more likely to confuse the issue than to protect servants and slaves. See Norton, *Founding Mothers and Fathers*, 132–33.

4. Hening, I, 254–55.

5. Hening, I, 440.

6. Hening, II, 117–18.

7. Hening, II, 118.

8. Snyder, *Brabbling Women*, 97.

9. Michael Dalton, *The Countrey Justice, Containing the Practice of the Justices of the Peace Out of Their Sessions* (London, 1661), 86, 88, 95. There were several editions of *The Countrey Justice* between 1619 and 1697. Dalton quoted Deuteronomy 24:14 "Thou shalt not oppress an hired servant, that is needy and poor" but left out the part of the verse about the fair treatment of "strangers." The guidelines did not apply to enslaved people.

10. ACCR, III, 3 March 1672/73, fols. 173–74.

11. YCCR, III, 2 May 1661 (recorded 26 August 1661), fol. 125; YCCR, III, 25 June 1661, fol. 121.

12. YCCR, III, 2 July 1661, fol. 123.

13. Ibid. Mary Hawthorne reported that she found the beating excessive and possibly life threatening. See YCCR, III, 2 July 1661, fol. 123.

14. YCCR, III, 2 July 1661, fol. 124. (Rawlins had not been living in the Russell household since Balgrave's first examination; the further bruising along her midriff and on her breast might have been indicative of some internal bleeding that did not manifest itself immediately.)

15. YCCR, III, 25 June 1661, fol. 121.

16. Snyder, *Brabbling Women*, 104.

17. YCCR, VI, 26 March 1683, fol. 479; YCCR,VI, 24 April 1683, fols. 493–94. John Wright was later accused of forcing his servants to work on the Sabbath, for which he was fined five hundred pounds of tobacco. YCCR, VI, 24 September 1684, fol. 602. Neglect of English indentured servants could also attract the court's attention: in 1689 William Mansfield's servant Mary Tabb was removed from his household when it became clear that she was lame and that Mansfield had not done anything to care for her or to affect her cure. YCCR, VIII, 24 September 1689, fol. 312.

18. YCCR, III, 24 October 1662, fol. 176.

19. Ibid. In a similar case before the York County Court a few years later, Hannah Langley and Andrew Hill were each sentenced to an additional year of service for "offering violence" to their mistress, Anne Batten. YCCR, IV, 26 February 1665/66. fol. 52. Gender seems not to have played a role in deciding the punishment of servants; in 1678/79 Mary Barrow tried to beat her mistress with a stick, which incurred the same penalty as John Shelton had received more than a decade before—an additional year of service. YCCR, VI, 24 February 1678/79, fol. 77.

20. YCCR, VI, 24 January 1682/83, fol. 455.

21. YCCR, III, 24 January 1658/59, fol. 46.

22. YCCR, III, Order regarding the coroner's inquest regarding the suicide of Daniel Tucker's unnamed servant, 21 December 1657, fol. 9; YCCR, III, Report of the jury of inquest regarding the suicide of William Bennett, 30 April 1658, fol. 25; YCCR, III, Report of the jury of inquest regarding the suicide of William Ayres (also a servant of Daniel Tucker), 24 October 1659, fol. 67; YCCR, III, Report of the jury of inquest regarding the suicide of Margaret Wynn, 24 October 1659, fol. 67; YCCR, III, Report of the jury of inquest regarding the suicide of Robert Peirson, 24 February 1659/60, fol. 74. Peirson hanged himself "with one bridle Reyne." YCCR, III, Report of the jury of inquest regarding the suicide of Mary Woddell, 24 July 1660, fol. 88; YCCR, III, Report of the jury of inquest regarding the suicide of Walter Catford, 25 June 1661, fols. 121-24. (Catford does not appear to have been an indentured servant.) YCCR, III, Order regarding the disposition of the estate of Ralph Heaton "who lately drowned himself," 31 October 1661, fol. 133. (Heaton does not appear to have been an indentured servant.) YCCR, III, Report of the jury of inquest regarding the suicide of Ursula Falls, 31 October 1661, fol. 135.

23. Pardon for Katherine Pannell, 17 October 1660, *BP*, 136, quotation from 136fn2.

24. YCCR, III, January 25, 1662/63, fols. 149, 150-51; Hening, II, 195, 204; *MCGC*, 511; Brown, *Good Wives*, 151.

25. Hening, II, 270.

26. Hening, II, 280-81.

27. Morgan Godwyn, *The Negro's and Indians Advocate, Suing for their Admission into the Church* (London, 1680), 83, 84, 85.

28. YCCR, V, 26 April 1675, fol. 110.

29. YCCR, X, 24 March 1696/97, fol. 377; YCCR, X, 24 August 1697, fol. 452; YCCR, X, 24 September 1697, fol. 464; YCCR, X, 24 February 1697/98, fol. 502.

30. Philip Alexander Bruce, *Institutional History of Virginia in the Seventeenth Century* (New York: G. P. Putnam's Sons, 1910), I, 226. Bruce thinks that Elizabeth Harris of London was the first Quaker missionary to visit Virginia.

31. "An Act For Tolleracon of Religion," Jamaica, 1674, National Archives at Kew CO 139/1.

32. YCCR, III, 15 August 1661, fols. 125, 127, 131.

33. Hening, I, 532-33; Hening, II, 180-83.

34. Bruce, *Institutional History of Virginia*, I, 229.

35. YCCR, III, Proclamation against Quakers, 10 September 1659, fol. 64.

36. YCCR, III, Proclamation against Quakers, 24 October 1659, fol. 66.

37. For these and other examples, see Bruce, *Institutional History of Virginia*, I, 226, 231-32; April Lee Hatfield, *Atlantic Virginia: Intercolonial Relations in the Seventeenth Century* (Philadelphia: University of Pennsylvania Press, 2004), 124-25.

38. Quoted in Bruce, *Institutional History of Virginia*, I, 222. The records of this trial were among those destroyed by the Confederacy in 1865; Bruce relied upon notes taken in the 1830s by George Bancroft.

39. Hening, I, 532–33; Hening, II, 180–83.

40. Rebecca Larson, *Daughters of Light: Quaker Women Preaching and Prophesying in the Colonies and Abroad, 1700–1775* (New York: Alfred A. Knopf, 1999), 8.

41. YCCR, VI, Presentments for not going to church, 24 January 1682/83, fol. 448; YCCR, VI, 26 February 1682/83, fol. 462.

42. YCCR, VI, 24 January 1683/84, fol. 546.

43. SCCR, IV, Militia lists, 24 October 1687, fols. 598–601; updated list dated October 1687, fols. 619–21.

44. SCCR, V, 16 August 1691, fol. 3; SCCR, V, 1 March 1691/92, fol. 30. Early in the eighteenth century, Quaker widow Mary Inman had a similar difficulty in probating her husband's estate; see SCCR, VI, March 1701/2, fol. 221.

45. Lefroy, II, 202, 249–50, 272–74.

46. Governor William Berkeley to the Justices of the Peace for Lower Norfolk County, 27 June 1663, *BP*, 199.

47. Hening, II, 198.

48. Edmund Scarburgh to William Berkeley, November 1663, *BP*, 213–18.

49. "To Friends beyond the sea, that have Blacks and Indian Slaves," in George Fox, *The Selected Works of George Fox* (New York: Isaac T. Hopper, 1831), 144–45. On Quakers and slavery, see also Jean R. Soderlund, *Quakers and Slavery: A Divided Spirit* (Princeton: Princeton University Press, 1985), 3.

50. George Fox, *To the Ministers, Teachers, and Priests, (so called, and so Stileing your Selves) in Barbadoes* (London, 1671), 5.

51. Godwyn, *The Negro's and Indians Advocate*, 4.

52. On Edmundson, see Soderlund, *Quakers and Slavery*, 3, and David Brion Davis, *The Problem of Slavery in Western Culture* (New York: Oxford University Press, 1966), 307–9.

53. George Fox, *Gospel Family-Order, Being a Short Discourse Concerning the Ordering of Families, both of Whites, Blacks and Indians* (London, 1676).

54. YCCR, III, 26 August 1661, fol. 125. On the gender implications of the order, see Brown, *Good Wives*, 143–44.

55. Hilary Beckles, *Black Rebellion in Barbados: The Struggle against Slavery, 1627–1838* (Bridgetown, Barbados: Carib Research and Publications, 1987), 37–38.

56. On events in Barbados, see Katharine Gerbner, "The Ultimate Sin: Christianising Slaves in Barbados in the Seventeenth Century," *Slavery and Abolition* 31, no. 1 (March 2010): 57–73, quotations from 58, 67. Gerbner notes that Fox's letter actually encouraged black and white Quakers to meet separately, which planters might have seen as a greater threat. Ibid., 68.

57. Hatfield, *Atlantic Virginia*, 129.

58. Norman Penney, ed., *The Journal of George Fox* (Cambridge: Cambridge University Press, 1911), II, 240.

59. Warren M. Billings, ed., "A Quaker in Seventeenth-Century Virginia: Four Remonstrances by George Wilson," *William and Mary Quarterly*, 3rd ed., 33, no. 1 (January 1976): 127–40; information on Wilson on 128–29, quotation from 136.

60. William Berkeley to Thomas Ludwell, 16 February 1675/76, *BP*, 498.

61. William Berkeley to Charles II, 24 March 1675/76, *BP*, 504–5.

62. For a succinct overview of the origins of the conflict, see Wilcomb E. Washburn, *The Governor and the Rebel: A History of Bacon's Rebellion in Virginia* (Chapel Hill: University of North Carolina Press, 1957), 17–39; *The Dictionary of Virginia Biography*, s.v. "Bacon, Nathaniel" (by Brent Tarter); Warren M. Billings, *Sir William Berkeley and the Forging of Colonial Virginia* (Baton Rouge: Louisiana State University Press, 2004).

63. Nathaniel Bacon, "Declaration of the People," August 1676, William Blathwayt Papers, vol. XIII, folder 1, Colonial Williamsburg Foundation.

64. Ibid.

65. [Ann (Hannah) Cotton], *The History of Bacon's and Ingram's Rebellion* (1675–76), also known as the Burwell Manuscript. The Virginia Historical Society owns the manuscript, which until 1867 had been housed in the Massachusetts Historical Society. The manuscript is probably an eighteenth-century copy of an earlier document. The authorship of the manuscript is uncertain; Wilcomb Washburn believes John Cotton wrote it, citing Jay B. Hubbell, "John and Ann Cotton of Queen's Creek, Virginia," *American Literature* 10 (1938): 179–201. See Washburn, *The Governor and the Rebel*, Essay on the Sources, 174. Terri Snyder revives the idea that Ann Cotton wrote the manuscript rather than her husband. See Snyder, *Brabbling Women*, 34, 152n47, 153n70. The manuscript is remarkably similar to but more detailed than a letter bearing Ann Cotton's name, so scholars have long assumed that, as Lawrence Wroth thought, that John Cotton, "taking up in a period of leisure, his wife's letter to an English friend and making it over into a history of the Rebellion found in the Burwell manuscript" (quoted in Hubbell, "John and Ann Cotton . . .," 183). It is odd that historians and scholars of literature have been so quick to assume that Ann Cotton wrote the letter but could not have written the history contained in the Burwell manuscript. It seems perfectly reasonable that Ann Cotton wrote both the letter and the later manuscript we have today, for if Ann was capable of writing the letter she could certainly write the history as well. Thus I agree here with Snyder, and attribute the manuscript to Ann Cotton rather than her husband. The manuscript and its attached letters and poetry should be reexamined by literary scholars to establish its authorship. Ann Cotton and her husband John had a plantation on Queen's Creek in York County, and they were probably successful enough that Bacon's Rebellion threatened their political and economic interests, but the Cottons' connection with Berkeley is unclear.

66. Cotton, *History of Bacon's and Ingram's Rebellion*, 4–5.

67. Ibid., 28.

68. Philip Ludwell to Secretary Coventry, before July 1677, Coventry Papers, vol. LXXVIII, Colonial Williamsburg Foundation Microfilm.

69. Cotton, *History of Bacon's and Ingram's Rebellion*, 26.

70. Ibid.

71. Nicholas Spencer to Secretary Sir Henry Coventry, 6 August 1676, Coventry Papers, vol. LXXVII, letter 170, Colonial Williamsburg Foundation microfilm.

72. Cotton, *History of Bacon's and Ingram's Rebellion*, 28.

73. "Declaration and Remonstrance," May 1676, *BP*, 527.

74. William Berkeley to Henry Coventry, 3 June 1676, *BP*, 531.

75. Edmund Morgan, *American Slavery, American Freedom: The Ordeal of Colonial Virginia* (New York: Norton, 1975), 269.

76. See ibid., 328–31; Brown, *Good Wives*, 184–85.

77. *Oxford English Dictionary Third Edition Online*, s.v. "milk-sop."

78. Cotton, *History of Bacon's and Ingram's Rebellion*, 35–36. The English had several stereotypes of the Ottoman Empire, including the idea that the sultan was a tyrant with absolute power who enslaved his subjects. In this context, Cotton's use of Janissaries is interesting: the Janissaries were technically slaves of the Sultan, though that unfree status meant something in the Ottoman polity very different from its meaning in colonial Virginia. Cotton's description of Bacon's and Ingram's followers as Janissaries implied a kind of slavish devotion to the every whim of their leaders.

79. Ibid., 37. Later claims against Hansford's estate were disallowed by the royal commissioners sent to investigate the rebellion and its aftermath, "the said Hansford haveinge noe Tryall or conviction by a Lawfull Jury." Petition of Thomas Palmer, Carpenter, in Michael Leroy Oberg, ed., *Samuel Wiseman's Book of Record: The Official Account of Bacon's Rebellion in Virginia* (Oxford: Lexington Books, 2005), 267.

80. Bruce E. Steiner, "The Catholic Brents of Colonial Virginia: An Instance of Practical Toleration," *Virginia Magazine of History and Biography* 70, no. 4 (October 1962): 387–409; Commission to Daniel Jenifer, *BP*, 403, 403n1.

81. Colonel Nicholas Spencer to William Blathwayt, 27 April 1689, William Blathwayt Papers, vol. XVI, folder V, Colonial Williamsburg Foundation.

82. Ibid.

83. Lord Thomas Culpepper to William Blathwayt, 10 June 1689, William Blathwayt Papers, vol. XVII, folder III, Colonial Williamsburg Foundation.

84. William and Mary, 1688: An Act for Exempting their Majestyes Protestant Subjects dissenting from the Church of England from the Penalties of certaine Lawes. [Chapter XVIII. Rot. Parl. pt. 5. nu. 15.] *Statutes of the Realm*, vol. 6: *1685–94* (1819), 74–76.

85. Hening, III, 171.

86. William P. Palmer, ed., *Calendar of Virginia State Papers and Other*

Manuscripts, 11 vols. (New York: Kraus Reprint Corporations, 1875–93; repr., 1968), I, 30 July 1742, 235.

87. Hening, III, 447–50, 298.

CHAPTER SIX: *The Children of Israel*

1. Thomas N. Ingersoll, ed., "'Releese us out of this Cruell Bondegg': An Appeal from Virginia in 1723," *William and Mary Quarterly*, 3rd ser., 51, no. 4 (October 1994): 777–82, esp. 781–82.

2. Ibid., 782.

3. Michael Anesko, "So Discreet a Zeal: Slavery and the Anglican Church in Virginia, 1680–1730," *Virginia Magazine of History and Biography* 93, no. 3 (July 1985): 259; Joyce E. Chaplin, *Subject Matter: Technology, the Body, and Science on the Anglo-American Frontier, 1500–1676* (Cambridge, MA: Harvard University Press, 2001), 289–95.

4. On the Indian College at Harvard, see Samuel Eliot Morison, *Harvard College in the Seventeenth Century* (Cambridge, MA: Harvard University Press, 1936), I, 340–60.

5. William P. Palmer, ed., *Calendar of Virginia State Papers and Other Manuscripts*, 11 vols. (New York: Kraus Reprint Corporations, 1875–93; repr., 1968), II, 1712–14, 311–12.

6. Lieutenant Governor Alexander Spotswood to the Council of Trade, 17 November 1711, in R. A. Brock, ed., *The Official Letters of Alexander Spotswood*, 2 vols. (Richmond: Virginia Historical Society, 1882–85), I, 122. For a broader look at Indians and the College of William and Mary, see Karen A. Stuart, "'So Good A Work': The Brafferton School, 1691–1777" (master's thesis, College of William and Mary, 1984).

7. Spotswood to the Bishop of London, 8 May 1712; Spotswood to the Bishop of London, 26 July 1712, in Brock, *Official Letters*, I, 156, 174.

8. Spotswood to the Bishop of London, 26 July 1712; Spotswood to the Archbishop of Canterbury, 26 July 1712; Spotswood to the Bishop of London, 13 June 1717, in ibid., I, 174, 176; II, 253.

9. Spotswood to the Bishop of London, 27 January 1714/15; Spotswood to the Bishop of London, 26 October 1715, in ibid., II, 89, 138. On the Indians at Fort Christanna, see also Owen Stanwood, "Captives and Slaves: Indian Labor, Cultural Conversion, and the Plantation Revolution in Virginia," *Virginia Magazine of History and Biography* 114, no. 4 (2006): 434–63.

10. *JHB*, VI, 7 September 1715, 167.

11. Stuart, "The Brafferton School," 21.

12. Hugh Jones, *The Present State of Virginia: From Whence Is Inferred A Short View of Maryland and North Carolina*, ed. Richard L. Morton (London, 1724; repr., Chapel Hill: University of North Carolina Press, 1956), 50, 51. On Jones's vital statistics, see John K. Nelson, *A Blessed Company: Parishes, Parsons, and Parishioners in Anglican Virginia, 1690–1776* (Chapel Hill: University of North Carolina Press, 2001), 313.

13. See, for example, Le Jau to the Secretary, 18 September 1708, in Frank J. Klingberg, ed., *The Carolina Chronicle of Dr. Francis Le Jau, 1706–1717* (Berkeley: University of California Press, 1956), 45, and Le Jau to the Secretary, 19 March 1715/16, in ibid., 175–76. On the antediluvian origins of the Indians, see Le Jau to the Secretary, 4 January 1712/13, in ibid., 106.

14. Journal of John Fontaine, 94, Colonial Williamsburg Foundation.

15. William J. Hinke, ed., "Report of the Journey of Francis Louis Michel from Berne, Switzerland, to Virginia, October 2, 1701 to December 1, 1702," *Virginia Magazine of History and Biography* 24, no. 2 (April 1916): 117.

16. Spotswood to the Bishop of London, 27 January 1714/15, in Brock, *Official Letters*, II, 91.

17. Le Jau to the Secretary, 15 September 1708, in Klingberg, *Carolina Chronicle*, 41. On Samuel Thomas and Francis Le Jau, see also Alan Gallay, *The Indian Slave Trade: The Rise of the English Empire in the American South, 1670–1717* (New Haven: Yale University Press, 2002), 226–37.

18. Stuart, "The Brafferton School," 54–71.

19. Reverend Thomas Bacon, *Sermons Addressed to Masters and Servants, and Published in the Year 1745, by the Rev. Thomas Bacon, Minister of the Protestant Episcopal Church in Maryland, now republished with other tracts and dialogues on the same subject, and recommended to all Masters and Mistresses to be good in their families by the Rev. William Meade* (Winchester, VA: John Heiskell, Printer, 1813), 11–12.

20. On numbers regarding slavery, see Philip D. Morgan, "The Black Experience in the British Empire, 1680–1810," in P. J. Marshall, ed., *The Oxford History of the British Empire* (Oxford: Oxford University Press, 1998), II, 468; Warren M. Billings, John E. Selby, and Thad W. Tate, *Colonial Virginia: A History* (White Plains, NY: KTO Press, 1986), 124–25, 206; Nelson, *A Blessed Company*, 259.

21. On Blair, see *The Dictionary of Virginia Biography*, s.v. "Blair, James, 1655–1743" (by Thad W. Tate); James B. Bell, *The Imperial Origins of the King's Church in Early America, 1607–1783* (London: Palgrave Macmillan, 2004), 71–73; Edward L. Bond, *Damned Souls in a Tobacco Colony: Religion in Seventeenth-Century Virginia* (Macon, GA: Mercer University Press, 2000), 225–35.

22. Henry Hartwell, James Blair, and Edward Chilton, *The Present State of Virginia, and the College*, ed. Hunter Dickinson Farish (Williamsburg, VA: Colonial Williamsburg, 1940), 65–67, quotation from 67. Though Hartwell, Blair, and Chilton wrote their description of Virginia in 1697, it was not published until 1727.

23. Michael G. Kammen, ed., "Virginia at the Close of the Seventeenth Century: An Appraisal by James Blair and John Locke ('Some of the Cheif Greivances of the Present Constitution of Virginia with an Essay towards the Remedies Thereof')," *Virginia Magazine of History and Biography* 74, no. 2 (April 1966): 141–69, quotations from 166.

24. Ibid., 167.

25. Samuel Clyde McCulloch, ed., "James Blair's Plan of 1699 to Reform the Clergy of Virginia," *William and Mary Quarterly*, 3rd ed., 4, no. 1 (January 1947): 70–86, quotation from 85.

26. "Heads of a Bill for the Conversion of the Negroes in America," Jervaise Papers 44M69/G2/144r, Hampshire Record Office. I am grateful to Noah McCormack for introducing me to this document. The "Heads" is undated but logically dates from between 1702 and 1710, when Thomas Jervaise's time in Parliament and Queen Anne's reign overlapped. Personal communication from Noah McCormack, 8 March 2010.

27. "A Draught of a Bill For Converting the negros &c In the Plantations" (Lambeth Palace Library, MS 941, 72), in Ruth Paley, Cristina Malcolmson, and Michael Hunter, eds., "Parliament and Slavery, 1660–c. 1710," *Slavery and Abolition* 31, no. 2 (April 2010): 272. Paley et al. date the "Draught" to 1711; Anthony Parent dates it to 1713; see Anthony S. Parent Jr. *Foul Means: The Formation of a Slave Society in Virginia, 1660–1740* (Chapel Hill: University of North Carolina Press, 2003), 243n13.

28. Travis Glasson, "'Baptism doth not bestow Freedom': Missionary Anglicanism, Slavery, and the Yorke-Talbot Opinion, 1701–1730," *William and Mary Quarterly*, 3rd ser., 67, no. 2 (April 2010): 279–318.

29. Jones, *Present State of Virginia*, 99.

30. *JHB*, VI, 7 September 1715, 167; 16 November 1720, 269; 18 May 1723, 368, 370.

31. William Gooch, Baronet, to Thomas Gooch, Lord Bishop of Norwich, 3 March 1743/44, William Gooch Transcripts, Colonial Williamsburg Foundation.

32. Le Jau to the Secretary, 18 September 1711, in Klingberg, *Carolina Chronicle*, 102.

33. Le Jau to Henry Compton, Bishop of London, 27 May 1712, in ibid., 116.

34. Le Jau to the Secretary, 11 December 1712, in ibid., 124–25.

35. Quoted in Parent, *Foul Means*, 246.

36. Jones, *Present State of Virginia*, 99.

37. Hening, IV, 126–35.

38. William Popple, Secretary to the Board of Trade, to William Gooch, 18 December 1735, William Gooch Transcripts, Colonial Williamsburg Foundation.

39. William Gooch to William Popple, 18 May 1736, William Gooch Transcripts, Colonial Williamsburg Foundation.

40. Edmund Gibson, *Two Letters of the Lord Bishop of London* (London, 1727), 10–11. Glasson notes that Gibson's youthful position on baptism and manumission was considerably more nuanced. Glasson, "Yorke-Talbot Opinion," 308–9.

41. [Anonymous], *A Letter to the Right Revered the Lord Bishop of London, from an Inhabitant of his Majesty's Leeward Caribee Islands, Containing some Considerations on His Lordship's Two Letters of May 19, 1727* (London, 1730), quotations from 34, 12, and 33.

42. See Glasson, "Yorke-Talbot Opinion"; Parent, *Foul Means*, 260. Glasson

argues convincingly that it was missionaries and their philanthropic allies, rather than planters and slave traders, who solicited the Yorke-Talbot opinion.

43. *JHB*, VI, 26 May 1730, 63.

44. William Black to the Bishop of London [undated response to the Bishop's queries, probably 1724 or 1725], Fulham Palace Papers, Virginia Colonial Records Project, Library of Virginia; "A List of Negroes baptized by John Garzia as rector of North-Farnham Parish, Richmond County, 1725–1732," Fulham Palace Papers, Virginia Colonial Records Project, Library of Virginia.

45. John Worden to the Bishop of London, 25 May 1725, Fulham Palace Papers, Virginia Colonial Records Project, Library of Virginia.

46. Hening, IV, 42–45.

47. Le Jau to the Secretary, 26 May 1712, in Klingberg, *Carolina Chronicle*, 112.

48. Adam Dickie to the Bishop of London, 27 June 1732, Fulham Palace Papers, Virginia Colonial Records Project, Library of Virginia.

49. Albemarle Parish Register, 1721–87, 101, Virginia Historical Society.

50. Le Jau to the Secretary, 30 August 1712, in Klingberg, *Carolina Chronicle*, 120.

51. Jack P. Greene, ed., *The Diary of Colonel Landon Carter of Sabine Hall, 1752–1778* (Charlottesville: University of Virginia Press, 1965), I, 4 May 1766, 295.

52. Ibid., II, 20 June 1775.

53. Reverend Samuel Davies to Mr. Forset, 1757, Colonial Williamsburg Foundation. (PH OO N.D. Davies L61|3|1.1).

54. Ibid.

55. Greene, *Diary of Landon Carter*, I, 31 March 1770, 378.

56. It would be possible to compare data generated in parish vestry books with Society for the Propagation of the Gospel reports to generate a number of baptisms. That would still leave us with an incomplete understanding of what baptism meant to slaves, though, thoughtfully used, numbers might be a way of conceptualizing the penetration of Christian beliefs in the slave community. For such an approach to the problem of conversion, see Annette Laing, "'Heathens and Infidels'? African Christianization and Anglicanism in the South Carolina Low Country, 1700–1750," *Religion and American Culture* 12, no. 2 (Summer 2002): 197–228. Robert Olwell estimates 3–5 percent of the enslaved population in South Carolina was baptized. See Olwell, *Masters, Slaves, and Subjects: The Culture of Power in the South Carolina Low Country, 1740–1790* (Ithaca: Cornell University Press, 1998), 118. Alexander Byrd argues that it would be difficult to find more than two thousand black Christians in Virginia, a claim complicated by competing definitions of what conversion meant. Byrd, *Captives and Voyagers: Black Migrants across the Eighteenth-Century British Atlantic World* (Baton Rouge: Louisiana State University Press, 2008), 161, 299n18. Morgan has argued, regardless of how enslaved Christians are counted, "The vast majority of eighteenth-century Anglo-American slaves lived and died strangers to

Christianity." Philip D. Morgan, *Slave Counterpoint: Black Culture in the Eighteenth-Century Chesapeake and Lowcountry* (Chapel Hill: University of North Carolina Press, 1998), 420. Jon Butler's assertion that the Atlantic slave trade constituted a "spiritual Holocaust" is another way of expressing the problem of understanding black Christianity before the American Revolution. Jon Butler, *Awash in a Sea of Faith: Christianizing the American People* (Cambridge, MA: Harvard University Press, 1990), 157.

57. Le Jau to the Secretary, 1 February 1710, in Klingberg, *Carolina Chronicle*, 69.

58. John Thornton, *Africa and Africans in the Making of the Atlantic World, 1400–1800*, 2nd ed. (Cambridge: Cambridge University Press, 1998), 249–53. Thornton also notes that African practice was strongly anticlerical and that African Christians believed that divine revelation was ongoing.

59. Herman Bennett has described learning about Catholicism and the law as an important part of developing a creole consciousness in colonial Mexico. Though the evidentiary base is decidedly less broad for eighteenth-century Virginia, it is probable that enslaved people in British colonies underwent a similar process. See Herman Bennett, *Africans in Colonial Mexico: Absolutism, Christianity, and Afro-Creole Consciousness, 1570–1640* (Bloomington: Indiana University Press, 2003).

60. Ingersoll, "An Appeal from Virginia in 1723," 781–82. "Seek ye first the kingdom of God" is a famous line from the Gospel of Matthew, and the letter writers were apparently familiar with the King James Version (Matthew 6:33).

61. William Gooch to Edmund Gibson, 28 July 1732, Gooch Papers, Colonial Williamsburg Foundation.

62. Philip J. Schwarz, *Slave Laws in Virginia* (Athens: University of Georgia Press, 1996), 71.

63. Lieutenant Governor William Gooch to the Board of Trade, 14 September 1730, Gooch Transcripts, Colonial Williamsburg Foundation.

64. Gooch to the Board of Trade, 12 February 1730/31, Gooch Transcripts, Colonial Williamsburg Foundation. On the estimate that three hundred enslaved people participated in the rebellion, see John Brickell, *The Natural History of North-Carolina* . . . (Dublin, 1737), 357. Brickell did not witness the rebellion himself, though he did claim to see the executions. Three hundred does seem like too high a number. Travis Glasson suspects that the rebellion might have been a figment of anxious imaginations and the planters' willingness to connect missionary efforts and obnoxious behavior from enslaved people. The reemergence of a connection between baptism and freedom in 1775 suggests that this might have been a long-cherished ideal among enslaved people that periodically surfaced in rebellions. See Glasson, "Yorke-Talbot Opinion," 301–2.

65. John K. Thornton, "African Dimensions of the Stono Rebellion," *American Historical Review* 96, no. 4 (October 1991): 1101–13; Mark M. Smith, "Remembering Mary, Shaping Revolt: Reconsidering the Stono Rebellion," *Journal of Southern History* 67, no. 3 (August 2001): 513–34; Parent, *Foul Means*, 159–62;

Charles F. Irons, *The Origins of Proslavery Christianity: White and Black Evangelicals in Colonial and Antebellum Virginia* (Chapel Hill: University of North Carolina Press, 2008), 30–32.

66. Thomas Hutchinson to the Council of Safety, 5 July 1775, in David R. Chesnutt et al., eds., *The Papers of Henry Laurens* (Columbia: University of South Carolina Press, 1985), X, 206–8. See also Sylvia R. Frey, *Water from the Rock: Black Resistance in a Revolutionary Age* (Princeton: Princeton University Press, 1991), 62–63.

67. David Patrick Geggus, "Slavery, War, and Revolution in the Greater Caribbean, 1789–1815," in David Patrick Geggus and David Barry Gaspar, eds., *The French Revolution and the Greater Caribbean* (Bloomington: Indiana University Press, 1997), 8–9.

68. See esp. Irons, *Proslavery Christianity*, 23–54.

EPILOGUE

1. Anonymous, *A Letter to an American Planter, from his Friend in London* (London, 1781), 20.

2. Lemuel Haynes, "Liberty Further Extended," in Richard Newman, ed., *Black Preacher to White America: The Collected Writings of Lemuel Haynes* (Brooklyn, NY: Carlson Publishing, 1990), 19 (emphasis in original).

3. "Petition of a Great Number of Negroes" to the Massachusetts House of Representatives, 13 January 1777, in Thomas J. Davis, "Emancipation Rhetoric, Natural Rights, and Revolutionary New England: A Note of Four Black Petitions in Massachusetts, 1773–1777," *New England Quarterly* 62, no. 2 (June 1989): 248–63.

4. Anthony Benezet, *A Serious Address to the Rulers of America* (London, 1783), 12.

5. The Pennsylvania Abolition Society to the United States Congress, 3 February 1790, www.franklinpapers.org.

6. Brunswick County to the General Assembly of Virginia, 10 November 1785, in Fredrika Teute Schmidt and Barbara Ripel Williams, eds., "Early Proslavery Petitions in Virginia," *William and Mary Quarterly*, 3rd ser., 31, no. 1 (July 1973): 143–44.

7. "To the honourable the General Assembly of Virginia, the Remonstrance and Petition of the Free Inhabitants of Amelia County," 10 November 1785, in ibid., 138–40; "To the honourable the General Assembly of Virginia the Remonstrance and Petition of the Free Inhabitants of Halifax County," in ibid., 145–46.

8. James Sidbury, *Plowshares into Swords: Race, Rebellion, and Identity in Gabriel's Virginia, 1730–1810* (Cambridge: Cambridge University Press, 1997), 76–82.

9. Quoted in Randolph Ferguson Scully, *Religion and the Making of Nat Turner's Virginia: Baptist Community and Conflict, 1740–1840* (Charlottesville: University of Virginia Press, 2008), 193.

10. Charles F. Irons, *The Origins of Proslavery Christianity: White and Black*

Evangelicals in Colonial and Antebellum Virginia (Chapel Hill: University of North Carolina Press, 2008); Christopher A. Luse, "Slavery's Champions Stood at Odds: Polygenesis and the Defense of Slavery," *Civil War History* 53, no. 4 (2007): 379–412; Colin Kidd, *The Forging of Races: Race and Scripture in the Protestant Atlantic World, 1600–2000* (Cambridge: Cambridge University Press, 2006).

11. Josiah Priest, *Bible Defence of Slavery, and Origins Fortunes, and History of the Negro Race* (Lexington, KY, 1852), 79, 92.

12. On the theological assault upon race in the twentieth century, see Kidd, *The Forging of Races*, 271–74.

13. Quoted in Jane Dailey, "Theology of Massive Resistance: Sex, Segregation, and the Sacred after *Brown*," in Clive Webb, ed., *Massive Resistance: Southern Opposition to the Second Reconstruction* (New York: Oxford University Press, 2005), 166.

ESSAY ON SOURCES

The county court records of seventeenth-century Virginia form the backbone of this book. I used records from Accomack, Northampton, Surry, and York counties because they have relatively complete seventeenth-century runs. Other counties with some seventeenth-century records are Charles City County (formed in 1634, fragments), Henrico County (formed in 1634, fragments after 1650), Lancaster County (formed 1651, records after 1652), Lower Norfolk County (formed 1637, fragmentary records from 1637–46), Middlesex County (formed c. 1669, records begin in 1673), and Old Rappahannock County (formed 1656, fragments after 1683). All of these records are available on microfilm at the Library of Virginia in Richmond. The Rockefeller Library at Colonial Williamsburg keeps a set of the York County microfilms; Linda Rowe maintains a set of transcripts, abstracts, and biographical files of people mentioned in the York records. Other counties that formed in the seventeenth century have no surviving seventeenth-century records. The laws of seventeenth-century Virginia were collected in the early nineteenth century; see William Waller Hening, ed., *The Statutes at Large, being a Collection of all the laws of Virginia* (New York: R. & W. & G. Bartow, 1819–23). (Hening collected almost all the seventeenth-century acts. A few missing statutes appear in Warren M. Billings, "Some Acts Not in Hening's *Statutes*: The Acts of Assembly, April 1652, November 1652, and July 1653," *Virginia Magazine of History and Biography* 83, no. 1 [January 1975]: 22–76, and Jon Kukla, "Some Acts Not in Hening's *Statutes*: The Acts of Assembly, October 1660," *Virginia Magazine of History and Biography* 83, no. 1 [January 1975]: 77–97.) Appeals and capital cases were tried at Jamestown; for fragments of these records, see H. R. McIlwaine, ed., *Minutes of the Council and General Court of Virginia* (Richmond: privately printed, 1924). Many of Virginia's seventeenth-century court records, including most of the Jamestown records, burned when the retreating Confederate army set fire to Richmond in 1865.

For the period before 1624, the most complete source is Susan Myra Kingsbury, ed., *Records of the Virginia Company of London*, 4 vols. (Washington, DC: Government Printing Office, 1906–34). For the initial two years of English exploration, see Philip L. Barbour, ed., *The Jamestown Voyages under the First Charter, 1606–1609*, 2 vols. (Cambridge: Cambridge University Press for the Hakluyt Society, 1969). The observations of William Strachey and John Smith overlap to some degree, but both are invaluable: William Strachey, *The Historie of Travell into Virginia Britania*, ed. Louis B. Wright and Virginia Freund (London: Hakluyt Society, 1953), and Philip L. Barbour, ed., *The Complete Works of Captain John Smith*, 3 vols. (Chapel Hill: University of North Carolina Press, 1986). For a solid set of papers spanning most of the seventeenth century, see Warren M. Billings, ed., *The Papers of Sir William Berkeley, 1605-1677* (Richmond: Library of Virginia, 2007). For useful comparisons to nearby places, see William Hand Browne, ed., *Archives of Maryland* (1883-1972, 1990-), at www .aomol.net/html/index.html, and J. H. Lefroy, ed., *Memorials of the Discovery and Early Settlement of the Bermudas Somer Islands*, 2 vols. (London: Longmans, Greene, 1877). Three good examples of the propaganda literature circulated by the Virginia Company are William Crashaw, *A Sermon Preached in London before the right honorable the Lord Lawarre, Lord Governour and Captaine Generall of Virginea, and others of his Majesties Counsell for that Kingdome, and the rest of the Adventurers in that Plantation* . . . (London, 1610); [Robert Gray], *A Good Speed to Virginia* (London, 1609); and [Robert Johnson], *Nova Britannia: Offering Most Excellent Fruites by Planting in Virginia* (London, 1609). Other printed sources form the company period are William Strachey, *For the colony in Virginea Britannia: Lawes Divine Morall and Martiall, &c* (London, 1612); Alexander Whitaker, *Good Newes from Virginia Sent to the Counsell and Company of Virginia* (London, 1613); and Edward Waterhouse's propaganda masterpiece, *A Declaration of the State of the Colony and Affaires in Virginia with a Relation of the Barbarous Massacre in the Time of Peace and League, Treacherously Executed by the Native Infidels Upon the English* (London, 1622). The writings of George Percy are always a good counterpoint or corrective to the writings of John Smith. See George Percy, *Discourse* [1608], in Barbour, *Jamestown Voyages*, I, and Percy, "A Trewe Relacyon (1625)," *Tyler's Quarterly Historical and Genealogical Magazine* 3, no. 3 (January 1922): 259-82.

Sources for late seventeenth-century and eighteenth-century Virginia are more plentiful. At the John D. Rockefeller Jr. Library of the Colonial Williamsburg Foundation, I found the William Blathwayt Papers (1631-1722), Fulham Palace Papers, Lambeth Palace, London (Virginia Colonial Records Project Microfilm), and the William Gooch Typescripts particularly useful. In chapter 6, I focus on William Willie's Albemarle Parish Register (1720-74) held in the Virginia Historical Society. I selected this register because of its long run and because one minister made most of the entries. There are, however, numerous published registers and vestry books. See, for example, C. G. Chamberlayne, ed., *The Vestry Book and Register of St. Peter's Parish, 1684-1786* (Richmond: Virginia State Library, 1937). Printed primary sources include Henry Hartwell, James Blair, and Edward Chilton, *The Present State of Virginia, and the College*, ed. Hunter Dickinson Farish (Williamsburg, VA: Colonial Williamsburg, 1940); Hugh Jones, *The Present State of Virginia: From Whence Is Inferred A Short View of Maryland and North Carolina*, ed. Richard L. Morton (London, 1724; repr., Chapel Hill: University of North Carolina Press, 1956); and R. A. Brock, ed., *The Official Letters of Alexander Spotswood*, 2 vols. (Richmond: Virginia Historical Society, 1882-85). For a comparative study with Carolina, see Frank J. Klingberg, ed., *The Carolina Chronicle of Dr. Francis Le Jau, 1706–1717* (Berkeley: University of California Press, 1956).

There are several good general histories of Virginia. An excellent starting place is Warren M. Billings, John E. Selby, and Thad W. Tate, *Colonial Virginia: A History* (White Plains, NY: KTO Press, 1986). On seventeenth-century Virginia, see Robert Appelbaum and John Wood Sweet, eds., *Envisioning an English Empire: Jamestown and the Making of the North Atlantic World* (Philadelphia: University of Pennsylvania Press, 2005); Warren M. Billings, *Sir William Berkeley and the Forging of Colonial Virginia* (Baton Rouge: Louisiana State University Press, 2004); Lois Green Carr, Philip D. Morgan, and Jean B. Russo, eds., *Colonial Chesapeake Society* (Chapel Hill: University of North Carolina Press, 1988); April Lee Hatfield, *Atlantic Virginia: Intercolonial Relations in the Seventeenth Century* (Philadelphia: University of Pennsylvania Press, 2004); James Horn, *Adapting to a New World: English Society in the Seventeenth-Century Chesapeake* (Chapel Hill: University of North Carolina Press, 1994); Edmund S. Morgan, *American Slavery, American Freedom: The Ordeal of Colonial Virginia* (New York: Norton, 1975); Anthony S. Parent Jr., *Foul Means: The Formation of a Slave Society in Virginia, 1660–1740* (Chapel Hill: University of North Carolina Press, 2003); and James R. Perry, *The Formation of a Society on Virginia's Eastern Shore, 1615–1655* (Chapel Hill: University of North Carolina Press, 1990). This list is hardly exhaustive but provides a good introduction. For Indians, see especially Helen C. Rountree, *The Powhatan Indians of Virginia: Their Traditional Culture* (Norman: University of Oklahoma Press, 1989). For the eighteenth century, see especially Rhys Isaac, *The Transformation of Virginia, 1740–1790* (Chapel Hill: University of North Carolina Press, 1982), and Philip D. Morgan, *Slave Counterpoint: Black Culture in the Eighteenth-Century Chesapeake & Lowcountry* (Chapel Hill: University of North Carolina Press, 1998).

The literature on race generally, and race and religion specifically, is voluminous. I have selected a few starting points. When this project began life as a seminar paper in 2001, the works of Michel Foucault on discourse and power were particularly germane to scholarly conversations about race. Though I ended up finding Foucault less relevant for this project, all serious students of race as an idea should begin with Foucault, *Discipline and Punish: The Birth of the Prison* (New York: Vintage, 1995). For the origins (or absence) of race in the ancient world, see Frank M. Snowden Jr., *Before Color Prejudice: The Ancient View of Blacks* (Cambridge, MA: Harvard University Press, 1983); Ivan Hannaford, *Race: The History of an Idea in the West* (Baltimore: Johns Hopkins University Press, 1996); Benjamin Isaac, *The Invention of Racism in Classical Antiquity* (Princeton: Princeton University Press, 2004). For medieval and early modern Europe, see George M. Fredrickson, *Racism: A Short History* (Princeton: Princeton University Press, 2002); David Brion Davis, *The Problem of Slavery in Western Culture* (New York: Oxford University Press, 1966); and Davis, *In the Image of God: Religion, Moral Values, and Our Heritage of Slavery* (New

Haven: Yale University Press, 2001). For race in the New World and especially in Virginia, begin with Winthrop Jordan, *White over Black: American Attitudes toward the Negro, 1550–1812* (Chapel Hill: University of North Carolina Press, 1968). See also Kathleen M. Brown, *Good Wives, Nasty Wenches, and Anxious Patriarchs: Gender, Race, and Power in Colonial Virginia* (Chapel Hill: University of North Carolina Press, 1996), and Kirsten Fischer, *Suspect Relations: Sex, Race, and Resistance in Colonial North Carolina* (Ithaca: Cornell University Press, 2002). Also enormously helpful is Joyce E. Chaplin, *Subject Matter: Technology, the Body, and Science on the Anglo-American Frontier, 1500–1676* (Cambridge, MA: Harvard University Press, 2001). All of the essays on the origins of race in the January 1997 issue of the *William and Mary Quarterly* are useful, but I am particularly fond of James Sweet's formulation of "racism before race." See "The Iberian Roots of American Racist Thought," *William and Mary Quarterly*, 3rd ser., 54, no.1 (January 1997): 143–66.

Three of the main chapters of this book address marriage, baptism, violence, and religious toleration. Some of the rich secondary literature on these topics include Nicholas M. Beasley, *Christian Ritual and the Creation of British Slaves Societies, 1650–1780* (Athens: University of Georgia Press, 2009); David Cressy, *Birth, Marriage, and Death: Ritual, Religion, and the Life-Cycle in Tudor and Stuart England* (New York: Oxford University Press, 1997); Will Coster, *Baptism and Spiritual Kinship in Early Modern England* (Hants, England: Ashgate Press, 2002); Jennifer Morgan, *Laboring Women: Gender and Reproduction in New World Slavery* (Philadelphia: University of Pennsylvania Press, 2004); David D. Smits, "'Abominable Mixture': Toward the Repudiation of Anglo-Indian Intermarriage in Seventeenth-Century Virginia," *Virginia Magazine of History and Biography* 95, no. 2 (1987): 157–92; Mary Beth Norton, *Founding Mothers and Fathers: Gendered Power and the Forming of American Society* (New York: Knopf, 1996); Ann Marie Plane, *Colonial Intimacies: Indian Marriage in Early New England* (Ithaca: Cornell University Press, 2000); Katharine Gerbner, "The Ultimate Sin: Christianising Slaves in Barbados in the Seventeenth Century," *Slavery and Abolition* 31, no. 1 (March 2010): 57–73, and Terri L. Snyder, *Brabbling Women: Disorderly Speech and the Law in Early Virginia* (Ithaca: Cornell University Press, 2003). On religious toleration in Virginia, see *From Jamestown to Jefferson: The Evolution of Religious Freedom in Virginia*, ed. Paul Rasor and Richard E. Bond (Charlottesville: University of Virginia Press, 2011).

Two of the toughest challenges I have faced with this book are convincing my colleagues that religion mattered in the Chesapeake and that Christianity mattered to enslaved people. For religion generally in Virginia, begin with Edward L. Bond, *Damned Souls in a Tobacco Colony: Religion in Seventeenth-Century Virginia* (Macon, GA: Mercer University Press, 2000). Bond's book should transform how scholars view Christianity in seventeenth-century Virginia, but it has not gotten the wide readership or the recognition it deserves. Recent scholarship has reevaluated Anglican spirituality, emphasizing the belief patterns that developed in the Chesapeake, which respected the church as an institution and allowed Anglo-Virginians to establish relationships with God that did not depend on regular church attendance or ministerial intervention. See Lauren Winner, *A Cheerful and Comfortable Faith: Anglican Religious Practice in the Elite Households of Eighteenth-Century Virginia* (New Haven: Yale University Press, 2010); John K. Nelson, *A Blessed Company: Parishes, Parsons, and Parishioners in Anglican Virginia, 1690–1776* (Chapel Hill: University of North Carolina Press, 2001); James B. Bell, *The Imperial Origins of the King's Church in Early America, 1706–1783* (London: Palgrave Macmillan, 2004); and as a general overview, John F. Woolverton, *Colonial Anglicanism in North America* (Detroit: Wayne State University Press, 1984).

Historians have tended to view the established Church of England in the eighteenth century as less a venue for the care of souls and more a site for reinforcing the hierarchical nature of southern and Caribbean colonial societies, which fulfilled the spiritual needs of neither poor planters nor African slaves. See especially Rhys Isaac, *The Transformation of Virginia, 1740–1790* (Chapel Hill: University of North Carolina Press, 1982); Jon Butler, *Awash in a Sea of Faith: Christianizing the American People* (Cambridge, MA: Harvard University Press, 1990). Recent scholarship has renewed conversations about the missionary proclivities of Anglican ministers. On Anglican missionaries and conversion schemes, see Travis Glasson, "'Baptism doth not bestow Freedom': Missionary Anglicanism, Slavery, and the Yorke-Talbot Opinion, 1701–1730," *William and Mary Quarterly*, 3rd ser., 67, no. 2 (April 2010): 279–318, and Glasson's *Mastering Christianity: Missionary Anglicanism and Slavery in the Atlantic World* (New York: Oxford University Press, 2012). Most historians have believed that only the New Light, low-church proclivities of the Great Awakening attracted black converts. See, for example, Sylvia Frey and Betty Wood, *Come Shouting to Zion: African American Protestantism in the American South and the British Caribbean to 1830* (Chapel Hill: University of North Carolina Press, 1998); Mechal Sobel, *The World They Made Together: Black and White Values in Eighteenth-Century Virginia* (Princeton: Princeton University Press, 1987), and her *Trabelin' On: The Slave Journey to an Afro-Baptist Faith* (Princeton: Princeton University Press, 1988). Although Sobel is right that new denominations gained many converts from among slaves after midcentury, before the Great Awakening, many enslaved people pressed for recognition of their conversion within the Church of England. On that point, see Nelson, *A Blessed Company*, 259–72. The notion that enslaved people thought about Christianity and incorporated it into their lives is beginning to take root in the historiography; see James Sidbury, *Plowshares into Swords: Race, Rebellion, and Identity in Gabriel's Virginia, 1730–1810* (Cambridge: Cambridge University Press, 1997), and Charles F. Irons, *The Origins of Proslavery Christianity: White and Black Evangelicals in Colonial and Antebellum Virginia* (Chapel Hill: University of North Carolina Press, 2008).

Lower Norfolk County, 103, 120, 124
Luke, 119–121

Manuel, 102–104
marriage, 51–52, 124, 138, 169; Anglo-
    African, 78, 82; Anglo-Indian, 65–67,
    69–70, 190n15; and Christianity,
    61–63; of Indians, 64; and law, 71,
    82–83, 85; and race, 50–51, 70, 82,
    85; of John Rolfe and Metoaka,
    50–55, 61–62, 66, 69–70
Mary I, 14–15
Maryland, 8, 30, 37, 69–70, 76, 80–81,
    91, 98, 125, 134–136, 144, 192n55,
    194n3
Massachusetts Bay, 7, 59, 120, 128, 141
Massacre of 1622. *See* Assault of 1622
Mather, Increase, 63
Menifye, George, 92, 103
Metappin, 103
Methodists, 7, 159
Metoaka, 41, 54–55, 61–62, 66, 186n62;
    conversion of, 49–53, 67; kidnapping
    of, 49–50; marriage of, 50–55, 61–62,
    69–70
Miles, Alice, 77–78
ministers, 22, 36, 46–48, 51, 56–57, 63,
    121, 144, 145–149, 153, 170. *See also
    individual names*
mixed-race people, 74–75, 78, 80–83,
    85, 101–102, 108–109, 138, 155, 162,
    164
Monacan Indians, 38, 69
Mongum, Philip, 95–96
monogenesis, 21–23, 25, 28, 34, 63–64,
    126, 167
Morley, Thomas, 116
Muslims, 4, 17–18, 32, 89, 177n2. *See
    also* Islam; Turks

Nansemond County, 91
Nansemonds, 42, 48, 69, 191n24
Nash, Peter, 119–121
Native Americans. *See* Indians
New England, 7, 59, 123, 129
Newman, Mary, 82–83
Newport, Christopher, 38, 41
Nicholson, Francis, 146
Noah (biblical figure), 3–5, 21, 25, 27,
    63–64, 142, 167

Noble, Rebecca, 78
Norfolk County, 165
Northampton County, 90–91, 96–97
North Carolina, 93
Nutting, Thomas, 120

Obama, Barack, 11
Opechancanough, 52–53, 56–57, 69
Ottoman Empire, 13, 18, 32, 133, 203n78

Pamunkey Indians, 136
Pannell, Katherine, 117
Paquiquineo, 37
Parker, William, 43
Paspahegh Indians, 42–43, 48
Payne, Francis, 95–96
Pennsylvania Society for Promoting the
    Abolition of Slavery, 171
Pepper, Richard, 155–156
Percy, George, 38–39, 42, 44, 183–
    184n34
Perry, William, 92
Pettway, William, 157
Phillip, John, 95, 104
Piscataway Indians, 69–70
Pocahontas. *See* Metoaka
polygenesis, 22, 107
Pope, John, 72
Porter, John, 124–125
Porter, Judith, 80
Portugal, 20
potential Christianity, 3, 29, 30–32, 34,
    107, 168, 169, 173; of Indians, 30, 31,
    32, 33, 34, 38, 46–47; of Muslims, 32
Potomack Indians, 49
Potomac River, 37, 135
Potts, Francis, 96–97
Powhatan (individual). *See*
    Wahunsonacock
Powhatan Indians, 24, 31, 33, 38, 55–56,
    103, 180–181n50; alliance with Eng-
    lish of, 40–41; encounter with Span-
    ish of, 37; inheritance practices of,
    52–53, 64, 187n74; politics of, 37–38,
    40–41; violent conflicts between Eng-
    lish and, 41–42, 49, 57–59
predestination, 15
Presbyterians, 7, 63, 88, 159
Princess Anne County, 165
Printer (slave), 155–156